The Shaman

Patterns of Religious Healing Among the Ojibway Indians

BY JOHN A. GRIM

UNIVERSITY OF OKLAHOMA PRESS
Norman

Library of Congress Cataloging in Publication Data

Grim, John.
    The shaman.

    (The Civilization of the American Indian Series; v. 165)
    Bibliography: p. 231
    Includes index.
    1. Shamanism—Comparative studies. 2. Shamanism—Siberia (R.S.F.
S.R. and Kazakh S.S.R.) 3. Shamanism—Great Lakes Region. 4. Chippewa Indians—Religion and mythology. 5. Chippewa Indians—Rites and
ceremonies. 6. Indians of North America—Religion and mythology.
7. Indians of North America—Rites and ceremonies. I. Title.
BL 2370.S5G75   1983   291.6′2   83—47834

ISBN: 978-0-8061-2106-2 (paper)

7   8   9   10   11   12   13

To
Emelia and Dee Forast, who reared me
Thomas, who helped me to see
and Mary Evelyn, with whom I journey

CONTENTS

ILLUSTRATIONS

Figures

Maps

PREFACE

IN January, 1982, I had the opportunity in Tokyo to discuss this book with Sevyan Vainshtein, Senior Researcher in the Soviet Institute of Ethnography. I was especially interested in his comments on my comparative patterns of shamanic experience derived from Siberian shamans and applied to the shamanic vocations among the Woodland Ojibway of North America. Moreover, I was eager to have his evaluation of my religious interpretation of the shaman.

In our conversations Dr. Vainshtein cited three areas that need further study in the field of Siberian shamanism. First, he pointed out that contemporary modes of Siberian shamanism are remnants of nineteenth-century practices that were significantly influenced by Mongolian Buddhism. What is needed, he indicated, is a study such as this, comparing Native American shamanic traditions and those of Siberian peoples, to identify ancient patterns that have endured in the later historical record. He stressed comparative ethnography as an important area of work in the studies of shamanism.

Second, he pointed out that, within nomadic and pastoral economic-cultural types, shamanic practitioners transmitted an ancient body of tribal religious lore. Thus the religious nature of shamanic activities is a significant focus for future comparative studies in the morphology of particular shamanic traditions.

Third, Dr. Vainshtein indicated a personal interest in the question of the domestic, or family, shaman and his or her relation to the development of the shamanistic profession. Dr. Vainshtein tied this issue to his ethnographic research on the origin and diffusion of certain crafts and animal-herding techniques from Siberia.

The meeting with Dr. Vainshtein was fortuitous because it reaffirmed my own thinking that Siberian shamanism may have a particular relationship to the shamanic activities of the native peoples of North America. That relationship may lie in the patterns of shamanic behavior that were formed before the Llano and Plano spearpoint hunters arrived on the North American continent approximately ten thousand years ago. Or the relationship may have been formed more recently by diffusion through boreal cultures. These questions need to be explored further, for an adequate understanding of Siberian and North American shamanism may well lie in comparative ethnographical and historical studies.

In interpreting the religious nature of the shaman, a variety of methodologies is helpful. No one discipline can be said to describe or explain fully such a culturally particular phenomenon. Thus I have tried to suggest, in my patterns of shamanic experience, how the methods used in the respective fields of mythology, sociology, anthropology, and psychology can help to elucidate the religious meaning of shamanism.

An explanation of the religious activities of the shaman may be important in understanding certain historical developments in the world's great religious traditions. Also, an investigation of the shaman as an archaic religious personality is useful in researching later traditions that focus similarly on the emulation of great religious figures. Thus this book undertakes a comparative typology of religious figures, such as the prophet, priest, yogi, and sage, to demonstrate the similarities and differences of the shaman compared to those religious personalities. The typology also emphasizes the particular motivation of the shaman, who, like other religious types, is tied not only to cultural particularity but also to an inner religious direction.

Dr. Vainshtein's third area of interest, namely, the relation of the domestic to the professional shaman, is not a central concern of this work. While there is a wealth of Ojibway source materials on that subject, I have not fully explored it. I undertook my studies of Ojibway shamanic activities because of a personal interest in Ojibway culture and religious practices. My understanding of the tribal religious practices is, of course, limited by my own cultural background, but I hope that the Ojibway themselves may find this work useful.

It is my privilege and pleasure to acknowledge those who have helped to make this book possible. Two individuals deserve special mention without whom I could not have produced this work. Professor Thomas Berry's special insight and presence have been an enormous inspiration to me and others who have visited him at the Riverdale Center for Religious Research. Our conversations there, under the great red oak by the Hudson River, were themselves shamanic training of a latter-day sort. My wife, Mary Evelyn Tucker-Grim, has given innumerable hours of assistance, both thoughtful and technical. Her suggestions and editing skills are rooted imperceptibly but firmly through the soil of this work. I also wish to thank those who have read and commented on the manuscript, namely, Professors Howard Anderson, Ewert Cousins, Tom Driver, Anne Feldhouse, John Heaney, and Richard Smith. In addition, I would like gratefully to acknowledge the painstaking editorial assistance of Sarah Morrison of University of Oklahoma Press. Ultimately, however, I alone am responsible for any errors in the work. I would also like to thank my mother, Mrs. Emelia Grim, and my brother, August, and his wife, Eileen, for their warm support during my many years of research. In that regard I am also indebted to my parents-in-law, Mr. and Mrs. William D. Tucker, Jr., for their continuing encouragement of many aspects of my work. Finally, my wife and I would like to express our appreciation to Professor and Mrs. Wm. Theodore de Bary for a memorable year at Hotokudō, during which I wrote much of this manuscript.

Nanabozho, the Ojibway trickster and culture hero, was given a dog to remind him of the sacred medicine ceremony, midewiwin. In a similar spirit some years ago I was given a dog, Mindy, by an Algonquian friend who is now gone. The ancient relationship of the human and the dog reflects the intimate presence of all living things on the earth to one another. I like to think that this relationship and the ceremonies that evoke it are never gone but linger in the deep recesses of our mind, waiting for a call to make it quick and responsive.

THE SHAMAN

1

INTRODUCTION

AMONG tribal peoples the shaman is the person, male or female, who experiences, absorbs, and communicates a special mode of sustaining, healing power. For most tribal peoples the vital rhythms of the natural world are manifestations of a mysterious, all-pervasive power presence.[1] This power presence is evoked by a shaman in ritual prayer and sacrifice to guide tribal hunts, perpetuate sacred crafts, and sustain human life in its confrontations with the destructive forces of the surrounding world. Although an emphasis on such power and its transformations is frequently associated with magic rather than with religion, it should be noted that religion does function at all levels of the human venture as a means of attaining both the psychic and the physical energies that are needed to respond creatively to the terrors of the human condition. The shaman responds to these urgencies of life by contacting and transmitting such efficacious power in a particular manner.

The transformative power that the shaman invokes is experienced as an all-encompassing presence that is mysterious but as real as the wind or as breath, after which it is sometimes designated as "spirit." It evokes the awesome feeling generally associated with the holy. Although for the most part seen as a benign force, this power is also feared when experienced in its terrifying aspects. Simultaneously fascinating as the sun's play on water and inscrutable as the deepening shadows of twilight, it evades articulate expression and remains ineffable. Yet, visible in dreams and visions, in memories of dead ancestors, in the fecund earth, and in the expansive sky, this mysterious power is so manifestly present that no explanation of it is adequate. Rather, it is itself accepted as the cause of those transformations in the life of the seasons, the animals, and the plants upon which tribal life depends.

The descriptions of Rudolf Otto are particularly insightful regarding the experiential qualities of the human perception of the holy. These qualities he summarizes in the term *numinous*,[2] which is derived from the Latin *numen*, signifying "divine will" or "divinity." It derives further from the Greek *neuein*, meaning "to nod or incline the head."[3] The simple act of bowing before the divine presence reveals a profound inner recognition of an overwhelming reality. This reality is simultaneously *mysterium tremendum*, or the repelling moment of the divine, and *mysterium fascinans*, or the alluring moment of the holy. In developing the word *numinous*, Otto emphasizes the transrational aspects of the mysterious power that tribal peoples recognize. Yet he insists that there is a rational element of the numinous that is often missing or unexpressed in the tribal world. Thus, he provides a contemporary context for a reexamination of the tribal shaman and his religious function.

The reaction of amazement *(scheu)* or awe[4] separates a particular person, place, or object from the normal flow of observation and marks it as sacred. The sacred is remarkably different from the routine or the mundane, and in the tribal world manifestations of the sacred bring human beings into contact with an order of reality that is different from their ordinary world. The sacred is not an epiphenomenon, or secondary expression of reality; it is the deepest aspect of reality and is attained by a direct human experience. In speaking of the Tlingit Indians, J. R. Swanton observed:

> This supernatural energy must be carefully differentiated from natural energy and never confused with it. It is true that the former is supposed to bring about results similar to the latter, but in the mind of the Tlingit the conceived difference between the two is

as great as with us. A rock rolling down hill or an animal running is by no means a manifestation of supernatural energy, although if something peculiar be associated with these actions, something outside the Indian's usual experience of such phenomena, they may be thought of as such.[5]

The particular experience suggested here is the intuition of the sacred. The mysterious presence referred to is so all pervasive in the tribal world view that even the profane is full of potential for becoming sacred. A stone or a tree has a basic relation to ordinary existence by its created presence, but a numinous manifestation, or "hierophany," will make it "wholly other," or sacred.[6]

The sacred has been appropriately described by a Dakota chief as a place where power rests:

Everything as it moves now and then, here and there makes stops. A bird as it flies stops in one place to make its nest and in another place to rest from its flight. A man when he goes forth stops when he wills. So the god (Wakan) has stopped. The sun, which is so bright and beautiful is one place where he has stopped. The moon, the stars, the wind he has been with. The trees, the animals, are all where he has stopped, and the Indian thinks of these places and sends his prayers to reach where the god has stopped and to win health and a blessing.[7]

Here the sacred is identified with the places where Wakan, the mysterious power, has stopped. A whole country with its lively and refreshing growth may provide a walking place for the god, Wakan, but there are special places, or hierophanies, where power becomes manifest with exceptional clarity and efficacy. Such stopping places are not static entities. Rather the power is apprehended here as a sacred presence by the visionary personality. The stopping place is experienced by the seer as a unique communication of sacred power.

A mountain might embody such a presence. So also certain rivers, groves of trees, birds in flight, or even the skillful acts of a craftsperson. All these may be understood as specific manifestations of a numinous reality. On occasion the numinous is experienced more subjectively, as in dreams, visions, and reflections on afterlife. In effect, a hierophany simultaneously produces a personal experience of the sacred and an encompassing cosmic feeling of awe. For as Van der Leeuw points out, such power has both a psychological significance and a cosmic character.[8]

Cultural experiences of a hierophany are frequently described in terms that mediate between the psychological and the cosmic dimensions of the power. Words such as *mana, wakan,* and *orenda* distinguish the sacred from the profane in the tribal world. Such expressions are not analytically defined; they spring from direct personal experience. The subjects bearing the power that the seer experiences are considered to be *spirits.*[9] For example, in Melanesia, *mana* is the power that is given will and form in the spirits: "This Mana is not fixed in anything, and can be conveyed in almost anything; but spirits . . . have it [power] and can impart it. . . . All Melanesian religion consists, in fact, in getting this Mana for one's self or getting it used for one's benefit.[10] Similarly, *orenda* or *oki* is the word used in the Iroquois cosmology,[11] *wakan* in the Sioux,[12] *coen* in the Athapaskan,[13] and *yok* in the Tlingit.[14] Among the Algonquian peoples of North America, *manitou* expresses the resonant relationship between the cosmic and human orders. As is evident in the following passage, manitou encompasses a wide variety of spirit presences:

The numerous manitou, of fairly equal rank, appeared as spirit prototypes of plants, birds, beasts, elemental forces and life circumstances such as Poverty and Motherhood. They included useful trees like cedar and birch; certain roots, plants and berries; hummingbird, woodpecker, arctic owl, golden eagle, bald-headed eagle . . . hawk, loon, lynx, sturgeon, beaver, moose, otter, deer, wolf, black bear, caribou, turtle; and the sun, moon, thunder, lightning, meteoric stones and winds of the cardinal points. The seasons might be personalized as supernatural; so also were extraordinary circumstances like cannibalism, the heedless self-assurance of elder sister or brother (represented in the mythic figure of Foolish Woman), the vulnerableness of the mighty (represented by the mythic hero, Nenabozho, called the White Rabbit). These Supernaturals possessed different powers but were esteemed similarly, unlike the dreaded *windigo,* the Water Monster and ghosts.[15]

The variety of natural occurrences and mythic personalities associated with the manitou indicate the power's richness and indeterminacy.[16] Such richness suggests that the experience of the sacred was widely distributed among the Algonquian peoples, and the indeterminacy of reference demonstrates the transformative quality of this power. The manitou concept seems to articulate the mutuality of exchange between the experiencer and the embodiment of power. Quite often the experience of such a power and its effects, or transformations, is not conceptualized beyond such mediating terms as *manitou.* Instead the experiences are evoked in expressions such as vision-songs and vision-dances. These intimate contacts provide some of the clearest insights into the relationship of power and its embodiment as a spirit.

The transition from an awareness of the sacred to a fully developed notion of spirits demonstrates the tendency toward personalization of the numinous. Spirits are needed as intermediaries between the cosmic power and the human beings receiving that power. The role of spirits is further explained by Van der Leeuw, who has observed that these spirits possess both will and form.[17]

Spirits provide human beings with a means of drawing on a sustaining energy as they face their own human inadequacy. A specific example sheds light on the function of spirits among tribal peoples. From the pre-Buddhist period in Japan manifestations of the sacred were expressed by the word *kami.* These kami became associated with specific places, objects, actions, clans, and individuals. As Motoori Norinaga points out, kami were associated with the deities of heaven and earth that appear in the ancient records. Concerning this concept of kami he observes:

It is hardly necessary to say that it includes human beings. It also includes such objects as birds, trees, plants, seas, mountains and so forth. In ancient usage, anything whatsoever which was outside the ordinary, which possessed superior power, or which was awe-inspiring was called *kami*. Eminence here does not refer merely to the superiority of nobility, goodness or meritorious deeds. Evil and mysterious things, if they are extraordinary and dreadful, are called *kami*.[18]

Furthermore in the development of the crafts, communication with the kami was essential before any article took its final shape. A sword did not have the proper charm unless it was executed by a craftsperson who contacted the kami.

Thus in Japan kami are spirits having a relationship to power similar to that of the mana among the Melanesians and the orenda among the Iroquois. They are the spirit intermediaries that may be contacted by persons competent to receive and transmit efficacious power. The sacred crafts, embody these spirit forces, which are intimately associated with the earth. Shinto crafts gradually developed into priestly traditions, whose practitioners passed on to successive generations the mnemonic chants and rhymes for contacting spirits.[19] This process is suggested in Langdon Warner's statement: "Knowledge of natural processes is the very basis of all arts which transform raw materials into artifacts. Possession of the mysteries of a craft means nothing less than a power over nature gods and it creates a priest out of the man who controls it."[20] The personal experience of spirit presence, however, is not usually associated with the priest but with the shaman. Thus it is to the person of the shaman that tribal peoples turn for aid in dealing with the urgencies of life.

The Experience of Power

A shaman receives his or her healing and vitalizing power from the spirits. After experiencing this power personally, he or she brings the sustaining energy to the community.

Such contact with the numinous is a gratuitous gift of the spirits. A person is called to such an encounter and introduced to such mysteries by the spirits. The spirits then become personal helpers of the shaman, who afterwards invokes their aid in a manner that is itself often prescribed by the spirits. Often the shaman becomes so intimate with the spirits that they possess him or her. In some instances the shaman journeys with the aid of his spirits; at other times he meditates, communing with his spirit helper. In all cases the shaman becomes a personal hierophany manifesting transphenomenal power.

A Goldi shaman related to Lev Shternberg the intimacies of his spirit contact, journey, and possession:

Once I was asleep on my sick bed, when a spirit approached me. It was a very beautiful woman. . . . She said: "I am the *ayami* of your ancestors, the shamans, I taught them shamaning. Now I am going to teach you." . . . She has been coming to me ever since, and I sleep with her as with my own wife, but we have no children. . . . Sometimes she comes under the aspect of an old woman, and sometimes under that of a wolf. . . . Sometimes she comes as a winged tiger. I mount it and she takes me to show me different countries. I have seen mountains, where only old men and women live. . . . She has given me three assistants—the "jarga" (panther), the "doonto" (bear) and the "amba" (tiger). They come to me in my dreams, and appear whenever I summon them while shamaning. . . . When I am shamaning, the *ayami* and the assistant spirits are possessing me; whether big or small, they penetrate me as smoke or vapor would.[21]

In this passage the *ayami,* or spirit, that embodies the power of the ancestors comes in a dream to the future shaman, a dream that connects this visible world with a transphenomenal reality. In a similar altered psychic state the *ayami* and her helping spirits work through the Goldi shaman to transmit a healing capacity. While this energy is transphenomenal in its source, it is efficacious in the world of time and change. Moreover, the shaman mediates the process through his own personal gifts and capabilities.

The shaman's experience of a spirit world can take place in the context of an inner journey, often acted out ritually by climbing a notched tree, sitting in a spirit-canoe, or tracing a prescribed path in dance. At other times the journey consists of an internal seizure resulting in a trance state. In either case, the journey is initiated by a call from a realm beyond the visible world. In this other world the shaman is taught certain symbolic gestures that are used later in ritual activities to impart a sustaining or healing energy to individuals or the community.

Each shaman needs his or her own personal experience of spirits, even though he or she may have acquired skills and techniques from an older shaman or a shamanic society. Shamans also need great personal inventiveness to adapt their communications to their particular life situations. Because of their spontaneity and inventiveness, shamanic rituals are usually less standardized and less traditional than the rituals carried out by priests. Although shamans may not be the only religious figures in the community, they are unique because of the immediacy of their personal encounter with the spirit world and the vigor of the forces that they command.

The ability to respond to the creative impulse is evident in these words of the Dakota shaman Lame Deer:

The *wicasa wakan* [sacred person, shaman] loves the silence, wrapping it around himself like a blanket — a loud silence with a voice like thunder which tells him of many things. Such a man likes to be in a place where there is no sound but the humming of insects. He sits facing the West, asking for help. He talks to the plants and they answer him. He listens to the voices of the *Wama Kaskan* — all those who move upon the earth, the animals. He is at one with them. From all living beings something flows into him all the time, and something flows from him. I don't know where or what, but it's there. I know.[22]

Oriented toward this mysterious flow of life, shamans respond to the ceaseless rhythms of silence and sound in the earth. Just as they are open to the dramatic moment of ritual contact with the spirits, so also are they ready to undertake inner, meditative journeys because these too are effective in healing. Aware of both hidden and manifest spirit presences, shamans maintain the purity of their communications with the spirit world by silence, ritual prohibitions, and other limiting activities that demonstrate the sacrificial nature of their vocation. Their meditative activities are as highly developed as their ecstatic journey rituals. Thus contemplation is as much a shamanic mode as ritualized trance.

The Shaman and the Community

Shamanic activity is generally a public function. The tribal community witnesses the dramatic encounter with the spirits and benefits from the ritual communications. In this sense, the shaman is for the tribe a vital link to those ineffable forces that are needed to transform individual and community life. The shaman is also a spokesperson informing the spirit world of the tribe's needs. Significant tribal activities, such as hunting and agriculture, are often undertaken only with the guidance and support of the spirits communicating through the shaman.

Despite the differences in the techniques used by various practitioners of the shamanistic art, there are certain characteristic shamanic ritual practices that can be identified and discussed as shamanism. In recent years the term *shamanism* has been used in such a broad sense that for some critics it has lost its meaning. Yet it is nonetheless appropriate to use it in investigating the personality and the practices of shamans in particular cultural settings. Thus shamanism serves as an explanatory context for investigation rather than as a definitive description of the phenomenon. Among the characteristic shamanistic practices are healing by means of a trance state, interpreting dreams and visions, guiding the souls of the dead, divination, prognostication, offering sacrifices to appease offended spirits, and the initiation of new shamans.

One of the primary rituals in shamanistic practice is the enactment of a journey to the spirit world. The dramatic quality of this ritual and its elaborate thaumaturgy focus the tribe's attention on the shaman's encounter with hidden forces. He allows each tribal member to share this encounter. Each person in the audience participates in the ritual and absorbs its meaning into his or her own life. The following is a typical description of a shaman centering the tribal psyche on his ritual:

The rhythmic music and singing, and later the dancing of the shaman, gradually involves every participant more and more in a collective action. When the audience begins to repeat the refrains together with the assistants, only those who are defective fail to join the chorus. The tempo of the action increases, the shaman with a spirit is no more an ordinary man or relative, but is a "placing" (i.e. incarnation) of the spirit; the spirit acts together with the audience, and this is felt by everyone. The state of many participants is now near to that of the shaman himself, and only a strong belief that when the shaman is there the spirit may only enter him, restrains the participants from being possessed in mass by the spirit. This is a very important condition of shamanizing which does not, however, reduce mass susceptibility to the suggestion, hallucinations, and unconscious acts produced in a state of mass ecstasy. When the shaman feels that the audience is with him and follows him he becomes still more active and this effect is transmitted to his audience. After shamanizing, the audience recollects various moments of the performance, their great psychophysiological emotion and the hallucinations of sight and hearing which they have experienced. They then have a deep satisfaction.[23]

In such chants and songs, either exuberant or hushed, shamans vocalize their spirits, calling them towards their people. By frenzied calls mimicking the wild shouts of birds or animals, shamans arouse their own desires for possession by their spirit helpers. Often drumbeats pace the chants; the steady rhythm creates the psychic mood necessary for entry into trance. Such a heightened atmosphere is maintained by tribal members for extended periods while the shaman journeys into distant regions of psychic experience. Some shamans visually manifest their spirit power by wearing masks and by dancing in a special manner. All such activities are significant for the tribe. They demonstrate the ability of the shaman to make present the power he represents, as well as to transform himself and others under the motivation of that power. Many native arts and ritual expressions are derived from a shamanistic source.[24] The effectiveness of these arts depends on the contact with an all-pervasive numinous presence that they express.

Tribal peoples generally join the sacred and profane aspects of life in one orientation toward higher power. "No man can succeed in life alone, and he cannot get the help he needs from men."[25] In this expression of an American Indian the need for a supportive power that is other than human is clearly stated. The shaman's ritual assures the flow of such vital energy into the community. The dramatic actions, the emotional chants, the terrifying masks, and the elaborate dances all bring about contact with a spiritual energy that sustains the society. The shaman dramatizes and makes visible the incomprehensible mystery of all existence.

Alternately, silent and sensitive to the coded pulse of the natural world or frenzied in yearning for the remembered moment of contact with the spirits, the shaman remains a paradoxical figure in many respects. He or she performs a vital function in the tribe and is a central figure in the community. Yet the experience that enables shamans to function in this manner also makes of them marginal or "liminal" people.[26] They cross the threshold into another world and return again to the conventional world. In this ambiguous position they move at times to the center of society and then return to the margins. They draw freely from tribal traditions and yet spontaneously create their own responses to new situations.

As Victor Turner has pointed out, "The shaman or prophet assumes a statusless status, external to the secular social structure, which gives him the right to criticize all structure-bound personae in terms of a moral order binding on all, and also to mediate between all segments or components of the structural system."[27] The liminal character of the shaman makes of him the major ritualist in the tribal rites of passage. He is the one best able to guide the neophyte through the mysterious transition leading from and returning to the structured tribal world. Having intimate knowledge of the threshold to efficacious power, the shaman is able to lead another across that boundary to an encounter with power and then back to the normal world.

If one considers the liminal position of the shaman, it is not difficult to understand how this tribal personality can contribute so much to the formation of a tribal culture and yet gradually fade when confronted by the structures of a foreign civilization. The tribal shaman has been somewhat eclipsed in many contemporary tribal communities. Yet ongoing investigations seek to reassess the meaning of shamanism in tribal society and to suggest its significance for our time.

Status of the Study of Shamanism

Shamanism as an academic study has had a varied history, from the late seventeenth-century ethnographic accounts to contemporary studies on extant shamanic practices. While the literature is voluminous, a morphological approach allows the examination of a few representative works to indicate major trends in shamanistic studies. Rather than categorize the sources simply as psychological, sociological, or ethnographical studies, we will use them to point toward a more interpretative study of shamanism. As Mircea Eliade has suggested, "In the last analysis, it is for the historian of religion to synthesize all the studies of particular aspects of shamanism and to present a comprehensive view which shall be at once a morphology and a history of this complex religious phenomena."[28]

After we examine the etymology of the word *shaman* and give a brief description of its passage into Western academic use, we will summarize the literature on shamanism in three phases: first, the early studies of shamanism which investigated the origin of religion; second, the anthropological efforts which collected ethnographic data from particular cultures; and third, the more recent hermeneutical studies, which interpret shamanism in a multicultural context.

The word *shaman* is a transliteration of the Tungusic word *saman* or *hamman*,[29] which functions as both a noun and a verb. As a noun it means "one who is excited, moved, raised"; as a verb it means "to know in an ecstatic manner."[30] The Tungus are a central Siberian tribe of which many divisions can be found from the arctic region to the Chinese frontier. Neighboring Asian tribes also have shamanic figures, who are called by a variety of names: *ojuna* (masculine) and *udoyan* (feminine) among the Yakut, *buge* and *utagan* among the Mongolians, *kam* and *utugun* among the Altaic, *tadibey* and *iduan* among the Finno-Ugric, and *baksy* and *duana* among the Kirghis.[31]

Western contacts with the Siberian tribes are recorded in the various travel accounts and missionary literature. An early reference to the word *shaman* was made by the Dutch diplomats E. Ysbrant Ides and Adam Brand. These men accompanied a Russian embassy sent by Peter the Great to China from 1692 to 1695. E. Ysbrant Ides's writings, published in 1698, describe the family shaman of a Tungus group.[32] Later several European writers used the word *shaman* to describe such aboriginal religious personalities in Siberia. In 1875, A. H. Sayce included the term in an article for the *Encyclopedia Brittanica*.[33]

During the nineteenth century a linguistic method was established by Max Muller and others for the comparative study of religions. This comparative method, when applied to the etymology of the word *shaman*, indicated to most

nineteenth-century orientalists an Indian Buddhist derivation from the Sanskrit *sramana* or Pali *samana*. In 1831,
however, W. Schatt objected to this linguistic identification
with the Buddhist term *samana*. He speculated on evidence
within the Tungusic language itself *which* suggested an indigenous development of the word *shaman*. These linguistic studies were continued by Dorji Banzarov in 1846, J.
Nemeth in 1914, and Berthold Laufer in 1917.[34] Briefly
stated, the linguistic studies sought to establish the indigenous origin of shamanism by deriving the descriptive term
shaman solely from tribal elements. They compared *saman*
with the analogous terms of several neighboring Siberian
tribes and conjectured that certain linguistic changes had
altered the word's original root. This root was traced back
to the Turko-Tartar word *kam*. Thus these researchers con-
cluded that shamanism had a central-Asian origin rather
than an Indic-Buddhist derivation.

Sergei Shirokogoroff reopened the question of Buddhist
influences on the formation of the Tungus word *saman* in
his work with G. Mironov in 1924. Shirokogoroff's later
work in 1935, *The Psychomental Complex of the Tungus*,
restated his linguistic arguments and proposed the formula
of a "shamanism stimulated by Buddhism."[35] Current researchers consider the etymological derivation of *shaman*
a moot question, agreeing with Shirokogoroff on possible
Buddhist influences but also emphasizing the pre-Buddhist,
indigenous characteristics of shamanism.

Most of the early studies of shamanism identify it as a
primordial religious experience. Weston La Barre, following this tradition, observes, "Essential shamanism is thus at
once the oldest and newest of religions, because it is the
de facto source of all religion."[36] Influenced by the etymological arguments and comparative religious research, the
nineteenth-century Russian ethnographers were the first
to recognize the antiquity and cultural particularity of
shamanic practice.[37] Gradually the recognition of similarities between the Siberian shaman and the American

Indian medicine man led to comparative ethnographic works. These early studies were the first significant approaches to shamanism.

Foremost among these studies are the *Reports of the Jesup North Pacific Expedition.* Franz Boas initiated this expedition in 1901, following his earlier ethnographic work on the native peoples of the Canadian and American Northwest Coast. Sailing slowly up the northern Pacific to Alaska and across the Bering Strait to Siberia, the expedition established contact with the tribes of the Northwest Coast, with Alaskan Eskimos, and with both Neo- and Paleo-Siberian groups.[38] The major fieldworkers, Waldemar Bogoras and Waldemar Jochelson, made extensive comments on the shamanic practices that they observed. Their published works are still a major source for the historical ethnography of the area.

Bogoras's and Jochelson's approach had several lasting influences on the study of shamanism. First, they considered shamanism to be archaic; that is, an early or primitive religious experience maintained in the tribe despite later religious developments. Second, they identified the family shaman (an individual shaman who traveled with an extended family) as having developed earlier than the professional tribal shaman. Third, they considered that shamanism originated in North Asia. Similarities with shamanic activities in North America were explained by the migration of an earlier period. Fourth, they made extensive observations of the pathological appearance of shaman candidates. These observations, which may constitute their most lasting influence, led them to conclude that the shaman is a psychopathic type who performs a specialized function in tribal society.[39]

American studies in shamanism were heavily influenced by the *Reports of the Jesup North Pacific Expedition.* Two other researchers stand out, however, and are appropriately included in this section, namely Robert Lowie and Paul Radin. Both considered shamanism to be a primordial religious expression offering important insights to the contemporary world.[40] Lowie's work, *Primitive Religion*, based on Plains and especially Crow Indian material, deals with what he considers to be the significant facets of primordial religion, among which he includes shamanism. Paul Radin based his comprehensive study, *Primitive Religion*, on his research among the eastern Woodland tribes, especially the Siouan Winnebago. His emphasis is on the social and economic factors in shamanism. He also discusses what he considers to be the neurotic-epileptoid condition of the shamans. Both Radin and Lowie contributed fictional stories to Elsie Clews Parson's ethnographical anthology, *American Indian Life*, and each of their stories narrates a shaman's vision. Lowie's piece is remarkable for its attention to the detail of a Crow shaman's ritual. Radin's story is a striking example of literary ethnology relating the transmigration visions of the Winnebago shaman Thunder-Cloud. The contemplative quality of these visions is remarkable, and Thunder-Cloud's depth of meditation suggests that Radin himself questioned the strictly pejorative interpretation of shamanism as psychopathic.

The quest for the origin of religion was dominant during this early phase of shamanistic studies. Although the major contributors on the question of origins (e.g., Edward Tyler, Robert Marett, Emile Durkheim, Konrad Preuss) did not use strictly shamanistic data, the ethnographers of this early phase often directed their research to conform with one or more of the origin theories. The exact relationship between shamanism and primordial religions remains an unresolved question. Several recent works have drawn from archaeological material to present a new argument for the paleolithic origin of shamanism. Foremost among them is an article by Horst Kirchner, "An Archeological Contribution to the Early History of Shamanism." Kirchner speculates on the meaning of certain Ice Age cave paintings, including the "stricken shaman" of Lascaux and the "horned shaman" of Trois Frères.[41] Using Kirchner's work,

Andreas Lommel attempts to reassert the primordial dimensions of shamanism in his study, *Shamanism: The Beginnings of Art*.[42] Lommel reflects the change in the psychological interpretation of the shaman's sickness. He considers that the psychotic intrusion constitutes a necessary stage, both for the shaman's creativity as an artist and for his or her sensitivity as a tribal healer.

While the specific origins of religion remain undefined, the impact of these earlier studies is still felt in shamanistic research. The tendency is to accept the shaman as a primordial religious personality that has persisted even to the present. Nevertheless, a more comprehensive interpretation of this archaic religious experience is still needed.

The second phase of shamanistic studies is associated with cultural ethnology. In many ways this is still the most acceptable manner of studying shamanism because these researchers insist on presenting shamanism in its particular cultural milieu. Gustav Rank has emphasized the importance of the cultural-historical method:

Equally important in research is the functionalistic viewpoint which when we investigate details helps us not to lose sight of the structural unity. All our efforts would be in vain if we were not able to place shamanism in a functional relationship with human existence in its widest sense, that is, with its social-economic system and religious ideas. Without such a holistic view of the matter, the question of origin and development is left floating in a theoretical vacuum, lacking any contact with reality.[43]

It is apparent from his remarks that the earlier concern to associate shamanism with the origin of religion is not to be completely ignored. Any interpretation of shamanism must begin, however, by situating the shaman in a particular cultural context.

The first ethnographer to be mentioned in this context is Franz Boas. Boas was trained in an academic environment that was concerned with the archaic nature of shamanism, but he chose to set aside the question of the origins of religion and evolutionary schemas of its development for a closer examination of cultural particularity. The influence of culture on an individual's actions, as well as the role of culture in shaping a person's thought, was of singular concern to Boas. He wrote:

> Notwithstanding incongruities that are never entirely absent, each culture is a whole, and its form has a dynamic force which determines the behavior of the mass of individuals. It is only from their thoughts and acts, from the products of their actions that we derive the concept of their culture. How far an individual is able to free himself from the fetters that culture lays upon him depends not only upon his individuality but equally, if not more, upon the culture imposed upon him.[44]

This awareness of the interaction of the individual and his or her culture has become significant in situating and describing shamanistic practices. The volume of works concerned with the shaman using such a cultural-historical method is extensive and still growing. Several journals, such as *American Anthropologist, Anthropos, History of Religions,* and *Numen,* regularly explore shamanic material using this methodology. Three anthropological ethnographers will be discussed here for their representative works on specific cultural forms of shamanism: Sergei Shirokogoroff, for his work on the Siberian Tungus; Knud Rasmussen, for his writings on the Eskimos of Greenland and North America; and Vilmos Dioszegi, for his studies on contemporary Siberian shamanism.

As mentioned earlier, Sergei Shirokogoroff proposed a significant thesis regarding the Buddhist influences on shamanism.[45] It was, however, another work of his, *The Psychomental Complex of the Tungus,* that described the unique Tungus development of shamanism. Shirokogoroff investigated Tungus shamanism, using social, economic, and religious data, to situate the shaman in the tribal context. His work is still a major source on the Tungus, for it deals with the shamanic practices of both the nomadic and the more sedentary division of the tribe.

Shirokogoroff speculated on the central issues regarding the shaman's psychic illness, spirit contacts, and trance techniques. While he based his comments on his extensive Tungus research, he tended to reduce the shaman to a psychopathic type. Thus his work is regarded as an important, although flawed, model of research in the field of shamanism using the cultural-historical method.

Some of the most readable ethnographic descriptions of shamanism are in the works of Knud Rasmussen. As a Greenlander, who had childhood contacts with Eskimo peoples, Rasmussen brought to his work a concern and a compassion for the Eskimo that lends a special sensitivity to his writing. Refraining from extended speculation on shamanistic theory, Rasmussen gathered ethnographic material on the Eskimo from Greenland to Alaska. His works are more than just delightful reading; they give us a picture of Eskimo shamanism during that crucial period of cultural transition from the 1920s through the 1940s, when Euro-American influences extensively penetrated these northern tribes. Having lived with the Iglulik, Netsilik, and Copper Eskimo tribes, Rasmussen reported firsthand on the conversations, ceremonies, and rituals in which he participated. This intimate cultural contact makes his work an outstanding source of information on shamanism.

The final ethnographer to be dealt with here is the Hungarian researcher Vilmos Dioszegi. A foremost scholar of Siberian shamanism, Dioszegi disagreed with such formidable Russian scholars as D. Zelenin and A. F. Anisimov, who predicted the dissolution of Siberian shamanism and its eventual evolutionary sovietization.[46] In research among the Buryat Mongols and Finno-Ugric Samoyed, Dioszegi found shamans active during the 1960s. Although Dioszegi followed the official government ideological position on northern Asian shamanism in his ethnographic work, he recognized a strong undercurrent of historical continuity

which distinguished Siberian shamanism. Thus he viewed
shamanism within the overall context of Marx and Engels,
who interpret religion as an economic force in history destined to end in cultural alienation, yet, he emphasized the
need to document the contemporary remnants of shamanism as valuable cultural records. He wrote:

> Today, shamanism already belongs to the past. Due to the
> propagation of science it had to become extinct. But for the sake
> of science, it must not disappear without trace: for the benefit
> of the researchers of Comparative Ethnology, Ethnogenetics and
> History of Religion it is indispensable that the authentic and de-
> tailed records of this vanished world be collected without delay.[47]

Dioszegi's work highlights both the contributions and the
limitations of this phase of cultural shamanistic studies.
While such studies have contributed significantly to the
accumulation of ethnographic data, they often simply cata-
log material without a comprehensive method of interpretation. Dioszegi is aware of both the need to record contemporary shamanic activity and the need to interpret its
social significance.

The third phase of shamanistic research is hermeneutical
studies. As the ethnographic literature on shamanism became more accessible, interpretations of it began to appear.
In 1939, Ake Ohlmarks presented his theory of arctic and
subarctic shamanism based on the presence of ritual hysteria.[48] The earlier works of J. L. Maddox, and W. T. Corlett were also interpretative, but they did not deal with all
of the essential issues in shamanism.[49] The current phase
of shamanistic studies introduced by those works is given
a more comprehensive treatment in the work of Mircea
Eliade.[50]

The title of Eliade's book, *Shamanism: Archaic Techniques of Ecstacy,* affirms the antiquity of the shamanic
experience. In his work Eliade deals with cultural expressions of shamanism, indicating his reliance on the second
major phase of shamanistic studies. Eliade's real contribu-

tion, however, lies in his hermeneutical insights into the ecstatic techniques used by shamans to contact the world of spirit power. He bases his interpretation of shamanism on the primacy of the ecstatic experience and the cultural milieu in which that archetypal experience finds expression. Considering central and northern Asian shamanism, Eliade stresses the flexibility needed to interpret the experience:

We must keep in mind the two essential elements of the problem: on the one hand, the ecstatic experience as such, as a primary phenomenon; on the other, the historico-religious milieu into which this ecstatic experience was destined to be incorporated and the ideology that, in the last analysis, was to validate it. We have termed the ecstatic experience a "primary phenomenon" because we see no reason whatever for regarding it as the result of a particular historical moment, that is, as produced by a certain form of civilization. Rather, we would consider it fundamental in the human condition, and hence known to the whole of archaic humanity; what changed and was modified with the different forms of culture and religion was the interpretation and evaluation of the ecstatic experience.[51]

While some scholars challenge his interpretation, Eliade's work does provide a hermeneutical context for shamanistic studies. Using the method of the history of religions, Eliade is concerned with understanding the religious meaning of shamanism, especially its northern Asian expressions. That he himself sees the difficulty in proposing ecstacy as the central experience is clear from the following statement: "The shaman's seance almost always has recourse to ecstacy; and the history of religions is there to show us that no other religious experience is more subject to distortion and aberration."[52]

The current phase of hermeneutical studies of shamanism following Eliade draws freely from a wide range of sources. A particularly representative work is I. M. Lewis's anthropological study, *Ecstatic Religion.* Lewis takes up the central issue of shamanic trance and spirit possession.

He is unwilling to ignore the religious dimensions of these shamanic activities and criticizes those anthropologists who do:

Once they have shown what for secular ends is done in the name of religion, some anthropologists naively suppose that nothing more remains to be said. Thus they leave largely unexplained the characteristic mystical aspects which distinguish the religious from the secular, and they totally fail to account for the rich diversity of religious concepts and beliefs. Although my ambitions do not extend to explaining these particularistic aspects of different ecstatic religions, I do seek to uncover some of the foundations, psychological as well as social, upon which the ecstatic response is based.[53]

Lewis's criticisms of shortsighted, overly analytical anthropologists bespeaks his comprehensive, hermeneutical approach.

Several other scholars deserve mention for their work in the hermeneutical phase of shamanistic studies. In his later work the Swiss psychologist C. G. Jung asserted the archetypal, multicultural dimensions of the shamanic personality.[54] In the early 1960s, Hans Findeisen and E. Stiglmayr responded to each other's articles in *Ethnos,* using the hermeneutical approach to discuss shamanism as a medium for spirit contact.[55] Similarly, the contemporary Swedish historian of religions Ake Hultkrantz draws extensively on the hermeneutical method for his discussion of North American shamanism.[56] The work of anthropologists Victor Turner and Clifford Geertz should also be mentioned in this context. Turner provides a useful interpretation of ritual process for discussing the personal formation of the shaman and his or her religious function. Geertz has critiqued the imprecise use of the word *shamanism,* arguing for a more particularized treatment of such personalities within the context of their ethos and world view.

Thus the hermeneutical method draws from a variety of academic disciplines, interprets the data in a larger cultural context, and proposes a significant explanation of the meaning of shamanism. Within this hermeneutical context and drawing primarily on cultural historical data, the present study proposes certain patterns of shamanistic experience to explain the type of shamanism practiced by various Siberian tribes. By applying these patterns and the methods that were used to identify them, we will investigate the shamanic practices of the North American Ojibway Indians. First, however, we will consider the significance of the shaman as a religious personality.

The Need for a Religious Interpretation of Shamanism

The shamanic experience has yet to be given adequate religious interpretation. Recent studies have moved beyond facile rubrics, such as primitive religion, occultism, or psychopathic aberration, but they still tend to be reductionist, as[57] they reduce the role of the shaman to a realm that is void of the mystery of power. They often concentrate exclusively on data that support only an anthropological, sociological, or psychological interpretation. The contributions of those disciplines are crucial in any analysis of the religious dimensions of shamanism, but it is also essential that any analysis assist in explaining how and why a people enter into such a communion with an ultimate mystery governing the universe.

The central focus of shamanism is the vital human contact with a transphenomenal power that it achieves by specialized techniques. The community that supports the shaman looks beyond his personal foibles or psychic aberrations. Such disturbances are generally considered necessary as a sign to the community of the unsettling ramifications of any numinous communication. The transvestite propensities of some shamans, their frenzied yells, or their solitary estrangement are often seen as spirit signs that assist the shamans in their ritual. The shaman's journey and his or her communication with the world of sacred power transcends such individual idiosyncrasies. Yet the possible use of such techniques for individual aggrandizement or manipulation of power raises the question of the shaman's dark side.

The egotistical use and control of spiritual power is a constant threat to the positive contribution of the shaman to the tribe. For, while such power is generally considered to be neutral by tribal peoples, the decision to use it for productive or destructive ends is the personal choice of the one who acquires it. Thus even the socalled "white" shamans are sometimes accused of malicious practices. This study focuses primarily on the beneficial aspects of shamans as healers, counselors, and guides. Yet we cannot overlook the dark side of shamanism, because the numinous experience of power, being both awesome and fascinating, sometimes leads its practitioners to ambivalent ends.

Even the extraordinary creative abilities of the shaman must be interpreted within a religious perspective. The shaman's costume and the drums, bells, flutes, and other sacred instruments are used to facilitate the religious encounter. Likewise, rhythmic chanters, the gestures of the shaman, and the entire setting of the ritual are all integral to the religious ceremony. An interpretation that does not see these activities as essentially religious obscures the central meaning of shamanism. Furthermore, the special psychic energies that shamans transmit to their tribes need to be interpreted in religious terms. Such a religious interpretation of shamanism not only demonstrates the importance of the shamanic experience to religious studies but also provides a meaningful context for understanding prior analytical research.

In religious studies of shamanism two methods can be contrasted: the first is phenomenological, the second is theological. The phenomenological method describes the manifestation that a thing considered sacred or religious makes of itself. Religious studies of a phenomenological nature are "concerned to let manifestations of the religious experience speak for themselves rather than to force them into any preconceived scheme."[58] The theological method, as known in the West, proceeds mainly from a given body of scripture that it interprets in consonance with an established tradition. Karl Rahner has further defined theology as "essentially the conscious effort of the Christian to harken to the actual verbal revelation which God has promulgated in history, to acquire a knowledge of it by the methods of scholarship, and to reflect upon its implications."[59]

The study of shamanism has significant implications for both of these fields of religious inquiry. As an ancient spirituality, shamanism provides phenomenological studies with valuable insights into the formative modes of religious experience. As contact with and presentation of a numinous presence, shamanism enriches theological thought in its articulation of the human experience of divine reality. Contemporary religious studies can draw on this resource in rethinking and creatively reexpressing the traditionally honored subjects of theology. Revelation is a case in point. Shamanism generally expresses a revelatory experience of transcendent reality. The archaic revelation of the shaman provides a pattern to aid in interpreting later forms of revelation, particularly that of the prophetic mode.

At the present time the entire field of religious studies is being broadened by an examination of the multiplicity of spiritual traditions within the human community. Included are the religious forms of the so-called higher civilizations as well as those of the tribal cultures. The more explicated traditions have been extensively influenced by one another and also by their interactions with earlier spiritualities. Yet formal academic study of theology in the West is just beginning to absorb and reflect upon the data from the Asian religions. The Oriental traditions are now providing essential source material for theological thinking concerning such themes as divinity, creation, the human condition, revelation, faith, sacrifice, sacraments, grace, incarnation, redemption, sacred community, spiritual perfection, and final beatitude.

While the volume of Western writing on Asian religions is large, and its influence is already evident, the scholarship on the tribal religious experience of the shaman, though extensive, has been given less attention. Yet many of the more important religious influences in recent times are taking place in the unconscious depths of the human psyche. Revealed in dreams and symbols that are akin to those of the tribal religions, these experiences cannot be fully explained by strictly rational principles. A broader view and a variety of methods are required.

The contribution of shamanism in the formation of the higher traditions is thus a subject of singular importance. Two observations present themselves immediately. First, there is the receptivity of a shamanic community to the introduction of the higher religions founded on a sacred personality. That is, a society that is already attuned to the mediation of the shamanic person is prepared to receive the healing message of a particular religious founder. Second, the characteristics of a shaman provide a compendium of traits found in tribal wisdom traditions. These traits have already been identified in religious founders such as Buddha. Pictured with an herb in his hand as a babe just come from the womb, he is called the "great medicine man."[60] Similarly, in the Chinese Confucian tradition the virtue of social responsibility is expressed by the term *ju,* which was used in ancient China to describe the shaman's advice given in divination.[61] Thus the Confucian scholar may have assumed the communal responsibility that was previously characteristic of the ancient diviner-shaman. While the shamanic personality is not proposed as the origin or source of these later religious and spiritual developments, it is suggested that studies of shamanistic phenomena provide an insight into the nature of religious experience both before and after the formation of the traditional, civilizational religions.

It was the Sophist Protagoras who said that man is the measure of all things. Now, however, in more ecologically minded times, we are becoming aware that the basic religious questions are those concerning the origin, structure, and function of the cosmos itself and the place of human beings within this emergent process. In this new appreciation of the relationship of religion to cosmology, the study of shamanism assumes a particular significance. The shaman interprets cosmological mysteries through ritual reenactment of his initiating experience. Thus any true understanding of shamanism requires an ecological perspective that has been obscured by the modern emphasis on mechanical processes based on our technological inventions.

Beyond Ethnology

Shamanism is not only characteristic of tribal peoples but also is an ongoing and irreducible mode of experiencing the sacred that is not limited to a particular ethnic group. Consequently, though the ethnological reports are valuable, the data reported require further interpretation. As a critical method for such an inquiry into the religious meaning of shamanism, this study has relied on a cultural-historical investigation of ethnographic material. From this investigation certain patterns of shamanic experience have been phenomenologically derived that are helpful in examining the power to which the shaman responds.

As a context for the experience of vital and necessary spiritual power, shamanism has a certain attraction for our times, when the more sophisticated, or more rationalized, modes of religious life are often so weak that they no longer communicate the power needed by contemporary man, who must resolve a new and overwhelming set of tensions in a creative manner. We experience in contemporary society a radical reassessment of institutionalized religion. Concurrent with the weakening of religious structures as they pertain to the individual and the community, there is a loss of efficacy in the rituals that formerly communicated a sustaining energy to individuals and to the community. With the rise of technology the natural world was considered a reality to be exploited under the rubric of progress. No longer valorized in ritual activity or recognized as integrally present in the natural world, numinous power was often inappropriately channeled into tangential, if not aberrant, forms. Those forms, lacking both historical and cosmological bases, tend to sustain themselves by a cultish emotionalism.

With the breakdown of traditional religious structures we find also a willingness to practice spiritual techniques that are not traditionally associated with conventional churches. These paths are no longer seen simply as exotic or Oriental but as viable alternatives readily available to contemporary society. Their practitioners are not always vague, cultish groups; instead they may be established religious movements, such as Krishna Consciousness, transcendental meditation, the Bahai faith, and Tibetan and Zen Buddhism.[62] The use of psychedelics and other consciousness expanding drugs has also created the need for an interpretation and critical evaluation of these altered states sometimes associated with religious experience.

This widespread contemporary religious search has produced several analytical interpretations. Anthony Wallace has utilized the term "revitalization movements" to describe "the deliberate, organized attempts by some members of a society to construct a more satisfying culture by rapid acceptance of a pattern of multiple innovations."[63] Victor Turner speculates on the liminal nature of contemporary splinter communities and interprets their positive function as a social dialectic.[64] Using the insights of Van Gennep and Turner, Raymond Prince likens the contemporary metaphysical climate to that of nineteenth-century Neo-Transcendentalism. He believes that these conditions can be considered as a "cocoonlike" stage in preparation for a new social order.[65]

This is but a cross section of the various explanations for the current experimentation with new modes of encounter with a transphenomenal reality. The search for a sustaining energy that can vitalize the human order is constant. Indeed, the subjective origin of religion seems to be largely a response to the fundamental inadequacy of human beings to deal with existence in an effective way. There is a need to establish a continuing relationship with a pervasive trans-earthly, as well as intra-earthly, power. We begin to realize that in such a dynamic relationship there is a potential for sacred manifestation in every earthly phenomena.[66]

Tribal peoples have long looked to the natural world for the experience of numinous power. The shaman looks to the earth for his vision of power and often contacts vital energies for his tribe through earth symbols. The Dakota shaman Lame Deer wrote:

> In order to be a medicine man one should find the visions there, in nature. To the west a man has the power from the buffalo. From the north he gets the power from the thunder beings. From the east his strength comes from the spirit horse and the elk. From the south he has the ghost power. From above, from the sky, he will receive the wisdom of the great eagle. From beneath, from the earth, he will receive the mother's food. This is the way to become a *wicasa wakan* [holy man, shaman] to learn the secret language, to speak about sacred things, to work with the stones and herbs, to use the pipe.[67]

Contemporary mystical personalities are beginning to re-discover this sense of relatedness to the earth, and, with this revalorization of natural processes, shamanism acquires a special significance. For shamanism acquaints us with particular experiences of sacred power as it manifests itself in the natural world. Although we must acknowledge that the experience of such power may be beyond description, we still can attempt to explain it and the responses that it evokes from humans. The meaning of shamanism lies in the depths of the human psyche, which is not yet fully known to itself but is partially manifest in particular human efforts to structure symbols as a way of knowing.

The following chapter presents ethnographic material on the classical shamanism of Siberia in order to develop some interpretative patterns of examination of the shaman's religious function. In subsequent chapters these patterns are applied to ethnographic data on North American Ojibway shamanism to provide a context for understanding the shamanic personality. Within the Ojibway tribe the shamanism that was an accepted mode of spiritual experience before contact with European civilization survives into the present. Several types of shamanism are evident in the tribe, many of which have passed through a sequence of transformations during the historical period.

2

SIBERIAN SHAMANISM

"MAN cannot rest content with mere life: he must seek sacred life, replete with Power."[1] The quest for sacred life is, indeed, at the heart of the human venture; the recurring contact with numinous power gives to life a mysterious richness amidst suffering and a meaningful direction amidst ambiguity. In both tribal and technological societies this sustaining power comes to the community through particular people, places, times, and events. The shaman is such a person who communicates numinous power in a particular manner. He is thus analogous to other religious personalities, such as the priest, prophet, yogi, or sage, who find communal support because of their ability to mediate between the source of power and their own community. The shaman is likewise an ancient religious personality who transmits a special power that is efficacious in the social system.

In describing the formation and function of the shaman, this chapter examines certain patterns that recur in shamanic activity: cosmology, tribal sanction, ritual reenactment, and trance experience. These patterns, which are exemplified in the classical shamanism of Siberia, are not presented to describe shamanism by means of limited categories. Rather, they are intended as a way of elucidating the religious dimension of shamanism.

Several factors suggest the Siberian experience as a basis for investigating these religious patterns. There is an extensive ethnographic literature on Siberia in which particular shamanic rituals are recorded. As indicated above, the ethnographic and anthropological research on Siberia has so influenced other regional studies that Siberian shamanism has been called "classical shamanism." Furthermore, because of the widely accepted hypothesis that Native American peoples emigrated from North Asia, an investigation of the Siberian shaman is helpful in understanding North American Indian shamanic activities. These American shamanic experiences are significant because these tribal societies are entering into a self-reflective stage after being confronted by modern technological society. Thus the American Indians are bringing this ancient religious experience to the emerging theological dialogue.[2]

The Tribal Picture

The many tribes in Siberia, their movements, and origin are the subject of an extensive literature, which we merely note. Yet it will be helpful to have a general familiarity with the prominent Siberian tribes and their locations. Siberia occupies the area from the Ural Mountains to the Pacific Ocean and from the arctic regions to a line that roughly coincides with the 50° north latitude, that is, approximately one-quarter of the continent of Asia. The region is divided into four subregions based on the presence of different races, languages, and geographical formations.[3]

Western Siberia extends from the Ural Mountains to the Yenisey River. It differs greatly from the frozen stretches in the north, as it extends south through swampy tundra, marginal forests, mountains, and the wind-blown steppe at Kirghiz. The resident Ostyak, Samoyed, and Nenet groups speak a Finno-Ugric language. Also in this region are the Turkish-speaking tribes of the Altai, Yakut, and Sagay. The shamanism practiced by these tribal groups exhibits local variations that are caused in part by geographic and climatic differences.

The central region of Siberia comprises the vast area between the Yenisey and Kolyma rivers. This region of

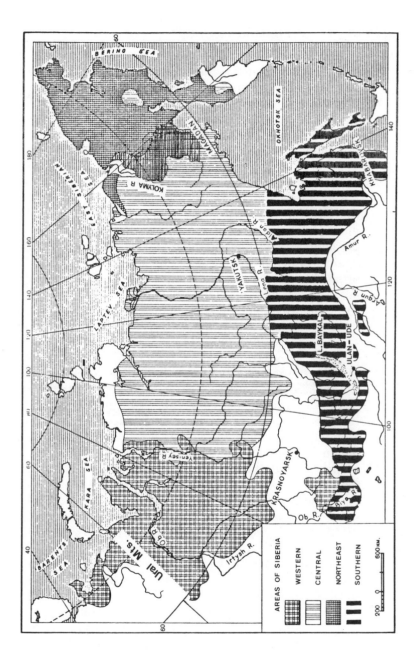

great rivers is much older geologically than the western Siberian land mass. Large stretches of fir forest link the tundra to the *tayga,* the grassy regions of bushes, dwarf birch, and willow trees. Like western Siberia, the central region has both newly arrived tribes, Neo-Siberians, and remnants of the more ancient peoples, Paleo-Siberians. The former include the Yakut and Tungus tribal groups, both of which have extensive subdivisions. The Paleo-Siberians are the Yukaghur and some Chukchee groups. Both the Neo- and the Paleo-Siberian peoples have intermarried.

The northeast region of Siberia, from the Kolyma River to the Bering Strait, includes the Kamchatka Peninsula. Cold, ice, and snow mark this area, and its forms of shamanism reveal the climatic adaptations of the resident Paleo-Siberian people. Their names are well documented in ethnographic research as the Chukchee, the Koryak, the Kamchadal, and the Asiatic Eskimo.

The southern region of Siberia includes the steppes west of Lake Baykal and extends eastward to the Amur River and Sakhalin Island. This area is warmer than the rest of Siberia, though it also is subject to dramatic climatic changes during the winter months. Lake Baykal is the heart of the region. In the west are the prominent Mongolian divisions of the Buryat, while in the east Tungus-Manchu tribal divisions predominate. Paleo-Siberian and Ainu peoples are located in the Amur and Sakhalin areas, where shamanism is still practiced. Indeed, in several reports it is often the only religious activity mentioned by pre-Soviet ethnographers.

While shamanism in Siberia is intertribal, each tribe has developed unique forms. Both the widespread presence of shamanism and its particularized traits in different tribes testify to its antiquity:

> The manner of distribution of a trait in a given territory can truly serve as an important indicator of its relative antiquity. Indeed, as a rule, ancient traits have a compact distribution. . . .

Compactedness does not in itself represent sufficient evidence of antiquity. We may assign antiquity to a trait only if, while occurring in a compact distribution, i.e., being distributed widely and continuously over a territory, it combines in various locations with other traits which differ from one another.[4]

Shamanism is such a compact phenomena among the Siberian tribes, though each local expression has distinct nuances. Currently, analysis of ethnographic and archaeological data ascribes the earliest shamanistic evidence to the transition period between the Neolithic and the Bronze Ages, approximately 6,000 to 2,000 B.C.[5] It may be possible, using the arguments of Karl J. Narr, Hans Findeisen, and others to push back this speculative date to an even earlier Paleolithic period.[6] Regardless of such specific dates, however, shamanism can undoubtedly be considered as early or archaic in its Siberian manifestations.

The Milieu of Shamanism

Although shamanic rituals are widespread among the Siberian tribes, the origin of shamanism is beyond the horizon of our present research. In addition, the historic manifestations of shamanism exhibit so marked a development that the ethnographic literature itself reflects a morphology of shamanism. In this first section we examine the cosmological milieu that gives rise to shamanism amidst cultural diversity.

It has been suggested that "animism forms the milieu of shamanism."[7] Undoubtedly, the animated spirit-world is an essential element of the shaman's dealings with the transphenomenal world. Yet the plethora of tribal spirits can be very confusing to the investigator unless a more comprehensive world view is formulated. Such a perspective is to be found in the tribe's cosmology, that is, their explanation of the world and its origins.

In the Siberian Yakut cosmology, called *olonkho,* the tribal singers, the *olonkhosut,* chant the epic tales that relate this tribe's understanding of the cosmic order.[8] The *olonkhosut* sing of three worlds: the upper world, or heaven; the middle world, or earth; and the lower, or under, world. The epic's emphasis, however, is on the earth, the beautiful middle region:

> The expanse across is unknowable — a broad and radiant country. The distance is unknowable — a limitless prospect of earth. . . . No shadows are visible — bright lakes; the milky lakes are covered with foam; the soil there is curds; the salt-flats stores of milk; the black boulders, oil with sour milk; the forest lakes of butter; the mountains of intestinal fat; the cliffs of lard.
>
> There is no winter, but summer reigns forever, in that country. There are no nights, but bright day stands always in that country.
>
> The sun never sets there, nor is the moon extinguished.[9]

The idealized images of a pristine earth are vibrant in that description. Moreover, this middle earth is not seen as the playground of chthonic spirits or ethereal gods. Instead, the lively images are all supportive of human needs and endeavors. The moment and manner of creation remains a mystery, but it is apparent that the middle earth itself is considered a blessing for humans.

Located at the center of the Yakut cosmology is the Tree of Life. This sacred tree unites the three worlds of the Yakut *olonkho*. Its roots reach down into the cold and filth of the underworld and bend back to the local spirits of the earth. The trunk is firmly established in the middle earth, while the branches rise up through tiers of heavens to the Yakut high gods. The Cosmic Tree symbolizes the flow of energy which sustains life on the middle earth:

> Nourished with the juices of this tree,
> Bathing in its enlivening flow,
> The weak grow strong,
> They grow, the small filled out,
> The sickly were made whole.
> Such was the purpose
> Of that, for the happiness of the living

Created, blessed
Regal tree.[10]

As we turn from the Yakut cosmology to their shamanic practice, a striking association is immediately apparent. Yakut shamans maintain close symbolic relations with the Cosmic Tree. The ancestral-shaman, a spirit personality, who initially chooses the Yakut shaman, is said to reside in the roots of a selected birch tree. This birch is given to the novice by elder shamans as his personal power symbol of contact with the Cosmic Tree.[11] The Yakut shaman's drum is commonly cut from a tree that has been struck by lightning.[12] Having been marked as extraordinary, the tree's wood provides an appropriate drum with which to ascend to the upper heavens or descend into the underworld. In these two examples, the spirit-ancestor tree and the ceremonial drum, a significant relation is established between the shaman and the Cosmic Tree.

The identification of the Yakut shaman with the Cosmic Tree finds further affirmation in his or her ceremonial costume, but with a different emphasis. The shaman's garb is heavy with iron discs and pendants, which make of the dress a jangling instrument as the shaman dances. The most important of these multivalent pendants is the *amagyat.* This copper plate with a man's figure in the middle symbolizes the shaman's ancestor-spirit and his or her contact with the mysterious regions. "The shaman can see and hear only with the help of his *amagyat*," said the Yakut shaman Tiuspiut.[13] It is handed down through generations of Yakut shamans. Its significance on the shaman's costume can be compared to a bird perched in the Cosmic Tree capable of flight to other regions. Indeed, the Yakut shaman's costume displays a complete bird skeleton of iron, amplifying this flight symbolism.[14] The shaman not only is symbolic of the Cosmic Tree but also performs the same function in the tribe's cosmology. Like the Tree of Life, the Yakut shaman's flight, or journey, maintains the relationship between the cosmic worlds.

As a human embodiment of the Cosmic Tree, the Yakut shaman functions in a highly symbolic manner as he points toward the other world, the world of spiritual power. Through ritual contacts with an ancestor-spirit the shaman evokes an efficacious power. In a very real sense, it is not the shaman alone or his activities in themselves that are, strictly speaking, religious, but the manner in which the shaman is able to connect the audience to cosmological power. "For the religious significance of an event," Ernst Cassirer wrote, "depends no longer on its content but solely on its form: what gives it its character as a symbol is not what it is and whence it immediately comes but the spiritual aspect in which it is seen, the relation to the universe which it obtains in religious feeling and thought."[15]

Thus, in this cosmic perspective, the Yakut shaman's function can be understood as intimately related to the tribal world view, for he or she communicates in a special manner between orders of reality. The first shamanic pattern to be identified is the presence of symbols of the tribal world view that create an appropriate milieu for shamanism. The Yakut story of the universe, which relates the interaction of the primal creative energies, is mediated through the shaman's contact with the numinous spirits. By evocation of these cosmologic mysteries the shaman transmits a healing and vitalizing energy.

The Shaman and the Tribe

The shaman's evocation of sacred power is achieved within the community. Shamans are formed by their particular cultural traditions, in as much as they draw on their cosmology, mythology, ritual, and symbols. They also help form tribal tradition through their own creative experiences. The shaman's personal call, subsequent retreat into meditative solitude, individuated trance state, and liminal stance toward the tribe are all indicative of his creative vocation. In this sense, the interior path of the shaman has certain parallels with that of the contemplative mystic. The difference is that a shaman's inner contemplative state finds expression in shamanic ritual rather than mystical union. And, ultimately, it is by the sanction of the tribe that the shaman's numinous experience achieves an efficacious form.

The mode of expression whereby the shaman relates to the social system is not standardized or ritually fixed. Rather it is a fluid response to certain critical situations. Of the Yakut tribe it has been said, "Shamanism is not the faith or religion of the Yakuts, but an independent set of actions which takes place in certain definite cases."[16] The tribal spokesperson here was not being obscure but was stating the tribal view of the healing event, namely, that the shaman calls on certain independent sets of rituals to respond to a variety of tribal needs.

The shaman purposely maintains a liminal stance in relation to the tribe in order to deal with a multiplicity of needs. Such a stance on the periphery of tribal activities allows the distance necessary for the healing vision. Yet the distance between a community and their shaman must be bridged before the flow of healing power can take place. The connection is of a practical nature for both the shaman and the community. The shaman establishes his or her vocation as a mediator of power, a position that is often rewarded by social prestige, while the community finds an interpretative instrument for its spiritual needs as it channels tribal energies into the shaman's creative art.

The tribe's sanction of the shaman is evident in its early recognition of the vocation of a potential shaman. In some tribes a formal initiation marks the tribe's approval of the shaman's personal rite of passage. In addition, the shaman's accessories provide a dramatic means by which the tribal audience can affirm and participate in the shaman's visionary experience.

Recognition of a potential shaman signified to the Mongolian Buryat the continued presence of spirit power within the tribe. The Buryat believed that a young shaman-to-be was educated by the spirits during periods of unconsciousness:

Usually the dead ancestors who were shamans choose from their living kinsfolk a boy who is to inherit their power. This child is marked with special signs: he is often thoughtful, fond of solitude, a seer of prophetic visions, subject occasionally to fits, during which he is unconscious. The Buryats believe that at such a time the boy's soul is with the spirits who are teaching him, if he is to be a white shaman, with the western spirits, if he is to be a black shaman, with the eastern spirits. . . . After enduring trials, the soul returns to the body. Year by year the tendency of the mind becomes more pronounced; the youth begins to have fits of ecstasy, dreams and swoons become more frequent; he sees spirits, leads a restless life, wanders about from village to village and tries to *kam* (shamanize).[17]

Seemingly lost and estranged from his tribe, the restless shaman wanders at the edge of his society. At this stage, he or she alternately experiences the reality of the tribal world and the dreamlike reality of the spirits. This ambiguous formative period is considered a crisis not only for the Buryat youth but also for the tribe. Regardless of whether the youth contacts harmful or beneficial spirits, the shaman's encounter with the numinous forces will enable the tribe to deal with crisis situations.

Such a crucial relationship between the shaman and the tribe is also typical of the Tungus peoples, who considered the death of their shaman a terrifying event. At the moment when the "spirit-watchmen" *(etan)* of the clan dissolved, evil forces were believed to be unleashed against the land and the tribe.[18] Only with the restoration of a new shamanic personality could this chaos be overcome and order be restored.

The most obvious sanction of a shaman is in the form of a tribal initiation. Having recognized the early visionary experiences, the tribe approves the shaman in his or her vocation:

The consecration of a Yakut shaman is accompanied by certain ceremonies. The old shaman leads his pupil up a high mountain or into a clearing in the forest. Here he dresses him in a shaman's garment, gives him a rattle, and places on one side of him nine chaste youths, and on the other nine chaste maidens. Then the shaman puts on his own garment, and directs the youth to repeat after him certain words. He demands of the novice that he shall give up all that is most dear to him in the world, and consecrate his life to the service of the spirits who shall come at his call. He tells his pupil where certain "black" spirits dwell, what diseases they cause, and how they may be propitiated.[19]

In this Yakut initiation the new shaman is not invested with drum, dress, or incantations. Instead, an elder shaman performs his personal ritual ceremony with the younger candidate. The two go together on an ecstatic journey in which the elder points out the topography of the mysterious regions.[20] This later initiation is a Yakut rite of passage acknowledging the shaman's earlier numinous encounter.

The shaman's accessories also reflect his or her paradoxical relationship of intimacy and distance with the tribe. The shaman's primary objects are his costume and drum. Both are sources of instruction and inspiration for the tribe, and both are highly symbolic of the shaman's spirit relations.[21] The costume, for example, can only be used by a particular shaman,[22] and the spirits will not listen to a shaman who neglects to wear his coat. When a shaman takes up his dress, he "receives supernatural power, which allows him to go to the upper and under worlds to meet spirits and deal with them."[23] An exact interpretation of the shaman's accessories requires some knowledge of the shaman's personal encounter with the numinous world. In fact, the symbolism of the shaman's dress instructs the audience that the wearer is one who has died and been brought back to life by the spirits. The movement of the costume is more than a musical event; it joins with the drum to produce an entrancing atmosphere for both the

A shaman of the Soyot, or Tuvinian, people of western Siberia, circa 1917. He is shown in shamanic costume, holding his drum. His bearing reminds one of Waldemar Bogoras's comment that the eyes of a shaman are "very bright, which gives them the ability to see 'spirits' even in the dark. It is certainly a fact that the expression of a shaman is peculiar—a combination of cunning and shyness; and it is often possible to pick him out from among many others" (The Chukchee, p. 116). Photograph courtesy of the Smithsonian Institution National Anthropological Archives.

shaman and the audience. The shamanic accessories thau-
maturgically recreate the drama of the shaman's sacred
encounter with the spirits. The reciprocity of the shaman
in trance with the entranced audience is central to the
shamanistic event. The costume, drum, and other accessories are essential aids both to the tribe and to the shaman
in structuring this mutually healing event.

This pattern of tribal sanction is the means whereby
the tribe approves the shaman's healing ceremony and
makes it available to the community. In the Siberian ethnographic data there is evidence of tribal recognition of a
young shaman, ceremonial initiation to acknowledge a shaman's vocation, and ritualistic approval of a shaman's costume and other artifacts. In Siberia these forms of tribal
approval effectively bridge the gap between the individual
shaman and the community.

The Numinous Encounter and Its Reenactment

The types of "calls" that bring a person to the shamanic
vocation are extremely varied among the many Siberian
tribes. The shaman may be chosen directly by the spirits.
On the other hand, he or she may inherit the ancestral-
spirit of a deceased member of the family or clan who
had been a shaman. There is also mention of self-made
shamans, though they seem to be a later development and
are considered to be lesser, or even fraudulent, shamans.
The distinguishing characteristic of the shaman's call is his
numinous encounter.

The direct call from the spirits to an unsuspecting person is generally recognized as a legitimate contact with
animating power in the universe. Strangely, the contact
with numinous power often produces an illness, whose
cure instigates the shamanic vocation. The following describes the call of the Yakut shaman Tiuspiut:

When I was twenty years old, I became very ill and began
"to see with my eyes, to hear with my ears" that which others

did not hear or see; nine years I struggled with myself, and I did not tell any one what was happening to me, as I was afraid that people would not believe me and would make fun of me. At last I became so seriously ill that I was on the verge of death; but when I started to shamanize I grew better; and even now when I do not shamanize for a long time I am liable to be ill.[24]

In this brief passage the salient features of the shamanic encounter with the numinous world are described. In illness Tiuspiut experiences confused images and chaotic forms that trouble and intimidate him. He appears to have been isolated gradually from the necessary solace of human contact and consequently becomes seriously ill. When he begins to shamanize, he experiences a healing. His confused sight and disordered hearing are thus given a meaningful direction.

A similar example can be seen in the Turkish-Sagay shaman Kyzlasov, who related his initial shamanistic experience to the Hungarian researcher Vilmos Dioszegi[25]:

I have been sick and I have been dreaming. In my dreams I had been taken to the ancestor and cut into pieces on a black table. They chopped me up and then threw me into the kettle and I was boiled. There were some men there: two black and two fair ones. Their chieftain was there too. He issued the orders concerning me. I saw all this. While the pieces of my body were boiled, they found a bone around the ribs, which had a hole in the middle. This was the excess bone. This brought about my becoming a shaman. Because, only those men can become shamans in whose body such a bone can be found. One looks across the hole of this bone and begins to see all, to know all and, that is when one becomes a shaman. . . . When I came to from this state, I woke up. This meant that my soul had returned. Then the shamans declared: "You are the sort of man who may become a shaman. You should become a shaman, you must begin to shamanize."[26]

Like many of his fellow shamans of Siberia, Kyzlasov's passive call was preceded by an illness. During this debilitating period he experienced the dream-vision that presaged his shamanic vocation. In no manner, however, were Kyzlasov's own efforts instrumental in securing his vocation. Healing came from a wholly other source. From a weak pathetic state he was revitalized by the spirits, in sleep he was given increased awareness, and from a bone that was formerly useless he received the power of penetrating sight.

The remaking of Kyzlasov was a central theme in his shamanic vision. In front of his ancestral-shaman Kyzlasov was "cut into pieces." This fragmented, dismembered state paralleled his illness. Through such a dismemberment a shaman was sacrificed and was therefore able to feel an identity with the suffering of the larger tribal community. Kyzlasov said, "You must take up shamanism so as not to suffer."[27] Thus Kyzlasov underwent dismemberment, fed the spirits with his cut-up flesh, and finally received his "excess bone" from his dream torturers. The bone symbolized the permanency of the inner transformative experience that enabled Kyzlasov to heal. When he "looked across" this experience, he began to see in a new way.

The symbolic complexity of Kyzlasov's vision has only been suggested here. A deeper analysis would lie in a cosmological treatment using Sagay ethnographic materials. Nonetheless, a cardinal point in the study of shamanism has been raised. By reflecting on his transformative dream, Kyzlasov was able to give form and order to a chaotic situation. Other Sagay shamans recognized what he had received in his numinous encounter. As a functioning shaman he could then evoke this transformative power for others.

The manner in which the shaman evokes transformative power can be clearly seen in the account of the Sagay shaman's drum.[28] Kyzlasov related that it is not the shaman himself but the ancestral-spirit who chooses the kind of drum that a shaman will use. In addition, the ancestral-spirit also determines its size, the kind of wood used in its construction, the animal skin stretched across it, and the designs painted on it. These instructions are pronounced by elder tribal shamans. The interaction between the new shaman and the established elder shamans provides some tribal control over these individualistic religious personalities. After several preliminary rituals the drum is ceremonially brought to life.

Although the drum might be finished, it is still unusable, first it must be given to a small child to play with for a few days and then the so-called "reviving" ceremony must be performed. The shaman must look for the spirit of the animal which gave its skin to be stretched over the drum. He must follow the path where the animal had wandered, right back to its birthplace, because only there can its spirit be caught. After that the drum "comes to life."[29]

Like most of the Siberian shamans' drums, this percussive instrument is a multivalent symbol for the Sagay. It simultaneously represents the shaman, the patient to be cured, and the spirits who communicate the healing power. The ceremonial construction of the drum parallels the shaman's vision of initiation. Just as the shaman was boiled and "played" by the spirits, so a child ritually plays with the drum. Just as the patient's life history must be known to the shaman, so the spirit of the animal skin stretched across the drum must be traced through its life path. His drum must resonate with this intimate knowledge. Kyzlasov continued:

When I got there, he [the ancestral-shaman], measured my drum, its circumference, its length and its height. He counted the pendants hanging from it. When he was ready, he gave me the men. (The shamans call their spirits "men".) They are my friends. Sometimes they come upon me unexpectedly, then they disappear again. They are rather unstable. It is to them I owe my well-being, it is through them, that when I hold the pulse of a sick person, it becomes clear to me, what is wrong with him. Then I begin to shamanize.[30]

Like Kyzlasov himself, Kyzlasov's drum must be taken to the ancestral shaman for approval and then invested with spirits. The drum becomes the insistent voice of the accomplished shaman, who, on the one hand, has intercourse with powerful supernaturals and, on the other, speaks of the ills that weaken his tribe. Thus, in Sagay shamanism the "reviving" of the drum reenacts the transformative experience of shamanic healing. Just as the patient's original vigor is renewed, so also is the drum invested with its unique energy.

This energy is also used by the shaman to aid his encounter with numinous spirits. When there is no patient to be cured, but an imbalance or loss is to be corrected through divination, the shaman still seeks an encounter with the "wholly other." As Rudolf Otto wrote, "Let us call the faculty, of whatever sort it may be, of *genuinely* cognizing and recognizing the holy in its appearances the faculty of *divination*."[31] The shaman's function is not only to heal but also to evoke the power to discern the meaning of particular tribal events. The drum is used by the shaman at each of these healing or divinatory ceremonies. For the drum has a central role in creating the transformative mood for the patient and the shaman. The repetitive beat of the drum effects the passage into the numinous world. In discussing ceremonial events in which instruments are used to establish contact with the spirits, Rodney Needham observes:

What is it that these events have in common? Obviously that they are *rites de passage*. In other words, the class of noise makers is associated with the formal passage from one status or condition to another. Once again, though, I am not saying that such rites cannot be accomplished without percussive noise makers, or that only such devices are used to mark them, but simply that there is a constant and immediately recognizable association between the type of sound and the type of rite. What I am proposing, namely, is that there is a significant connection between percussion and transition.[32]

Through a rhythmic drumming, then, the shaman induces a trance state in which he begins to evoke transformative powers. The drum is both symbolic of the shaman's initial passage and the instrument for reenacting that rite of passage.

The dimensions of this trance reenactment in shamanism have been developed by other researchers. For example, Claude Lévi-Strauss describes the experience of the shaman by using the psychoanalytic term *abreaction:*

> The shaman does not limit himself to reproducing or miming certain events. He actually relives them in all their vividness, originality, and violence. And since he returns to his normal state at the end of the seance, we may say, borrowing a key term from psychoanalysis, that he *abreacts.* In psychoanalysis, abreaction refers to the decisive moment in the treatment when the patient intensively relives the initial situation from which his disturbance stems, before he ultimately overcomes it. In this sense, the shaman is a professional abreactor.[33]

According to Lévi-Strauss, when the shaman abreacts, he relives the patient's problems not his own initial experiences. The difference between Lévi-Strauss's abreaction and the reenactment pattern described here is one of emphasis. The shamanic ceremony is, in both cases, a transformative experience. What is proposed here is that the shaman depends upon the help of the spirits even for what Lévi-Strauss labels abreaction. The "journey" to the source of the patient's illness cannot take place unless the shaman has undergone the initial trauma of his own dismemberment and the subsequent healing experience. This initial trauma establishes his relationship with certain helpful spirits. Thus the shaman evokes his spirits by reenacting his initial call.

The Shamanic Trance

The effectiveness of the shaman lies in his ability to enter into the trance state. It is not merely the pathos of his initiation, the tribal cosmologic symbols of his dress, or his dramatic thaumaturgy that make the shaman efficacious. Authenticity for the shaman means establishing contact with the powerful spirits. Consequently, trance is the technique that most distinguishes the authentic shaman. It is through his entrancing vision that the shaman transmits healing energies.

The crucial moment of the shamanic ritual is the shaman's encounter with the spirits. Indeed, the spirits are often so overwhelming that certain precautions are taken to prevent total disruption of the ceremony:

> In the northern part of the Yakut district the host chooses the best latchets (straps) and forms them into a loop, which is placed round the shaman's shoulders and held by one of those present during the dance, in order to prevent the spirits from carrying him off.[34]

The striking figure of the restrained and costumed shaman undoubtedly fixes the attention of the tribal audience on his role as mediator of the spirit presences. Rhythmic drumming, ritual chanting, and the jangling pendants of the shaman's dress heightened the tense atmosphere of the ceremony. Before the expectant audience, the shaman gradually passes into an altered state, in which he identifies himself with the power that he evokes:

> The shaman slowly takes off his shirt and puts on his wizard's coat. . . . The music swells and rises to the highest pitch, the beating of the drum becomes more and more vigorous, until the two sounds combine in one long-drawn crescendo. The numberless small bells ring and clang, it is not a storm—it is a whole cascade of sounds, enough to overwhelm all the listeners . . .; at last, the voice of the shaman chants the following obscure fragments:
>
> "Mighty bull of the earth . . . Horse of the steppe!"
> "I, the mighty bull . . . bellow!"
> "I, the horse of the steppe . . . neigh!"
> "I, the man set above all other beings!"

"I, the man most gifted of all!"
"I, the man created by the master all-powerful. . . ."[35]

Such a chant is not an expression of egoistic pathology; rather, here the shaman in trance becomes the autoplastic molder of himself. The shaman sheds his ordinary identity to pass through a succession of impersonations. He becomes the spirits to whom he calls for supernatural aid, the patient who seeks healing, the drum that is fragmented and reassembled, and the entranced seer of appropriate techniques for healing.

The trance, as presented in this Yakut shaman's ceremony, becomes a deeply meditative activity, as the shaman enters into a profound communion with both a numinous reality and the patient who is being treated. Mediating between the two realities, he or she invokes the symbolic presences of the ecstatic vision, trying to induce these power configurations across the threshold of the shamanic imagination into the healing atmosphere. Thus the trance is a type of fluid meditation that is constantly reshaped to evoke the encountered power.

One of the most puzzling aspects of the trance state is the shaman's communion with the spirits:

In the ensuing prayers the shaman addresses his *amagyat* and other protective "spirits"; he talks with the *kaliany*, asks them questions, and gives answers in their names. Sometimes the shaman must pray and beat the drum a long time before the spirits come; often their appearance is so sudden and so impetuous that the shaman is overcome and falls down. . . .

When the *amagyat* comes down to a shaman he arises and begins to leap and dance. . . . Those who hold him by the leather thongs sometimes have great difficulty in controlling his movements.[36]

The trance swoon and the ecstatic dance bring the shaman into intimate contact with the mysterious spirits. No one interpretation can entirely explain what *spirit* means to the Yakut shaman or, indeed, any shaman. The spirits are continually described as mysterious and revelatory, alternately fascinating and repelling. That the spirits are tied to tribal cosmology and thus to the historical reality of the tribe is readily acknowledged. The historical and sociological implications of the spirit presence vary with each tribe. What we seek here is the comprehensive religious meaning that we may ascribe to the particular developments. In this sense, the Yakut shaman provides us with a context for interpretation in his trance encounter:

At last he knows all he desires; he is acquainted with the cause of the misfortune or disease with which he has been striving; he is sure of the help of the beings whose aid he needs. Circling about in his dance, singing he approaches the patient.

With new objurations he drives away the cause of the illness by frightening it, or by sucking it out with his mouth from the painful place: then, returning to the middle of the room he drives it away by spitting and blowing.[37]

The trance encounter of the shaman is the accumulation of an intuitive knowledge, a way of seeing. The deeply unconscious trance state and the encounter with powerful spirits have a practical result, namely diagnosis and treatment. The shaman's healing techniques are appropriate to the individual illness. For example, tube-sucking may be used to draw out physical objects, herbal remedies for internal imbalances, and sudden trauma for psychic depression.[38] These therapies arise out of the shaman's trance dialogue with the archetypal spirits.

The healing trance draws on the shaman's own early initiation experience. Shamans are able to constellate the psychic elements of spirit power that healed them and transmit those energies in the trance state. Their extraordinary impact on the tribe is due to their ability to induce an unconscious state, or trance, that communicates a healing and revitalizing energy.

The discussion above distinguishes four significant patterns in the Siberian shamanic experience: a particular world view, tribal sanction, ritual reenactment, and trance experience. Yet this chapter by no means exhausts the possible patterns to be found in Siberian shamanism. Rather, from selected sources, it presents some of the more salient patterns that elucidate the formation and function of the shaman. Also it is apparent from this sampling that shamans play an indispensable role in the religious life of tribal Siberia. While they are not the only religious functionaries in any of the tribes, they can be described as centering personalities.

The person and the art of the shaman are a concrescence of the Siberian peoples' encounter with a numinous reality, but the patterns that are shaped by the Siberian context are not limited to that ethnographic area. Rather, they suggest ways of interpreting shamanic practices in other cultures and in other historical periods. They give us a cosmological, sociological, anthropological, and psychological means of understanding this ancient religious experience.

The first pattern, the tribal cosmology, defines the animated milieu in which shamanism arises. Shamanism is formed from the particular tribe's understanding of the relationship between the living and life-giving worlds. The phenomenal and the spiritual realms are seen as interlaced rather than completely distinct from one another. Thus, in investigating a specific shamanism, one must first examine its mythical world view. The second pattern, tribal sanction, constitutes a sociology of shamanism, for the shaman functions in a particular relationship with his or her society rather than apart from it. While often transforming his society through creative activity, the shaman is inseparable from his particular tradition and culture. Indeed, the shaman's expression of his society is validated by his society's approval of his religious function. The third pattern, the reenactment of the shaman's numinous encounter, gives us an anthropological perspective on shamanism. Here we see the human condition understood as the ac-

cumulation of primal power that must be ritually reinter-
preted by the shaman. Tribal activities, such as hunting
and herding, are directed with the help of powerful spirits
evoked in particular ceremonies. So also are sickness and
guilt alleviated through the intervention of vital energy
in ritual. The pattern of ritual reenactment thus highlights
the basic resonance between the shaman and the tribe.
The final pattern, the shaman's trance encounter with the
spirits, relies on a psychological method, as the psychic
realities that convey sustaining power are contacted in
profoundly altered states of consciousness. In order to adequately appreciate the archetypal dimension of the shaman's experience, a psychological framework is indispensable.

Thus we can approach shamanism from a cosmological
perspective, from a sociological perspective, from an anthropological perspective, and from a psychological perspective. Each perspective functions in relation to the other,
allowing a comprehensive picture of the shaman's religious
role to emerge.

3

OJIBWAY SHAMANISM AND ITS HISTORICAL BACKGROUND

THE Ojibway, one of the largest tribes on the North American continent, are located in the woodlands of the Great Lakes region. This chapter presents the historical background of Ojibway shamanism and the religious milieu in which their shamanic vocations and techniques arise. In the four following chapters Ojibway shamanism and its religious functions are further investigated by applying the patterns of cosmology, tribal sanction, ritual reenactment, and trance experience derived from the classical context of Siberian shamanism.

Despite centuries of interaction between the Ojibway and Euro-American cultures, detailed knowledge of this tribe is limited. Until recently the Ojibway survived in remote, isolated groups that were protected from intrusive cultural influences. The first field studies of an anthropological nature were conducted in the 1930s, when A. I. Hallowell and Ruth Landes began their research. As late as 1939, Alfred Kroeber could write that the Apache and the Ojibway were "the least known" of the surviving North American groups.[1]

While a voluminous literature describes earlier contacts by various missionaries, traders, military officers, and travelers, the ethnohistory of the Ojibway has only recently been assembled.[2] Henry Schoolcraft, for example, observed the Southeastern Ojibway during the nineteenth century, but the Southwestern and Northern Ojibway remained relatively isolated until recent decades.

The four main divisions of the tribe are described as the Southeastern, Southwestern, Plains, and Northern Ojibway. The Indians in each of those geographical areas are further divided into bands, which range from small family groups to cross-clan villages. While various dialects are spoken in each area, the Algonquian language is common to all Ojibway bands.

The major bands of the Ojibway tribe currently reside in the Great Lakes region of southern Ontario, Michigan, Wisconsin, and Minnesota.[3] In addition, significant bands of Plains Ojibway are located in Manitoba, Saskatchewan, North Dakota, and northeastern Montana.[4] The Ojibway are occasionally called by the name of a particular band, such as the Saulteaux, who received that designation after an early encounter at the falls of Sault Sainte Marie with the French, who thereafter called them the "people of the falls."[5] The Bungi are named from the Ojibway word *punki,* meaning "a little." The name was given them by the traders at York Factory and Fort Severn because they begged supplies.[6] The Leech Lake band are known as the Pillagers from an incident in 1781 when they pillaged a trader's wares.[7] Collectively, the Ojibway are also widely known as the Chippewa, from the name given to the southwestern bands in government treaties.

To clarify our historical presentation, we use three terms to refer to the Ojibway through history. The nomadic tribal ancestors who crossed the Bering Strait and eventually moved toward the Atlantic Ocean are referred to as the *Paleo-Ojibway.* The sedentary stage of Ojibway village life on the Atlantic Coast is designated by the tribal term *Anishinaubag.* The totemic clan villages of the time of the first European contact are called *Proto-Ojibway.* Some of those seasonal villages, located at the Straits of Mackinac in northern Michigan, are identified in Reuben Gold Thwaites's *The Jesuit Relations and Allied Documents.*[8]

The Paleo-Ojibway were part of the "American Indian complex" that Herbert Spinden conjectured was descended from the Mesolithic-Neolithic cultural center at Mal'ta in the Lake Baikal region of Siberia.[9] Soviet anthropologists

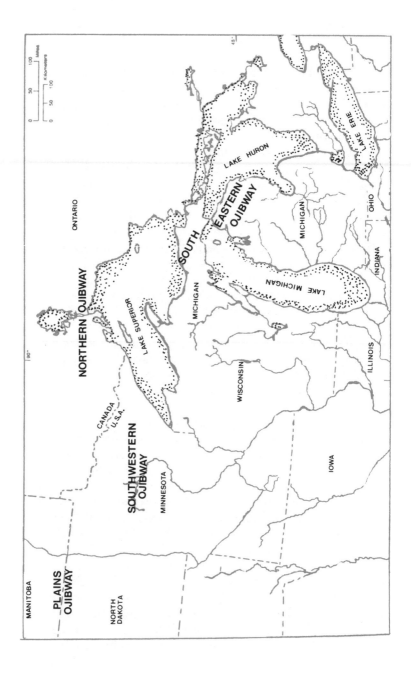

have suggested that the nearby Volgul and Ostyak tribes have physical characteristics similar to those of the Algonquian people.[10] The Paleo-Ojibway were possibly among those early peoples who left archaeological evidence of their presence in North America during the final stages of the Wisconsin glaciation. After a period of nomadic movement following the big game animals, they apparently established their sedentary villages in the eastern woodlands and coastal areas of North America. Archaeological study of early Woodland sites attests to the shift that these peoples made from nomadic to village life.[11] During this period the nomadic hunters abandoned the atlatl and became sedentary groups, who continued to hunt but did so with bows and arrows instead of throwing-sticks. Those village groups left identifiable pottery remains.[12]

Ojibway tribal historian William Warren records the oral tradition of descent from the *Anish-inaubag:*

Respecting their belief of their own first existence, I can give nothing more appropriate than a minute analysis of the name which they have given to their race, *An-ish-in-aub-ag.* This expressive word is derived from *An-ish-aw,* meaning without cause or "spontaneous," and *in-aub-a-we-se,* meaning "the human body." The word, *Anish-inaubag,* therefore, literally translated, signifies "spontaneous man."[13]

The *Anish-inaubag* are described in mythical lore as living in villages along the Atlantic coast. This growth of Neolithic village life was probably accompanied by Woodland cultural developments,[14] many of which are similar to those of widely separated tribes near the polar regions. Some of the shared implements and practices are snow shoes, birchbark canoes, conical lodges, game drives, hunting territories, and skin drums. In addition, certain parallel beliefs can be seen, namely shamanism, bear ceremonialism, scapulimancy, a "soul-loss" theory of illness, and the earth-diver motif in the tribal cosmologies.[15]

These similarities have led to speculation regarding an

archaic culture, which is variously labeled "inland boreal,"[16] "caribou,"[17] or "circumpolar."[18] While these ethnological questions are not directly related to our discussion of Ojibway tribal lore, they do indicate the probable direction of cultural influence on this Woodland tribe. The *Anish-inaubag* seem to have been only minimally influenced by southern cultural developments, among, for example, the Adena, Hopewell, and Temple mound-building peoples. More immediate cultural borrowings, however, took place between the Laurentian Iroquois and the Algonquian village groups.[19]

According to Ojibway oral tradition and the birchbark pictographs of tribal lore, the *Anish-inaubag* suffered an extended plague in their Atlantic coastal towns.[20] A migration took place that separated the Proto-Ojibway, Ottawa, and Pottawatomi from their eastern Algonquian kin. This migration, considered to be a response to a sacred call, is dated at approximately 1400 A.D.[21] By the seventeenth century the Proto-Ojibway had settled in seasonal villages along the streams and rivers that disgorge into the confluence of Lake Superior and Lake Huron. Early contact with European missionaries and traders has preserved the totemic names of several of those villages.

The Proto-Ojibway consolidated their tribal structure as they continued their westward migration from the rapids at Mackinac in Michigan around Lake Superior. This late seventeenth-century migration was undertaken largely because of pressure from tribal bands that were fleeing the devastating expansion of the Iroquois Confederacy. The migration was, however, experienced by the Ojibway not only as a historical expediency but also a continuing sacred call that had been delivered initially to the *Anish-inaubag.*

Two major migrations proceeded around Lake Superior. The Northern Ojibway, usually distinguished as the Bois Fort, Bungi, and Saulteaux bands, settled on the north shore of Lake Superior and on the high plains near Winnepeg, Manitoba. The ruggedness of the often inhospitable country that these bands occupied enabled them to preserve their archaic hunting culture amidst the surrounding Euro-American civilization.

As the Ojibway moved along the south shore of Lake Superior, they encountered stiff resistance from the Ouda-gamie (Fox), Winnebago, and Santee Dakota tribes. The achievements of Ojibway warriors during those two centuries of intermittent warfare forms the core of tribal heroic legends. Indeed, from the struggle over the Indian settlement on La Pointe Island, Wisconsin *(Moning wuna-kaun-ing)*, to the expansion through North Dakota, southern Ontario, and northeastern Montana, the Ojibway demonstrated a tribal élan comparable to that of the Iroquois Confederacy or the Cherokee civilization. Peaceful relations with the governments of the United States and Canada eventually enabled the Ojibway to become the largest American Indian tribe north of Mexico in 1972.[22]

The Religious Milieu

It is not possible to describe fully the particular forms of shamanism during each of the three phases of Ojibway tribal development. Knowledge of shamanistic activity among the Paleo-Ojibway is fragmentary and identifiable only through pictographs and later oral traditions. For material on the religious practices of the *Anish-inaubag,* we rely on tribal traditions and comparative ethnology. In studying the Proto-Ojibway, we enter into the historical period of European records. Although those records are often biased in their theological perspective and limited in their presentations of Ojibway shamanism, they remain our most extensive source for investigating shamanism among the Woodland tribes.

It is significant to note that the Paleo-Ojibway figure of the horned shaman, which is found on both stone and birchbark, can be compared to similar Siberian petroglyphs and bronze-disc figures.[23] Comparisons can also be made between this Ojibway figure and similar horned drawings *(t'ao-t'ieh)* on Chinese Shang bronzes (1600–1027 B.C.).[24] More extensive investigation of the similarities between Siberian, Chinese, and Ojibway figures must be undertaken, however, before a clear statement can be made regarding the exact function of these figures.

The *Anish-inaubag* are remembered in the tribal oral tradition and the mnemonic birchbark records as the primordial ancestors of the Ojibway who lived in villages along the "great salt sea." The stories that tell of the *Anish-inaubag* are considered sacred stories, *atisokanak*. As such they are distinguished from profane tales of daily life, *tabatcamowin,* and are narrated only during the approved winter months.[25] Traditionally connected with the origin moment, the mythic *illud tempus* of creation, the *Anish-inaubag* are associated with the most sacred beliefs of Ojibway tribal life, namely, *dodem, manitou,* and *midewiwin.*

The *dodem,* or totem, of the Ojibway is a mythical and psychobiological symbol of the ancestral life forces. It is expressed as an animal progenitor that comes to each tribesperson at birth through his or her male lineage. Tribal lore tells of the first five totemic figures who appeared to the *Anish-inaubag.*[26] Since then the Ojibway have determined blood relationships and marriage eligibility by these totems, which have increased in number to about twenty-one.[27] The totem symbols promoted social cohesion among the *Anish-inaubag* and at the same time united disparate groups by requiring exogamous marriages. The totem also affirmed the patrilineal and "corporate" character of the Ojibway bands, which have been described as "atomistic."

Thus the totem had both a social and a religious function. It evoked from the solitary Ojibway family a particular clan-relatedness that welded together the village bands. Complimentary to that idea, and perhaps even stronger than the clan ties, was the natal kinship with the powers of the earth that the totem imparted to each tribesperson.

Ojibway mythology attributes the creation of the first people, *Anish-inaubag,* to *manitou,* which in the Ojibway language means the presence and manifestation of numinous power (the word is used as both a noun and a verb). The Ojibway tribesperson's individual contact with manitou power usually occurs through the vision fast, which is undertaken before puberty and is the most important act in an Ojibway childhood. Having rubbed a child's face with charcoal, as a sign of sorrow, the family elders lead him or her to an isolated place to obtain a manitou dream or vision.[28] The fasting and the humbling experience of the child are expected to attract the attention of a spirit power. If the quest is successful, the manitou usually greets the child by saying, "My grandchild, I come to pity you."[29] Thus a lifelong contact is established with the spirit, who "pities" and adopts the young Ojibway.

Other Indian tribes encourage multiple vision quests, but the Ojibway generally undertake this sacred ritual only once. The effect of the encounter is deepened during the remainder of the individual's life.[30] That the Ojibway encourage this ritual contact during childhood, when the imaginative faculties are especially acute, suggests an appreciation for the lasting effect of childhood impressions in later life. The vision fast provides the individual Ojibway with the means to initiate contact with the surrounding spirit power. No longer isolated or alienated from the environment, the visionary's psychological response becomes intimately related to his surroundings. The following narrative vividly portrays the character of the vision experience, which can establish an ongoing sacred relationship between an Ojibway youth and his environment:

While singing, I heard the winds whistle, saw the tree waving its top, the earth heaving, heard the waters roaring, because they were all troubled and agitated. Then said he [the *manitou*], "I am from the rising sun. I will come and see you again. You will not see me often." Thus spoke the spirit, and then turned away towards the road from which he had come. I told my father my dream, and after hearing all, he said, "My son, the god of the winds is kind to you; the aged tree I hope, may indicate long life; the wind may indicate that you will travel much; the water which you saw, and the winds, will carry your canoe safely through the waves."[31]

In the contact with spirit power the initiate also receives prohibitions against certain actions or foods. These prohibitions express the will of the manitou, just as the vision gives the spirit a form. The ritual prohibitions sustain the initial sacrificial aspect of the fast and manifest the ongoing personal relation of the manitou and the initiate. Furthermore, the initial manitou contact, the continuing supportive power, and the ritual prohibitions all help to elaborate the mythic identity associated with the spirit patron. The person who undergoes the vision fast experiences the same cosmological milieu that is described in the sacred legends. This participation in the religious milieu often is mediated by numinous figures from the mythologies, which are felt as real and immediate presences.[32] The sacred legends and the events of the vision quest are narrated only at certain times and with great caution because of the thaumaturgic power that they evoke.

The manitou has a distinctly personal nature. Although the word *power* is repeatedly used in this work to describe it, the manitou is not an impersonal, magical, or vague supernatural force. Instead particular persons, places, or things reveal the sacred energies. The manitou are special hierophanies in which the individual participates by receiving symbolic communications from the spirit world. Thus in a particular situation the term manitou refers to a phenomenal reality that has a transphenomenal significance. In Ojibway use, the term means that a spirit has been transformed into a phenomenal appearance.[33] In this way the natural world reveals personal manitou presences that impart strength to individual tribal members.

After this initial contact with the transphenomenal spirits, a young Ojibway continues to learn the manifestations of manitou power in the cosmos. Such an individual might become a shaman. Indeed, the vision quest has been called "democratic shamanism" because the same power presences are contacted in dreams and visions as in the shamanic rites.[34] Further training, by both the manitou spirits and the elder shamans, is necessary, however, before one can command the ritual power of a shaman.

Various shamanic vocations and techniques were developed from such training. Among the Ojibway, shamanistic techniques are distinguished from the work of professional shamans because the techniques are received in a vision or by purchase from a visionary and are applied to a specific problem. The shamanic vocation, on the other hand, is a gratuitous gift from the manitou. Although shamanic training can be purchased from experienced shamans, the disposition to learn and the ability to secure the means of purchase are considered a manitou blessing.[35] Generally, the shamanic techniques are considered to be temporary powers. Most significant among them are naming *(o'gwime)*, herbal brewing *(nenan dawiiwed* and *mashgigiwaboge)*, tatooing *(ayhassowe)*, bloodletting *(patchichaowe* and *paskkweige)*, vomiting *(shigagoweiwe)*, and weather control.[36]

Among the Ojibway a shamanic vocation is ascribed to individuals who undergo a unique experience of manitou power and then train for a career as a shaman. The four major shamanic vocations that seem to have been active among the *Anish-inaubag* and the Proto-Ojibway are the *tcisaki,* or shaking-tent diviner; the *nanandawi,* or tube-sucking shaman; the *wabeno,* or fire diviner; and the *meda,* or family shaman. Later the development of the Midewiwin was a continuation of these shamanic specialities.

Ojibway Shamanistic Expressions

The *tcisaki* shaman is usually a male diviner who "reveals hidden truths" while in communication with the manitou in a shaking tent.[37] The shaking-tent ceremony revolves around the contact of a solitary *tcisaki* with particular

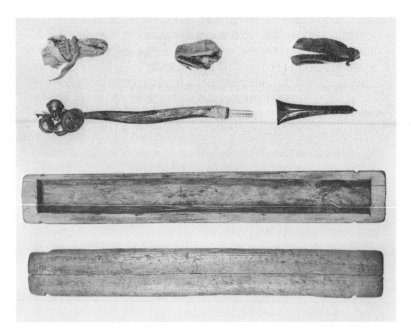

Carved wooden container and top, 11.75 inches long, for storing tatooing equipment. Tatooing was a shamanic technique applied as a cure for lameness and rheumatism. This box contains needles that are decorated with wrapped strands of cloth and brass bells. On the right is a tiny elm-bark rattle. Above are birchbark packets of seeds and small buckskin paint pouches. The container and its contents were collected from the Ojibway of Thunder Bay, Michigan. Courtesy of Museum of the American Indian, Heye Foundation.

manitou who aid his search for lost objects or tribespeople. In some performances of this ceremony the *tcisaki* may be bound and suspended within the conjuring lodge.[38] The shaman contacts his helping manitou, who loosen his bonds as they reveal the desired information. The tent shakes violently with spirit presences, hence the name of the ceremony.

The *nanandawi* shaman is the tribal doctor. He cures by

evoking his manitou patron, who locates the cause of the illness and directs the shaman in removing it. The shaman does so by ritually applying small bones to the affected area. He either sucks or blows into the bones, depending on the manitou direction. The *nanandawi* may also use herbal prescriptions and other shamanistic techniques, but the major part of his shamanic vocation is his skill in "talking with the spirits" to determine the cause of the illness and the subsequent sucking cure with bones.[39]

The *wabeno,* or "men of the dawn sky," manipulated fire in order to interpret dreams, guide novices through spirit contact, and heal the sick.[40] They use a herbal preparation to protect themselves from the fire. This allows them to briefly seize hot coals without being affected by the burning. They heal the sick by manipulating the fire near the patient's body. The *wabeno* act as mediators of the power which they contact in a trance and which they manifest in their manipulation of fire. They also interpret dreams by entering into the trance state, which often is induced by singing special chants and staring fixedly into the coals of a fire. The *wabeno,* at one time, formed a society similar to the Midewiwin.

The *meda* shaman is the family healer who "sounded the drum" for sick members of the isolated Algonquian hunting groups.[41] The *meda* also maintained dream contact with the manitou to assure success on the hunt and to predict the movement of enemy groups. From these ancient activities the *meda,* or family shaman, most probably developed other shamanic techniques, such as herbal healing and naming.[42] During the crucial period of the tribal consolidation and migration from northern Michigan, the *meda* probably developed into the secret society of shamans, the midewiwin. Since the late seventeenth century the word *meda* has been used to refer to an individual shaman initiated into the esoteric lore of the midewiwin.[43]

Three aspects of *midewiwin* must be identified. First, the word is used to refer to the Ojibway shamanic society, which has also been called the Grand Medicine Society and, in more recent times, the Mide Society. Henceforth, when referring to that organization, we shall call it the *Mide Society*. Second, midewiwin describes the ceremony of the Mide Society. This ceremony was seasonal, occurring usually in the spring and late summer, though a midewiwin could be performed at any time for anyone in acute need of curing. This ritual will be referred to here as *midewiwin*. Third, midewiwin means the Ojibway tradition, as taught by the Mide Society. The narration of this traditional lore implied for the Mide visionary, or shaman, the recreation of a mythic event. The society tradition shall be referred to here as *Midewiwin*, with a capital letter to distinguish it from the ceremony, midewiwin.

The midewiwin ceremony is both a healing ritual and an initiation rite into the shamanic vocation. It is performed among the Ojibway by a prescribed number of ritual officers, who are selected from among the shamanic personalities within the tribe.[44] The Mide Society hierarchy comprises four earth and four sky degrees, which are achieved by learning the Midewiwin lore and undergoing the ritual cure. The ancient shamanic vocations, such as *tcisaki* (diviner), *nanandawi* (curer), *wabeno* (fire manipulator), and *meda* (family healer) are a part of the Mide Society. Thus these individual shamanic vocations were incorporated into the Midewiwin status terminology.

The word *midewiwin* derives from *mide*, meaning "sound of the drum," and *wiwin*, meaning "doings."[45] The healing power of the ceremony comes from the dramatic reenactment of the primordial midewiwin by the assembled manitou.[46] The eight ritual days of midewiwin are set aside for specific actions and recitations that involve both the patient to be cured (or a proxy) and the Mide Society shamans, who represent the mythic powers. Although midewiwin was usually celebrated during the spring maple-sugar gathering, it was also proper for a midwinter midewiwin to be performed for those in urgent need. The ritual pre-

*Portrait of the shaman Main'ans with the ethnologist Frances
Densmore, 1908. Main'ans, or Little Wolf, was a Mide Society
leader of the Mille Lac band. His shirt is a fine example of the
beaded floral patterns that incorporated Midewiwin teachings,
herbal lore, and artistry. Miss Densmore was a noted ethnologist
who recorded Ojibway customs and history in the late nineteenth
and early twentieth centuries.* Courtesy of the Smithsonian Institution National Anthropological Archives.

scriptions regarding the number of Mide shamans and instruction periods could be curtailed by taking up the pipe,
smoking it, and engaging in "mystic talk" with the manitou.[47]

The Midewiwin tradition is considered sacred and secret
by its Ojibway practitioners. It is believed to be sacred by
virtue of its origin among the manitou. Indeed, the ceremonial talk, or "mystic doings," of midewiwin is the narration of its own formation during the sacred time of mythic
lore. Midewiwin is secret because of the tribal prohibition
against profane mention of sacred matters. Yet, Midewiwin
can be openly purchased, for the payment of a fee constitutes acknowledgment of its sacred worth to the Ojibway.[48]

A significant function of the Mide Society is its ceremonial activity for the dead, which is called *Dzibai,* or "Ghost
midewiwin."[49] Ostensibly, Midewiwin tradition addresses
itself to giving life and curing disease, but the mythic vision
of the Mide Society provides for an after-death ceremony.
Ghost midewiwin is believed to aid the dead one on his
way to the western land of Nanabozho and to bring a person into the Mide Society who did not go through the ceremony while he was alive. The Ghost midewiwin lodge is
oriented north-south, in contrast to Life midewiwin's east-
west. Although the origin myth still figures prominently in
the ritual, talk of souls and their death routes are prominent in the elaborations of the Ghost midewiwin.[50] While
a proxy takes the place of the dead person, it is explained
that the soul, or "aura," departs from the fleshy body and
wanders in its familiar habitats until it is placated and begins the dangerous journey to the ghost world. Usually little
or no fee accompanies the performance of a Ghost midewiwin. Larger payments imply increased ritual activity, and
the family is usually anxious that the dead soul reach the
Ghost world as quickly as possible. Therefore the fees are
kept to a minimum. Although the rites are much the same
as in Life midewiwin, the tone is more somber, and hysteria
is not uncommon when grief overcomes members of the

family. The following passage suggests the uncertainty with which the recently dead are addressed by the Mide Society shaman:

> You are ready to leave me now; be sure not to look back for the glance draws us with you. Look straight ahead as you were told by the Chief Mide. We live here as long as we are supposed to. Never wish for us to hasten and join you. For you will find your brothers there, and your mother, father and grandparents there also. Do not trouble us; we will do all you requested before you died.[51]

The shaman encourages the dead soul to join his ancestors and not to long for his living relatives. He helps to mitigate the grief of the family by ritually assisting the soul into the Land of the Ghosts. In performing this religious function the ghost midewiwin harkens back to the early shamanistic practices of the *meda,* or family, shaman, who assuaged the terror of death in isolated family groups. Midewiwin incorporated this significant shamanistic function so thoroughly that the individual shaman as guide, or psychopomp, of the dead is not attributed to any of the Ojibway shamanic vocations.

The historical origins of midewiwin provide insight into the religious meaning of the Mide Society. As we shall demonstrate, the society retains the characteristic forms of the older Ojibway shamanism. The Midewiwin lore also reflects its ancient origins by situating the ceremony's inception among the primordial ancestors, the *Anishinaubag.* Yet no historical records mention a midewiwin ceremony among the totemic villages of the Proto-Ojibway.[52] Nor is the Mide Society found among the eastern Algonquian tribes.[53] This evidence would suggest that midewiwin originated among the consolidating Ojibway clans of the late seventeenth century.

The discrepancy between the historical evidence, which suggests that midewiwin developed after European contact, and the tribal lore, which claims an earlier origin, can be explained by examining the shamanic ethos that is central to midewiwin ritual. As a healing ceremony midewiwin reflects the traditional shamanistic milieu of the Ojibway tribe. This tribal milieu recognized the forces of life in nature as potential sources for personal power. The shamanistic activities among the Ojibway were acknowledged as contacts with these manitou powers. Midewiwin continues the contacts by structuring the society around the origin story. Rooted in the early shamanistic practices, midewiwin was appropriately considered a sacred and ancient rite passed down from the mythic times of the oldest tribal ancestors.

Thus Midewiwin origin lore recounts the sacred migration of the *Anish-inaubag* from the Atlantic Coast to the interior woodlands. By retelling the ancient migration accounts, the Mide Society gave direction to the tribe through the transitional crises of the seventeenth-century migration. These intense crises must have arisen because of the prolonged warfare with the Iroquois, the forced movement through the territory of hostile tribes, the depletion of the fur-bearing animals by overtrapping, and the continual intrusions of the French colonial trade.[54] The tribal shamans who formed the Mide Society confronted their despiritualized situation by appealing to the cosmological vision inherent in the migration symbol.

Midewiwin responded to these historical crises by providing a transindividual, transclan vision focusing on the primordial ancestors common to all the Proto-Ojibway bands. Midewiwin was not expressly a vision of future tribal unity but rather a vision of the tribal heritage, guided by the manitou and transmitting shamanistic healing power. Thus Midewiwin revitalized the shamanic ethos of the Ojibway and provided a justification for future movements. In their interpretation of the seventeenth-century crises, the Mide Society shamans brought about a new understanding of the Ojibway people's relation to their cosmology. This ritualized world view attempted to counter the despiritualizing crises mentioned above by establishing a shamanistic society open to all initiates, a healing ceremony for combating sickness and death, a record of the archaic shamanistic practices of the tribe, and an awareness of the Ojibway people's common ancestry.

4
COSMOLOGY

OJIBWAY cosmology is presented in both the tribe's sacred stories, called *atisokan,* and the Midewiwin lore.[1] The word *atisokan* means "grandfather," an indication both of respect and of relationship. It applies to the characters in the mythologies, as well as to the myths themselves. The stories are narrated *(atisokanak)* only during the winter months, when the life forces are considered to be still.[2] In that way the power connected with the mythic stories is not needlessly invoked. On the other hand, the Midewiwin cosmologies, the stories of the tribe's origin and migration, are recited at the Mide Society cures and during preliminary instruction.[3] It is to the symbols in these mythic legends that we turn for a clear presentation of the Ojibway world view. The cosmological stories and symbols provide the Ojibway tribesperson with a unique way of knowing the universe, an ethnometaphysics.[4]

Because the majority of Ojibway sacred stories develop the creation theme, they are correctly labeled cosmogonies.[5] These legends provide the tribe with a story of the earth's origin and continuation in seasonal cycles. They answer the questions "Where did this phenomenal world come from?" "What maintains its continued abundance?" "What relation does the human person have with the surrounding universe of beings?" Cast in mythic cycles of great fantasy and imagination, the Ojibway cosmology enables the tribesperson effectively to interpret changes in the natural world and their psychic significance. Thus the Ojibway world view is the interpretative context that informs all dimensions of tribal life.

The Ojibway world is one of personalistic power. The universe is perceived as having vital personal energies that can be invoked by individual members of the tribe. Both the aggressive skills of the solitary Ojibway hunter and the domestic duties of a tribal woman find support in the cosmology. By contacting the manitou powers described in the cosmology, a hunter can enter into the deep personal relationship with them that is necessary for a successful hunt.[6] For a successful household economy a woman must contact these forces, in a vision fast or in childbirth,[7] so that her work will be assured of powerful patronage. The tribal world view valorizes these contacts with the manitou.

Several examples from the Ojibway cosmology illustrate the tribal world view and its function in interpreting the natural world. For example, the story of winter's defeat demonstrates the personification of natural forces and expresses a particular confidence in the interaction of the human and the natural world:

Finally Old Man Winter came. Oh, how the cold came when he came! Everything grew cold. The trees cracked and the forests cracked. The Indians kept on making the food hotter with hotter and hotter coals. Old Man Winter kept on eating and eating and growing warmer and warmer and perspiring more and more. At last, Old Man Winter said, "You've got me. I believe I'll go."

He walked out into the north and disappeared. When the Indians looked out, they saw green grass and fields and fruit trees and birds. But they heard Old Winter-Maker calling, "I'm coming back; I'm coming back!"[8]

This simple myth tells how Winter-Maker is defeated at a grand banquet and forced to retreat north. The personalization of natural forces in the Ojibway cosmology encourages the conviction that all reality is animate.[9] The

universe is not an impersonal objective reality in the Ojibway world view, but distinctly personalistic. Thus the story
of winter enables the Ojibway to interact with the harsh
climate of their surroundings in a context of mutual personal relationships. The powers are understood to be both
beneficial and harmful. Yet the forces are unequivocally
real, and, structured as ethnometaphysics, they are the
context within which the Ojibway shamans function.

In giving order and meaning to the chaos of events,
the Ojibway world view articulates a cosmic structure that
is at once highly differentiated and centrally oriented. Differentiation in the Ojibway cosmology is evident in the
multilayered universe, the plurality of the manitou spirits,
and the ongoing elaborations and alterations of the cosmological stories themselves. Yet this differentiation is not
just diffused. There is also a central understanding of manitou power unifying the Ojibway cosmology, which is what
we characterize as the tribal world view. Profound encounters with this personalistic power are the special prov-
ince of the Ojibway shaman. It is because these shamanic
personalities, their actions, and their artifacts are charged
with cosmological symbolism that they evoke the differentiated spirits and transmit a multivalent energy.

The tribe's shamans are special individuals who have
deepened their dream and vision experiences of the cosmic forces by extensive learning and solitary meditation.
The Ojibway shaman's personality, actions, and artifacts
must be interpreted within the framework of the tribal
cosmology, which explains the shaman's use of cosmic symbolism. Four characteristic elements in the Ojibway cosmology that are prominent in the tribe's shamanic expressions are the multilayered universe, the axis of the universe often symbolized as a cedar tree, the mediation of
the manitou, and the character of Nanabozho. While these
aspects of the cosmological milieu do not exhaust the complex elements dealt with in Ojibway shamanism, any inter-

pretation of this shamanic experience must give special consideration to these particular symbols.

The Multilayered Universe and Cosmic Axis

In Ojibway cosmologies the present *flat-earth* is located between two cosmic zones referred to as *earth* and *sky*. Each of these regions is multilayered, and each of the layers has a ruling manitou presence. A cosmological story of the Ojibway at Lac du Flambeau in Wisconsin describes the universe in this manner:

> The Indians say that this earth has four layers. The bottom layer does not look like the one we are on now. It is night there all the time. That is where the manitou is who is the boss that rules the bottom of the earth. He rules all four layers. There is no special name for him or for the different layers. . . .
> The sky has four layers too. In the top layer of the sky there is a manitou who is equal in power to the manitou at the bottom of the earth. It is always day there. It is never night. This manitou has no name, but you can call him *Gicimanitou* (Great Spirit). There is no name for the top layer. We're right in the middle in between the four earth layers and the four sky layers.[10]

From the profound night of the deepest earth layer to the constant illumination of Gicimanitou's layer, the Ojibway cosmology expresses a regard for the variety and mystery of the universe. The four layers of both earth and sky further suggest a fullness of cosmic extension in the number four and a hierarchy of power. The Ojibway shaman Chingwauk indicated this hierarchy when he described the sun, Gicimanitou, as the highest blessing sought by the most powerful shamans so that they might "see everything on the earth."[11]

The many evil manitou are not located in the earth or sky regions but in the cosmic waters that separate our flat-earth from the earth below us. The principal malevolent force, personified as Michibissy or Matchi manitou, is a great underwater lion or feline being with horns and an encircling tail. Matchi manitou not only assails the human order with disease, storms, and other intrusions but also takes possession of certain shamans, who then claim this manitou as their patron spirit.[12] Thus the forces of evil are assigned a location in the cosmography as manitou.

The concept of the multilayered earth is a recurring theme in Ojibway shamanism. Through this symbol of the mysterious regions of the universe, the Ojibway shaman structures his communication with manitou power. Communication with those regions is, in effect, a transmission of energy from the noumenal to the phenomenal world. In the following selection from the mide shaman Hole-in-the-sky, the sound of the drum penetrates the many layers, symbolizing the shaman's own journey through the cosmic regions:

Then one (drum) sliver our Grandfather (Bear) took. Then, far, far above (from the bottom layer of Earth to the top, fourth layer of Sky) he (the drum man) stretched himself, so that he reached the Sky. Halfway up the Sky he spread four limbs (now the sliver had turned into a tree, Grandmother Cedar). To the ends of the Sky he spread his four limbs. Four holes did our Grandfather (Bear) make (through the drum) and said, "Here is where the Indian will state his wants." Four times he stretched his legs to the ends of the Earth: "From here (i.e., universally) they (manitou) will attend to the Indian's wants."[13]

The shaman's drum, representing the mythic cedar tree, becomes the cosmic axis that penetrates the mysterious regions and provides a path for the solicited healing power.[14] The impact of these cosmological concepts is especially striking when one considers the archaic *meda,* or family shaman. The isolated Ojibway band often depended on their family shaman to cure the sick, divine for the hunt, and generally meet all the pressing needs that were beyond a tribesperson's own spiritual ability. The *meda* would sound the drum and, as the passage above indicates, open the way to the mysterious regions. The drum itself, and by extension the family shaman who "sounds" it, becomes the very axis of power that reveals the universe to an otherwise isolated individual.

In the same vein, the archaic diviner-shaman, or *tcisaki,* constructs his conjuring lodge of tree poles according to the instructions of his spirit patron.[15] One tree with its branches extends higher than the others, suggesting the path by which the *tcisaki* may see into the cosmic regions and the manitou may enter the conjurer's lodge. Fig. 1 shows a typical representation of the *tcisaki*'s lodge in birchbark pictographs.[16] Like the *meda,* the *tcisaki* draws upon the tribal cosmology to establish contact with the personalistic powers in the universe.

The later Ojibway shamanism of Midewiwin also uses certain cosmological symbols to structure its ceremony. In the following account the origins of Midewiwin are described. The ceremony simultaneously ascends from the earth layers and descends from the sky regions. It is guided along the cosmic axis by the manitou powers to the interface of the cosmic regions, namely, flat-earth:

The Great Spirit advised him (Shell, the deepest earth manitou): "Tell us when you are ready (to bring midewiwin from its birthplace in the bowels of earth). You (and Bear) be the first ones to lift it out. We will come at the last." They commenced to move it. Earth made a great rumbling. As they came through successive layers to the top layer of Earth, the rumbling grew louder. Then they came out. At that time also he up above (Great Spirit), the mide manitou, and other manitou commenced to move it (the mide ceremony). The noise came down the layers of mide Sky. At the last layer of Sky they paused, then met at the mid-point between Earth and Sky and there was a terrible noise for a long time, indeed, a great noise. Thus it was when midewiwin assembled from Earth and Sky.[17]

Because its origin is described in these cosmological terms, the midewiwin ceremony is established as a unique event of cosmic centration and participation by the assembled personalistic powers. Midewiwin is ritually presented as the

Lodge especially constructed for a tcisaki, *or shaking-tent diviner, at Lac Courte Oreille, Wisconsin, in 1899. The lodge has the traditional pine tied to one corner, as well as a string of bells and a canvas cover.* Courtesy of the Smithsonian Institution National Anthropological Archives.

Fig. 1. The *Tcisaki*'s Lodge

accumulated force of the multilayered universe, which thus is brought to the place of healing. The locus of power is wherever the midewiwin lodge, *midewigan,* is constructed.

The Ojibway shamans throughout their history have drawn upon the cosmological symbol of the multilayered universe to situate the source of their manitou power. The initial entry into the cosmic layers can be termed an entry into mythic origins. The origin moment of the tribal cosmology parallels the individual tribesperson's sacred dream. The Ojibway shaman is the specialist who ritually moves in both of these symbolic worlds. The central axis, the mythic cedar tree, is variously identified with the shaman's drum and the midewiwin path. It becomes the symbol whereby the Ojibway shaman channels his dynamic art. Thus the breakthrough of spiritual energies into the present flat-earth and the human order is invoked through the symbols of the cosmology. The tribe views

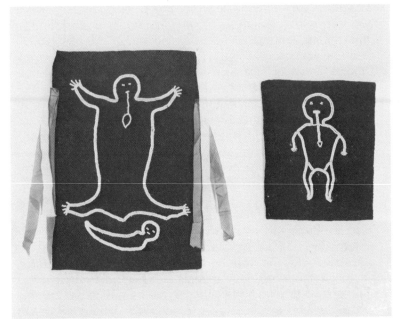

Beaded vision designs on cloth that were part of the medicine bundle of a Midewiwin dancer of the Bungi Ojibway band in Manitoba, Canada. The piece on the left is 9 inches by 2.75 inches and shows a Mide healer with power line, invoking his or her spirit power for the benefit of a patient. Courtesy of the Museum of the American Indian, Heye Foundation.

these energies as personalistic powers, whose appropriation and use are sanctioned by the tribal ethos of aggressive individualism.

Manitou

The Ojibway world view especially centers on the cosmological concept of the manitou as the embodiment of personalistic power. There are three general categories of manitou. The first are described as having existed before

the creation of the flat-earth. They are the anthropomor-
phic manitou of the multilayered earth and sky, such as
Gicimanitou, or Kitshi Manitou (the sun), Shell (the earth),
and Bear (the emissary of strength). The second category
of manitou are life forces of specific natural phenomena
such as certain waterfalls, trees, rocks, or unique atmo-
spheric events. The third kind of manitou are the extraordinary qualities manifested by some humans, such as a
warrior's bravery, a hunter's skill, and a diviner's art. The
concept of manitou includes both the life forces in general
and dramatic centrations of those life forces in special
entities and people.[18] As concrescences of the Ojibway
world view, manitou have both cosmic dimensions and personalistic qualities.

The manitou often act as mediators to bridge the gap
between the cosmological layers and the flat-earth. The
widespread practice of the vision fast among the Ojibway
attests to the significance of the manitou as intermediary
figures for those seeking spiritual strength. The manitou
dream or vision and the invocation of the spirits *(manitou
kazo)* are the means by which the power of the mythic
realms is experienced in the phenomenal world.[19]

The following is a description by a French official in the
early eighteenth century of the healing arts of a shaman-
juggler, or *nanandawi.* The shaman first contemplates his
tutelary manitou for guidance in seeing and treating the
illness. Before carrying out his healing art, however, he
makes a sacrificial offering to the manitou:

They offer up one or two of them [dogs] as a sacrifice to the
sun or the moon, that pity may be taken on the sick person.
This order is only given after prolonged contemplation, for the
jugglers . . . never attribute the cause of sickness to the ail-
ments or accidents which came upon the human body, but pre-
tend that a spell has been cast upon the sick person by the
spite and malignity of some enemy. Now they give out that it is
a guardian spirit, that is, a god whom they have invented by
their imagination, who reveals to them and teaches them how

and by what means the poison and spell have been cast upon the man who is sick.[20]

Despite his skeptical tone this French official, named Antoine de la Mothe, emphasizes the importance of manitou contact for the shaman's healing performance. The prolonged encounter enables the shaman to see what would ordinarily be hidden from view. The manitou is simultaneously the power needed to see the intrusive illness and the all-pervasive mystery that cures.

In the cosmology narrated during midewiwin, Bear establishes the cosmic axis along which he brings the ceremony to flat-earth. While bringing midewiwin, he situates manitou at the threshold of the cosmic regions. As in the following description of the ritual, entry into the mythic space becomes possible by means of these manitou:

> He (Shell) told our Grandfather Bear he was to handle that (gift of midewiwin) himself and bring it to the Indian. Bear reared himself (with his pack of mide rites). He turned around once, and he was black. He found near him a mide (cedar) tree. He pushed the mide tree up through earth's layers. He reached up through the layers of Earth pushing the tree through, and made a hole where he built a manitou wigwam. There he placed two manitou. "Now you must reach out and satisfy the Indian, giving him anything he requests."[21]

This brief episode from the Midewiwin cosmology is varied ritually in the ceremonial recitations. According to the degree of the midewiwin being performed, the storyteller can elaborate the number of turns made by Bear manitou, his color, the manner of selecting the mide (cedar) tree, the direction he faced when he emerged, or his look upon emerging from the earth layers.[22] This origin myth is elaborated in ritual reenactments in order to evoke a unique personalistic power for the individual patient-candidates.

From this cosmological episode the tribe understood that

Bear had established manitou at the interface between the layers of power and human need. The manitou at this interface of divine-human reality are a revelatory force for the Ojibway, and as such they mediate a healing medicine. The shaman is singularly predisposed to this revelatory force because of the intensity and frequency of his manitou encounters. Furthermore, it is not uncommon among the Ojibway for an accomplished shaman to claim the status of a manitou.[23] Such a claim was sanctioned by the tribe. For, just as the manitou mediated between the numinous zones and flat-earth, the Ojibway shaman emanated an awe-inspiring terror because of his access to those numinous regions.

Nanabozho: Trickster and Culture Hero

The most provocative cosmological symbol in Ojibway shamanism is the character of Nanabozho. William Warren recognized his importance for the Ojibway in his tribal history: "The history of their eccentric grand incarnation—the great uncle of the red man—whom they term Manabo-sho [Nanabozho], would fill a volume of itself, which would give a more complete insight into their real character, their mode of thought and expression, than any book which can be written concerning them."[24]

Nanabozho is variously interpreted in Ojibway tradition as a buffoon, sexual aggressor, breaker of traditional patterns, and demonic originator of death. Yet he is also considered a model of independent behavior, a lawgiver, a manitou personality, and the savior of his people.[25] All of those interpretations are supported by specific episodes from the cosmological stories. Overall this mythic figure is highly ambiguous, and usually Nanabozho is characterized as a trickster. His playful side indicates the culture hero's healthy regard for the incongruities of life within the tribal ethnometaphysics; whereas his dark, or destructive,

aspect reflects the individual's drive for self-aggrandizement. These trickster qualities are manifest in much of
Ojibway shamanism. For the use of personalistic power by
the aggressive Ojibway shaman is not restricted to beneficial practices alone.

The character of Nanabozho illustrates many of the cosmological concepts discussed above. For example, just as
the multilayered cosmography indicates a plurality and
hierarchy of manitou powers, so also does Nanabozho gradually develop intimate relations with many personalistic
powers as animal-manitou through his adventures. Furthermore, just as the symbolic cedar tree indicates a path
at the center of the cosmos, so also does Nanabozho pro-
ceed through various chaotic experiences that progressively
center his conscious awareness. Finally, just as the manitou
mediate sacred energies to a spiritually impoverished humanity, Nanabozho is said to have revealed the original
midewiwin healing rite to humans.

Besides mirroring the Ojibway cosmology as he does in
those examples, Nanabozho's actions also reflect the Ojibway tribal ethos of aggressive individualism. For Nanabozho does not simply rely on his relation to the personalistic powers of the universe; he displays a special kind
of self-reliance in accomplishing his tasks.[26] His ambiguous
attributes may, in fact, be due to a literary combination
of different story cycles.[27] Nanabozho has a variety of per-
sonas, which are especially evident in his dual guise as
trickster and cosmic person. Yet the overall presentation
of him as a mythic figure suggests a significant insight into
the paradoxical nature of the Ojibway cosmological milieu.

The trickster aspect of Nanabozho is extensively developed in numerous ribald stories. Nanabozho dupes several
animals into extraordinary predicaments and is himself
duped by other animals.[28] In the following passage the
ambiguous trickster threatens to disrupt the earth that he
himself has made because the evil underwater manitou
have caused his wolf companion's death:

One day, when he [Nanabozho] was walking alone by the ocean, he happened to remember the time when those [manitou] made him angry. Then Wenebozo [Nanabozho] just sat down by the beach with his feet nearly in the water, and he hollered and cried. He sat there crying, remembering the [manitou] who made him angry, and thought of what he would like to do to those [manitou]. He spoke to the earth and said, "Whoever is underneath the earth down there, I will pull them out and bring them up on top here. I can play with them and do whatever I want with them, because I own this earth where I am now.[29]

Nanabozho does not differentiate between the beneficient earth and sky manitou and the malevolent underwater manitou. He holds all manitou responsible and threatens them accordingly. His threatening tone, however, is more like that of a petulant child seeking willful vengeance rather than the commanding tone of a powerful culture hero.

This same trickster element marks the episode in which Nanabozho brings death to the human family. In this story he is supposedly motivated by altruistic concerns for limiting the size of the population, but his deceitful actions are without regard for their eventual repercussions in bringing suffering and death to the human community.[30] Again his deeds suggest a child's play, with childlike tantrums.

Yet the Ojibway see his actions as ultimately beneficial for humanity. They feel that, by causing human death, Nanabozho did indeed prevent overpopulation and depletion of the game animals. Similarly, in the first episode mentioned, Nanabozho's threat to the manitou ironically led to the important creation of midewiwin for later humanity. The Ojibway cosmological stories present the contradictory nature of Nanabozho as the interplay of divine and demonic elements. Nanabozho reflects the tribal world view that personalistic power is both beneficial and harmful. The contradictory elements are seen as coexisting without the need to eliminate one another.

Nanabozho's aggression and dark ambiguity are variously interpreted by prominent scholars. Some consider that the trickster reflects the development of human consciousness or the growth of sexual awareness.[31] Others see him as personifying the movement from nomadic groups to village culture[32] or the transition from religious individualism to community ceremonialism.[33] There is a further interpretation of Nanabozho in relation to the Ojibway shamanic experience.[34] For the shaman, like Nanabozho, manifests certain contradictory attributes in his use of power.

Like Nanabozho the Ojibway shaman is fascinated with manitou-power. In the tribe the visionary is described as being "amused" or distracted by the manitou in an otherwise somber and difficult world. Thus at times shamans escaped the rigors of the tribal hunting life and were "amused" by their guardian spirits' powers.[35] The Ojibway recognize that it is possible for a person to be overwhelmed by personalistic powers, yet they consider that the pursuit of personalistic power is a means of alleviating the inherent weakness of the human condition. The ideal personality is one who becomes so powerful that he can claim to embody the manitou himself, like Nanabozho, who boldly pursued power and brazenly claimed equal status with the manitou.

In the Ojibway tradition the possessor of power was respected and feared. The allure of power could overcome even the best of intentions, and the chief temptation of the shaman was to use manitou for personal gain. For example, the *tcisaki* conjurer could abduct souls during his ceremony.[36] Midewiwin medicine men could use their skills for deadly purposes. Indeed, one Ojibway expressed the ordinary tribesperson's fear of the shaman by saying:

He's wicked, a sinner, he kills! He's a bad medicine man! That's why he's mide! Oh, oh you must be good to him or he'll work love medicine, or paralyze you. Don't take a thing to eat or drink from him, it'll hold poison. You aren't safe from the mide people.[37]

This wooden figure, 14 inches high, with eagle down at its base, was used as evil "medicine" to summon harmful manitou power against another person. It is from a medicine bundle of Ojibway at Lake Winnipeg, Canada, and dates from the second half of the nineteenth century. Courtesy of the Museum of the American Indian, Heye Foundation.

Aged Ojibway shamans were also perceived as being vulnerable to seizure by their own powers. This psychic sickness was personified as the *Windigo,* a cannibalistic ice monster who caused its victims to devour their own family members.[38] The prospect of this deathly possession did not diminish, however, the active pursuit of power by the more formidable shamans.

The trickster's ambiguity thus offers significant insights into Ojibway shamanism. Although ideally the shaman's medicine was to be used only to promote health and harmony, in actuality, the possession of the medicine could harm the practitioner, or he or she could become perverted into seeking personal gain. Communication with the numinous regions did not guarantee a beneficial use of manitou power. Thus the Mide Society itself was often suspect. One researcher observed that the evil medicine tradition "was so deeply rooted in Ojibway society that a conflict persisted all through its history: menacing the good name of the midewiwin from its emergence, never purged from the cult even in its heyday, and threatening to submerge it altogether in the latter days of the mide decline."[39]

In addition to being the trickster, Nanabozho was also significant as the culture hero of the tribe. In this more positive aspect he can be described as the Cosmic Person, as defined by Thomas Berry.[40] That is, Nanabozho centers the universal forces in his own person and transmits that centration to the human community in the form of Midewiwin. He becomes the cosmological symbol of the profoundly spiritual dimensions of the natural world. This status is exemplified in his transformative mode and his sacrificial role in Midewiwin. Both functions are developed by Ojibway shamans.

In the Ojibway cosmology Nanabozho's appearance is repeatedly transformed into that of a variety of animals, such as a beaver and a wolf. In one of the more famous stories he changes himself into a stump in order to take revenge on the evil manitou for killing his wolf companion:

On warm days the (evil) manitou from under the water came up to bask and sleep on the beach by the lake. [Nanabozho] went to that bank and stood on the top of the hill nearby. He decided to become a tree stump that had been burned a long time ago. When [Nanabozho] looked at himself, that's just what he looked like—an old stump. [Nanabozho] also asked for warm sunshine for four days, so that it would be good and hot with no wind. That's how it was for four days.[41]

His transformation into a tree stump enabled him to wound the evil manitou, but ultimately he had to kill a shamanic healer and don her skin in order to overcome the manitou. This transformative mode of Nanabozho is particularly characteristic of Ojibway shamanism.

Alteration, or metamorphosis, of one's appearance is continually described as the special capability of the Ojibway shaman.[42] Midewiwin continues this practice in the symbolic transformation of individual shamans into the assembled manitou of the primordial midewiwin ritual.[43] The meaning of the shamanic transformation is not confined to a change in the shaman's external appearance. Rather, a unique inner transformation occurs in trance as the shaman evokes his or her helping spirits. The *tcisaki,* for example, does not become the spirits that come to his shaking tent, but he is uniquely related to them and to their communications in trance. So also the *nanandawi* does not become the manitou, but his inner identity undergoes a change, which allows him to heal the patient. In this sense, as A. Irving Hallowell wrote, "metamorphosis to the Ojibway mind is an earmark of 'power.'"[44]

Nanabozho's power and that of later Ojibway shamans is also manifest in their sacrificial mode. In Midewiwin lore Nanabozho undergoes the first midewiwin cure.[45] He is "shot" dead by the manitou and revived by the ceremony's medicine. By sacrificing himself, he transmits the healing rite to the later Mide Society. He initiates the healing communion with the natural forces that are centered on the patient undergoing midewiwin. In Midewiwin,

Nanabozho completes the ritual work of the highly differentiated manitou spirits and transmits a unified energy. He is the Ojibway prototype of the Cosmic Person, who, in sacrificing himself, assures the continuing interrelation of power to the animate universe and restores the original communication with the spirit sources of that power. As in Berry's definition, "In the end the Cosmic Person reestablishes the compactness of the original status of man within a higher form of unity and differentiation."[46]

Thus Ojibway shamanism in its many vocational expressions and techniques effectively incorporates the Ojibway cosmological symbols in ritual activities. While every tribesperson has access to the sacred world through the vision fast, the Ojibway shaman is a specialist in gaining access to that world by virtue of his sacred calling. This call to the shamanic vocation, in effect, grants the shaman an entrée into the cosmic regions of mysterious, personalistic power. Each of the four cosmological symbols we have discussed, namely, the multilayered universe, the cosmic tree as axis, the manitou, and the character of Nanabozho, is an abiding symbol to Ojibway shamans of their special relationship with efficacious power. This relationship is the basis for further development of the cosmology in the shaman's dreams, which elaborate and expand the mythic legends.[47] It also is the basis for the tribal sanction of the shaman. It is to this interaction with society that we now turn for a more extended presentation of the shamanic experience among the Ojibway.

5

TRIBAL SANCTION

AMONG the Ojibway, traditional shamanic activity is sanctioned by the local group rather than by formal initiation ceremonies. Such a corporate sanction reflects the social context that fosters the shamanic activity. Ojibway shamanism must be considered in relation to that particular style of life, or ethos, that is unique to the tribe. A diorama of Ojibway shamanism is suggested in which the shamanic experience is identified against the background of the tribal ethos.

Ethos here means the collective actions of the tribe, both conscious and unconscious.[1] In this sense, ethos is the tone, quality, character, and mood of the people's life-style.[2] To investigate the manner in which the shaman is sanctioned among the Ojibway, we will explore the nature of their tribal ethos and discuss some of its particular features. Then we will focus on three significant expressions of social recognition of Ojibway shamanism: dreams and visions, healing and divining, and, finally, status and sanction.

Tribal Ethos

The Ojibway were most readily identified in their formative period as a tribe by their hunting and warrior ethos. The style of Woodland life encouraged isolated village groups centered around family units. Both the huge expanses of forest and the means of economic survival determined the form of the tribal ethos. Because of the rigor of hunting life and the need for individual endurance, the ethos became one of *aggressive individualism,* which Ruth Landes vividly described as follows:

> The elemental conflict of man against a hostile nature has nowhere been enacted more dramatically than in the experience of the Ojibway Indians of southwestern Ontario and northern Minnesota, where the hunter, isolated by his vast lands and frozen winters, felt himself a soul at bay, against cosmic forces personalized as cynical or terrorizing. Out of this confrontation with a stark and hostile environment the Ojibwa Indians shaped a distinctive society and cosmology, both emphasizing individualism.[3]

Although the Ojibway appear to have become consolidated as a tribe in the seventeenth century, early historical records describe their separate village groups as gatherings of hunting and fishing people.[4] These early groups preferred the mobile, individual economy of a hunting family rather than the settled, collective life of an agricultural village. The northern woodlands, in which the Ojibway have lived for centuries, required that individual families maintain an aggressive pursuit of game animals. The current debate regarding the social structure of the Ojibway before European contact can be summarized in the terms *atomistic* and *corporate.* The atomists focus on the small family hunting groups and isolated village bands,[5] while proponents of the corporate theory argue that the Ojibway gathered in larger groups even before European contact.[6]

In any case, the ideal Ojibway male was expected to be an independent, aggressive hunter and a dominant personality in the village. The women also were influenced by the tribal ethos. As Landes has pointed out, their work was generally performed individually rather than in groups.[7] Preparing and sewing the furs, cooking, weaving, and, most importantly, raising the children were their principal occupations. While aggressiveness was not specifically recommended to women, it was not unusual for them to take up the customary masculine occupations, such as hunting or trapping. The path to advancement and improved status

An Ojibway woman, named She-Who-Travels-in-the-Sky, in the north woods of Minnesota, 1908. The birchbark baskets were used for a variety of purposes, such as collecting maple syrup, gathering berries, or boiling liquids by means of hot pebbles. Courtesy of the Smithsonian Institution National Anthropological Archives.

for Ojibway women often followed the traditionally male-oriented vocations of the hunter, the shaman, and even the warrior.

The heroic personality is celebrated in the folktales of the Ojibway and has been documented in various ethnographic sources.[8] The following ethnographic description of an Ojibway youth identifies those particular characteristics of aggressive individualism promoted in the tribal context:

A boy's independence as a hunter comes quite early, by increasing degrees. At nine years Albert had killed enough furs of good quality to sell to the Hudson's Bay Company. By twelve years he had his own hunting and trapping grounds, and cooked for himself. Every few days he returned to his parent's home, bringing furs and hides for his mother and sisters to cure. He sought his father, brother, and brother-in-law for a ritual hunting feast in honor of a bear he had slain (but was not yet strong enough to move alone). His family was proud of him. His sisters' conventional respect for him was sharpened by the fact that he was not only economically independent, in male terms, but that he was also socially independent for he lived as a "stranger" in his own trapping lodge. He needed only a wife to be fully a man—at twelve![9]

Although this youth was rather exceptional, he nonetheless epitomized the ideals fostered by the Ojibway hunting ethos. The notoriety of such a youth would spread among the Ojibway people during intervillage visits. He would be extolled as an exemplar of a maturing warrior in this male-dominated society.

The tribal ethos of aggressive individualism is dependent upon a ritual propitiation of the manitou. This reverent solicitation of spirit power counterbalances the assertive characteristics fostered by the ethos. For example, in approaching the manitou during a vision fast, the docility and humility of the Ojibway supplicant contrasts sharply with the independent behavior idealized by the tribe. Furthermore, the hunting ethic recommended a respectful treatment of animal bones so that the animal could be reborn and hunted again.[10] This ecologically compassionate act established a reciprocity between the hunter and the manitou of each species, thus safeguarding the Ojibway hunter's pursuit of game.[11]

Besides the hunting ethic, the clearest expression of the Ojibway ethos was the aggressive individualism of the warrior.[12] Whether the stimulus was revenge or simply the pursuit of fame, the Ojibway heroic ethos culminated in individual honors on the warpath. The warrior's songs of bravery and his artistic badges celebrated his prowess and signaled his individual commitment to battle. In this way, he embodied the powerful qualities of his guardian spirits for assistance in battle.

The Ojibway were able to raise large war parties because of the inspiration of individual tribal chiefs, as well as the individual commitment to the heroic manifestation of manitou power. In the late eighteenth century John Tanner observed, "An Indian chief, when he leads out his war party, has no other means of control over the individuals than his personal influence gives him. It is therefore necessary that they [the warriors] should have some method of rousing and stimulating themselves to exertion."[13]

The war party was composed of similarly motivated individuals who retained their personal freedom to withdraw at any moment. What held them together was the revenge motif, their own individual drive to attain the heroic honors of the warrior, and the persuasive influence of a singular leader. Thus both the hunter's activities and the pursuit of the warrior ideal indicate the highly individualistic and assertive dynamics of the tribal ethos.

Political Organization

The Ojibway hunting economy and the warrior's independence both fostered and were fostered by the political organization of the isolated villages. The aggressive individualism of tribal members was stimulated by their isolated-village system. Thus a brief discussion of this system is suggestive for understanding the persistence of shamanism among the Ojibway.

The style of life that can be identified as Ojibway varies between the groups north of Lake Superior and those south of the lake.[14] But generally the nucleus of political organization, in both the northern and the southern areas, is the village, which is composed of closely related families. A cluster of these isolated villages is designated as a band. On the north, however, the villages that comprise a band are very loosely organized. Landes wrote,"Almost any circumstance may cause people to drift to a given village or to leave it."[15] This social mobility among the northern Ojibway has worked against a central organization. Consequently, the sense of tribal authority is weaker north of Lake Superior.

In contrast, the southern Ojibway of Wisconsin and Minnesota are more tightly organized. Here the village is also the main social unit, but the formation of bands has developed to a more pronounced degree. The numerous wars of the migration period gave the southern villages a greater sense of tribal unity and a regard for social mechanisms that promote this tribal solidarity. One researcher maintains that the formation of the Ojibway tribe and the Mide Society was due to the challenge to the tribal ethos by Euro-American contacts during the migration period.[16]

Differences in the tribal marriage system, especially in the early twentieth century, also reflect a north-south dichotomy. The remote northern groups, who have conserved the archaic tribal life-style, continued the cross-cousin marriage alliance, in which the children of a brother in one village married the children of his sister in another band-village. In the southern Ojibway groups cross-cousin marriages declined, and a taboo developed on marriage between relatives, perhaps because of increased village populations, which eliminated the need for the older corporative practice. The demise of the practice may also have been caused by contact with Dakota groups or acculturative pressure from Euro-American groups.[17] Whatever the causes of the change, an understanding of them may provide significant insights into the rise of Midewiwin and the continuance of Ojibway shamanic traditions in both the northern and the southern group.

While the political structures of the northern and southern groups can be distinguished by the greater degree of organization in the south, the individual village was the basic unity of Ojibway social life in both areas. Indeed, the isolated Ojibway villages with their strong kinship ties have led observers to describe the Ojibway social order as atomistic. The small village groups, composed of parents, offspring, and friends, grew into larger cross-clan villages. This more centrated development from the eighteenth century onwards had ample precedent in traditional tribal gatherings. Before Euro-American contact the socalled atomistic villages congregated in seasonal sugar-making and fishing camps. Thus the Ojibway social order maintained its roots in the family and in villages of extended families — which gave rise to another description of Ojibway society as "corporate." The larger bands and the tribe seemingly developed in response to the migration of families and their need for mutual protection. It is interesting to note that, though the term *Ojibway* is now used to designate the tribe, they earlier identified themselves by means of band or village names. Some of the more prominent bands were the Saulteur, or "People of the Falls"; the Noquet, or "Bear"; the Marameg, or "Catfish"; the Mikinah, or "Turtle"; the Amikwa, or "Beaver"; the Auwase, or "Fish"; and the Mandua, or "Marten."[18]

The atomistic view of the isolated Ojibway family groups and totemic bands seems to correspond to the Ojibway ethos of aggressive individualism. Recent arguments for the corporate character of these village bands suggest, however, the possibility of a more close-knit social structure than was formerly realized. Furthermore, the relationship of Ojibway shamans to their manitou may also be said to reflect such a corporate social structure. Although shamans individually and aggressively pursue manitou-power, they at the same time enter into a bond with the manitou that incorporates mutual obligations and restrictions. The relation of shamans to manitou is not merely the coalition of atomistic entities but also the acknowledgment of reciprocal bonds that affect both parties. The corporate theory of Ojibway social structure also stresses the periodic gatherings of isolated village bands during the seasonal sugar-making and fishing camps. These gatherings of kinship villages might also help to explain the development of the professional shamanic vocations from the visionary techniques of the family shamans. The *meda*, or family shamans, may have developed into professional shamans as their talents became known and valued by different kinship villages.

The Ojibway kinship village was both the center of social organization and the bestower of game rights. Hunting and trapping rights were also influenced by the ethos of aggressive individualism. The kinship group, or extended family, had the right to hunt, trap, and fish certain wildlife in a certain area bounded by specific geographical markers.[19] An early nineteenth-century observer remarked: "It is customary for them [the Ojibway village] in the beginning of winter to separate into single families, a precaution which seems necessary to their very existence, and of which they are so sensible that when one of them has chosen a particular district for his hunting ground, no other person will encroach upon it without a special invitation."[20] Family hunting rights were further segmented because of individual claims of inheritance or acquisition by force, purchase, or extended use. Any violation of this land and game hunting tenure by trespass or poaching was punishable by immediate death or shamanistic revenge.

The individual Ojibway was expected to resort to aggressive measures in protecting his game rights. It was the source of his family's livelihood, and the tribal ethos affirmed his singular right to inherit and use them. The following passage succinctly expresses the Ojibway attitude towards economic goods and property:

> The scale of property rights is graduated thus: the absolute owner of property is the individual, regardless of sex or age. He lives most intimately with his domestic family but does not yield his ownership rights. He shares goods with his spouse and immature children. He has sentimental ties with his bilateral family, to whom he extends courtesies respecting his property. Beyond this he personally extends his ties in any direction he will. Throughout the rights of the individual are stressed.[21]

The right to share or conserve economic goods is given to the individual head of the family. Yet the individual is intimately tied through kinship to a larger incorporated group. Any aggressive behavior to protect his land and animal use is not arbitrary but set in the context of kin relationships and individual prerogatives.

Even the language used to express the bonds of kinship reflects the aggressive individualism of the tribal ethos. An extensive amount of data could be adduced to demonstrate how the classificatory kinship terms themselves suggest the Ojibway ethos. For example, among the Ojibway a complete stranger is aggressively identified by a kinship term after the initial introduction of his or her name and gens. The terms used to classify the stranger are bilateral and extend throughout the tribe.[22]

The relation between the tribal ethos and the Ojibway shaman can also be seen in the shaman's ability to interpret dreams, perform healing ceremonies, and maintain a certain status in the tribe. It is in these particular activities that the shaman demonstrates his or her special skills in dramatizing the tribal ethos and thereby is sanctioned by the tribe.

Dreams and Visions

The individual Ojibway's self-reliance and aggressive pursuit of heroic ideals is dependent upon contact with spiritual power in dreams and visions.[23] Although the vision fast is not the sole manner of encountering the manitou, it is considered one of the most effective means of invoking the patronage of the supernatural. Dreams are also considered to be revelatory of the numinous regions because the dreamer experiences the mythic world in a unique manner. As the early French observer, Raudot, commented:

> [They] are much given to dreams and are so well persuaded that it is their spirit who gives them to them, that they absolutely must carry them out. It is dreams which oblige them to undertake wars, to make great voyages, to abandon war parties which they have undertaken against their enemies and to return from them to their cabins. It is also these dreams that give them their spirit, or to use their term, their manitou, which they imagine takes care of them in all the acts of their lives.[24]

Thus the isolated Ojibway bands, composed of extended-family members, held within themselves the means to meet crisis situations with the confidence of personal dream power.

This numinous contact in dreams provided the Ojibway with both personal spiritual orientation and the ability to confront the rigors of life. Once the individual had received a sacred dream, he was formally initiated into the values of the traditional heritage. This heritage was an oral history consisting of myths and dreams preserved by the tribe. As the contemporary Ojibway spokesperson and author Gerald Vizenor has observed, "The past was a visual memory and oratorical gesture of dreams plaiting an endless woodland identity between the conscious and unconscious worlds of the people."[25] This poetic expression affirms the singular interaction of daily Ojibway life with the tribal heritage of myths and dreams. The numinous revelations of dreams that weave together the interior and exterior experiences of the tribe become the means for a life-long elaboration of the traditional tribal ethos.

The sustaining values of the tribal ethos are transmitted in the manitou dream, but the symbols and images by which these values are conveyed remain the exclusive possession of the individual. Indeed, the Ojibway tribesperson is largely responsible for the interpretation of his own dream.[26] The sacred dream, unlike the more ordinary dream, is not the subject of casual conversation. Such a dream represents the formal establishment of an interior teaching relationship with a manitou patron. This new teaching, or learning, relationship manifests itself in the behavior of the dream recipient. Landes observed, "People who received visions turned more away from simple, warm relations with their kind, partly because of the new manitou intimacy, partly because visions had to be kept secret to conserve their power."[27]

The significance of dreams as a rudimentary form of education among the Ojibway is demonstrated in the following statement recorded by Frances Densmore: "In the old days our people had no education. They could not learn from books nor from teachers. All their wisdom and knowledge came to them in dreams. They tested their dreams, and in that way learned their own strength."[28] Although the tribe did develop other forms of pedagogy, they consistently extolled the dream as the hunter's guide, the source of the warrior's strength, and the most profound revelation of wisdom. It is in this context of dreams that the formation and development of the Ojibway shaman takes place. The shaman's vocational call in a dream distinguishes him from other tribesmembers as *primus inter-pars* in the tribal fast for a vision. While all the Ojibway have access to power through dreams, the scope and depth of the shaman's vision identifies him as a singular vehicle of manitou power. Furthermore, the special ability to implement the spiritual revelation given in dreams marks certain individuals as shamans with a unique capacity to heal. Both the receipt of a sacred dream and the implementation of the manitou revelation in that dream earns the

Ojibway shaman the tribal sanction.

An Ojibway shaman could receive his "call" from a manitou at any age, but often such a dream or vision occurred
during the puberty fast. With the call the individual received the spiritual power needed to assert his shamanic
vocation. The shaman Hole-in-the-Sky explained his initial
vision as an experience that had lasting imagistic import,
as well as distinct physical manifestations.

> When I was a boy of six, I was always dreaming about snakes,
> that wherever I went I was being covered by them. One summer
> when I was about nine, Someone (in a vision) told me to strip
> and sit under an oak. I was just foolish enough to do that. I
> sat there with a cloth around my middle. Two (garter) snakes
> came near, then more, and more, and pretty soon they were
> crawling all over me—you couldn't see my skin. After a while,
> they left except for two around the front of my middle, who
> stayed with their heads nearly meeting.
>
> I heard a Voice say (in vision), "You will have this till you
> die." So these are my two manitos (in the body). When they get
> sick, I get sick.[29]

By this experience Hole-in-the-Sky was initiated into his
shamanic vocation, which was amplified in later visions
and subsequent interpretations. The snakes were revealed
as his source of power, which could be either destructive
or creative. His mature understanding of this dream determined the manner in which he used the snake power. In his
shamanizing Hole-in-the-Sky would draw upon the imagery
of the snakes and the physical sensation around his abdo-
men to evoke his manitou patron. The presence of the
snakes in his body was a continual reminder of his responsibility to his shamanic vocation. Any offense against the
manitou snakes within him caused him physical illness.

Although the vision also becomes the artistic inspiration
for the regalia needed to shamanize,[30] the Ojibway shaman's exterior dress, interior embodiment of the manitou,
and ritual reenactment of his dream all dramatize the tri-

bal ethos. They are acts of individual power that are aggressively applied to a healing situation. The tribal audience responds to the shamans' thaumaturgy because they understand his dream appointment and sanction his ritual expression of that vocation.

Thus the individual Ojibway shaman's dream has both an immediate quality and a lasting impact. It often initiates the shamanic call and signifies the type of shamanic vocation. Although shamanic dreams vary greatly, there are recurring images and songs that are interpreted as a specific vocational call. This call may be either to a lifelong shamanic role or to a temporary shamanic technique to meet a crisis situation. The *nanadawi*, for example, is given his tube-sucking technique in a dream or vision.[31] The *wabeno*'s vocation is signified by a dream of a certain horned manitou who teaches him healing and divining songs.[32] The *tcisaki* must receive the dream call four times from Mistabeo, the master spirit of the conjuring lodge, before his vocation is confirmed.[33] Similarly, entrance into midewiwin is usually initiated through a dream call.[34]

The dream call to one of the various shamanic vocations affirms the Ojibway tribal ethos, for the dreams issue an individual mandate that must be aggressively pursued lest inattention to the call become a source of illness. Shamans must dramatize their initiation dreams for the benefit of the tribe. Their presentations are an open revelation of their contact with the numinous regions through dream. Unlike other tribal members, they are mandated to reveal their dreams in rituals, and thus they open themselves to tribal sanction.[35]

In narrating or dramatically presenting their initiation dreams, Ojibway shamans evoke the power that has been given to them to heal, divine, facilitate rites of passage, control the weather, and so on. Ideally, the "medicine" that they exhibit will be used for the tribal welfare. For that reason the ritual invocation of their dream power brings them widespread approval of their ceremonial acts.

Healing and Divining

After receiving their appointments in dream, Ojibway shamans develop their ability to invoke the manitou patron. An extended effort is required of the shaman candidate to learn to invoke and control this power effectively. The tribe's sanction of the shamanic ritual involves more than appreciation of a dramatic spectacle. Rather, the tribe acknowledges the shaman's effectiveness in drawing from the manitou a response to their tribal needs.

The inherent need and weakness of the human condition, according to the Ojibway, is the cause of constant crises. The individual tribesperson is subject to an unremitting series of problematic situations: the possible lack of game to hunt or trap, the fickleness of social relations, the intrusion of illness, the attack of aberrant shamans, the inclemencies of the weather, and the caprices of unbridled cosmic forces. The fears of the isolated individual can only be warded off by the intervention of the powerful manitou. As A. Irving Hallowell expressed this Ojibway belief: "Human beings are conceived of as being in constant need of help, from birth to death. So essential is such help that no performance of any kind is interpreted as due to an individual's own abilities or efforts."[36]

The mediation of such strengthening energies in the human condition occurs in personal dreams and in the healing and divining ceremonies of the tribe's shamans. Through the shamanic rituals the individual Ojibway has the means to assert some independence from the isolating, sometimes terrifying environment. The role of the shaman is thus central to the maintenance of the ethos of aggressive individualism. The shamans themselves are formed by the tribal ethos, and, in turn, they provide the members of the tribe with the ritual means to aggressively foster their own independent existences. For example, the presence of a *meda* enabled the isolated family group to meet the exigencies of their woodland life with the confidence of supernatural aid.

The need for manitou aid to strengthen the human condition led to the development of a variety of healing and divining practices among the Ojibway. While the healing rituals themselves are highly individuated, they can be identified by the techniques used. Some of the most significant healing practices are tube-sucking, herbal brewing, bloodletting, naming, chanting, fire manipulation, and tatooing.

Tube-sucking *(nanadawi iwe winini)*, a classic shamanic art, is a prominent healing practice among the Ojibway. While this art is initially authorized in a manitou dream, the person who seeks to learn the *nanandawi* vocation is usually taught by elder shamans.[37] This apprenticeship does not confer tribal sanction, but it does dispose the young *nanandawi* to develop his or her healing art in a traditionally accepted manner. The skill of the *nanandawi* is suggested in the following passage, which describes a tube-sucking cure performed by a Wisconsin Ojibway shaman. The passage records an event when an Ojibway youth, Tom Badger, was treated for severe pains in his left side by a *nanandawi* shaman, Old Man Hay.

In the evening Old Man Hay started to doctor me. He used those bones to doctor me. First he told me to lay on my left side. Then he put the bone right on the place where my pain was. He pushed his head down close and kept pushing as hard as he could on that bone. When he pulled the bone away finally, the skin there pulled back. That's when it hurt most of all. He started twice to doctor me. The second time he did the same thing he did the first time. When a sucking doctor starts to cure, he first tells the people there about the dream he had at the time he was fasting. Old Man Hay did that. Then my father beat a War Dance drum. Old Man Hay shook a rattle while he doctored me. He put a little dish next to him, with a little water in it.

The two bones were lying there. They were about one and a half to two inches long. He didn't touch them with his hands but picked them up with his mouth. He didn't even have to pick them up with his mouth. His power was so strong that when Old Man Hay leaned over the dish, the bones stood up and moved towards his mouth. He swallowed the bones twice and coughed them up again. Then he put the bone to my side. After he'd finished sucking, Old May Hay drew out some stuff and spat it into a dish; it looked like blood. Old Man Hay showed it to me and to the others and then threw it into the fire. If he hadn't drawn the blood out, it would have turned to pus. And sometimes, when the pus burst inside, the person dies. My father drummed all the time that Old Man Hay was doctoring me. He didn't sing, but Old Man Hay sang a little bit at the beginning of every time he doctored me. He put the bone to my side four times and got blood each time, but the last time he doctored me there was very little blood. It was the same every time he doctored me. All we gave him was a piece of cloth and some tobacco, and gave him his meals. After he had finished doctoring me, Old Man Hay said to my father, "One time they had a medicine dance. You took the hide that Tom got in the medicine dance and gave it to someone else. You promised to give him another one in place of the one you took from him. Sometimes he thinks about it. That's why he is sick now."[38]

This narrative description is particularly interesting because of its elaborate detail. It provides a schema with which to interpret the Ojibway shaman's healing art because certain stages in his curative practice can be observed. First, there is the *invocation,* which Old Man Hay performed by reciting the dream that came to him at his vision fast. In this invocation he called upon his healing patron to grant him the special sight needed to "see" the illness and prescribe the necessary "medicine." Moreover, the invocation implied that the summoned power was strong enough to destroy the cause of illness.

Next, Old Man Hay executed the *craft* of healing, which in this case was tube-sucking. The presence of spiritual power was thus accompanied by a physical action that effected the passage of strength from one level of reality, that of the manitou, to another level, that of the patient in need of healing on the flat-earth.

Meanwhile, during the performance of the technique, the shaman and available assistants (in this case, Tom's father) maintain a *therapeutic field* by drumming, rattling, chanting, and magical feats.[39] This healing context is a significant psychophysiological control used to ease the patient and promote a curative atmosphere. The repetitive drumming, rattling, and chanting help to create a trance state for both the shaman and the patient. The impressive feats, such as causing the bones to move before touching them, increases the patient's confidence in the shaman's ability. These magical feats are often central to the maintenance of a field of healing during a curative ritual. In the description above, several magical feats are mentioned, such as, swallowing the bones, talking while they are in the throat, and coughing them up again. Likewise, the blood sucked from the patient's side may be seen to contain small worms or insects, which are offered as proof of the intrusion of an object causing the illness. These demonstrations of power are necessary both to bolster the shaman's self-image and to create the desired effect on the patient. Indeed, the whole healing performance is a demonstration of the shaman's power. The payment by Tom's family appears to be of secondary importance to the shaman, compared with the opportunity to exhibit his healing powers.

The final stage, namely, *the diagnosis of the underlying cause* appears to be peripheral to the healing ceremony itself, but it is, of course, necessary for a complete cure. This stage recalls the initial stage of invocation, in which the shaman calls upon the manitou to open the illness for inspection. In the passage above Old Man Hay diagnoses the pains as due to an inner preoccupation with the loss of an animal hide. The physical symptoms of pain and "bad blood" arise from this obsessive brooding. The underlying cause of such a sickness might also be traced to the vengeful attacks of another shaman. Whatever the diagnosis may be, this final stage reveals the individual's subsequent role in assuaging or avenging the cause of illness. Thus the shaman's healing art combines various techniques of divining in his diagnosis and prognosis.

The schema of invocation, healing craft, therapeutic field, and diagnosis of underlying cause can be helpful in investigating the other shamanic healing practices listed above. In all of them the shaman is especially sanctioned by the patient and by the tribe to perform his healing ritual. The shaman's healing performance is approved because it introduces the power of the manitou in a controlled form. The shaman deduces the individual's cause of illness and describes the appropriate retaliatory action. In this manner the actions arise within the context of the aggressive individualistic ethos, and consequently the shaman is tribally supported.

For the Ojibway divining is the ability to forecast future events or to elucidate certain contemporary occurrences. In the past shamans predicted the success or failure of war parties. Now they discern, for example, the meaning of a particular dream or determine the health or the location of distant relatives or the arrival of seasonal game animals.

Divining has certain similarities with healing in the Ojibway understanding. Like the healing ritual, the divining ceremony is the property of an individual. The divining shaman may have sharpened his skills by learning from elder shamans, but his prognosticating art requires the appropriate initiation dream. Divining rituals are also used for curing purposes because they create contact with manitou and thus bring increased strength to the patient.[40] The most prominent Ojibway divining shaman was the *tcisaki*. Even in the following brief description of the shaking tent ceremony, the schema of shamanic healing may be recognized, namely, invocation, craft, divinatory field, and diagnosis of underlying cause:

The patient or a delegate approaches the doctor with the request for his services, and exhibits a pile of dry goods, blankets, etc., tobacco, and perhaps some food. Depending on his habit, the doctor then instructs the patient to prepare a sweat tent. Into this, the doctor retires alone, and communes with his guardian turtle, *mikinak*. The following night the doctor enters the divining tent which he has ordered the patient to construct for him. He asks his guardian turtle to summon the other supernaturals for consultation. The people outside the tent hear the tones of this colloquy, although they cannot precisely distinguish the words. Each manitou has a distinctive intonation which is traditional. Thus, the turtle has a shrill voice, the eagle has a "gentle" (pleasant) voice. The spirits make a great noise when they enter and leave the tent; and at these times the tent shakes with fearful violence. From his consultation with the spirits, the doctor learns what he seeks.[41]

This *tcisaki's* initial consultation with his guardian spirit, *mikinak*, and the call to the "other supernaturals" to assemble can be considered the invocation. Again, the emphasis is on the need for a power presence to effect the desired end, in this case, prognostication. The craft of the conjuring lodge is based on the *tcisaki's* communication with the assembled manitou. The essential power exchange is by virtue of the *tcisaki's* conversation with these spirit powers. The tribal audience hears this conversation, though its meaning may be unclear to all but the shaman.[42]

The divinatory field created by the shaman and his or her assembled manitou makes this ceremony extremely impressive. For the spirits, according to traditional belief, cause a wind to circulate within the lodge, thus creating a violent shaking motion.[43] Another magical aspect of the divinatory field is the projection by the shaman of many different voices and animal sounds to the open area at the top of the lodge. Often the *tcisaki* drums and chants between periods of communication with the manitou. These actions contribute to an impressive performance that manifests his or her power and skill.

Finally, the divining ceremony reveals the underlying cause of the tribesperson's problem or the answer to his or her question. After invoking the manitou and requesting them to investigate the tribesperson's questions, the shaman later announces what the spirits report. The tribespeople often recognize a spirit's voice and wait for the report of a favored spirit. Such a manitou was *mikinak,* the turtle. Interestingly, the manitou turtle, the slowest of creatures, symbolized quick communication.[44] It might be that the tribal ethos celebrated the dogged persistence of the turtle to assert his painstaking deliberation.

Other shamanic rituals of divining among the Ojibway followed the schema presented but varied in the techniques by which the shaman practiced his or her prognostications. For example, the *wabeno* shaman divined by gazing at the coals in the fire, and dream interpreters predicted the future by analyzing the symbols in a person's dream. Regardless of the techniques used, however, the effectiveness of the rituals affirmed the tribal ethos. The shaman's divining provided a means for the individual Ojibway tribesperson aggressively to transcend the limitations of his life. The subsequent sanction of the Ojibway shaman by the tribe followed from this basic interaction, which had both a theoretical and practical aspect.

Theoretically, the tribal sanction of the shaman comes as a result of his contact with manitou power. Because the Ojibway traditionally view the human condition as weak, there is a positive need for such an intervention of power. The personalities supplying that need are the shamans, who are distinguished by their specific techniques of divining and healing. The theories of power manifestation, the weakness of the human condition, and the requirements of the tribal ethos provide the theoretical sanction of the shaman's vocation.

Shamans are also sanctioned because of their practical effectiveness in healing and divining. Their actions are tried and tested by the tribal tradition. Although there is a strong visual and emotional component to the shamanistic rituals, the shamans are respected not simply as dramatic personalities but also as astute healers and diviners. The tribe's approval arises largely from these pragmatic considerations. Thus, despite personal aggrandizement by some Ojibway shamans and outright sorcery by others, the tribal sanction of shamanism has remained largely intact throughout Ojibway history.

Status and Sanction

Status is a term that designates the social position of individuals in relation to their society. An individual's status is defined by his or her rights and obligations in the social group.[45] Among the Ojibway the tribal shamans are designated by specific terms, such as *meda, nanandawi, wabeno,* and *tcisaki.* Each of these terms indicates the technique used by the shaman to heal or divine. The isolated family shamans are called *meda* for the sound of their drum or rattle, with which they contact their guardian manitou.[46] *Wabeno* signifies the "red dawn sky," indicating both the symbolic color of the fire that these shamans handle and the length of their dance rites, which last through the night to the dawn.[47] The *nanandawi* is named for his sucking cure.[48] The etymology of *tcisaki* has not been verified, but the term is consistently used to indicate the shaking-tent diviner.[49] The practice of such shamanic techniques is the shaman's right, which is given to him or her by a dream or vision experience.

Certain obligations are also enjoined upon the dream-validated shaman by his or her manitou patron. Usually the obligations involve prohibitions against eating the animal species that are protected by the guardian spirit. Other, similar restrictions of behavior are sacrificial acts that identify the shaman with the tutelary spirit.[50] The execution of both rights and duties confers on the shaman a distinct social position and status in the tribe.

The status given to an Ojibway shaman can be investigated from these two perspectives, namely, the rights and the duties that define his status. Investigations among Ojibway shamans reveal, however, that both aspects of status are dependent on the shaman's unique, personal experience of supernatural forces. Thus the status of the shaman has a specifically religious dimension.

The tribe recognizes this religious dimension when a person begins to assume the characteristic shamanistic rights and duties. This initiative is seen by the tribe as a sign that the shaman-to-be has received a manitou dream. Accordingly, the tribe confers upon him a distinct social position as a potential shaman.

This initial status granted a shamanic visionary is the social compensation for the many hours of solitude needed to develop the relation with the manitou. The candidate's status, moreover, is not rigidly fixed but develops with the growing authority of the shaman. As he gradually learns to direct the manitou energies, his own power is correspondingly increased. This maturing process is evident in the following passage:

manitou "pity" stays only with the youth who is modest and reflective, who seeks more and more visions, in order "to learn" and to secure mystic protection, until by his early middle age the "power" has matured. Hence, the mighty shamans are "old" and always termed so in deepest respect and fear. To say "old man" was synonymous with saying "great shaman of midewiwin," in Minnesota and Ontario during the 1930's.[51]

When a shaman is called "old man," his social position as one who interacts with manitou power is acknowledged. Such an interaction marks the shaman as one who embodies the highest values of the tribe. In a similar manner, the shaman of an isolated village is usually termed "our wise man" *(n'gittci anicina beminan)*.[52] This phrase connotes both the respect and the fear of the members of his village. They recognize his authority in tribal matters, yet fear his potential for self-aggrandizement. Regardless of the shaman's personal predilection for beneficial or harmful medicine, his social position is unquestioned. It is based on his favored relation with the "levels" of awesome power that is sanctioned by the tribal ethos.

The rights and duties that define the status of the shaman are not entirely esoteric or hidden from the tribe. Although these rights and duties differ widely according to the particular shamanic vocation, the tribe can infer from the shaman's restricted behavior which manitou have empowered him. The public character of the shamanic vocation can be seen most clearly in Midewiwin.

Midewiwin represents a departure from traditional methods of shamanic sanction, for the initiates are not necessarily called to their vocation by a manitou dream. Yet Midewiwin does confer a distinct shamanic status on its initiates by virtue of the rights and duties that the initiates undertake. These rights and duties are mandated by the unique contact with the supernatural power that validates this shamanic practice. Thus, although the method of call and development of spirit contacts differs from the other shamanic vocations, the ultimate test of Midewiwin sanction remains the repeated experience of power. A brief discussion of the origin of Midewiwin indicates the singular importance of manitou contact in validating the Mide Society's shamans.

Midewiwin arose as a response of Ojibway shamans to the loss of spiritual vigor during the early colonial period when the Ojibway coalesced as a tribe. The most significant causes of this despiritualization were the challenge of Euro-American cultural intrusion, the overkill of animals stimulated by the fur trade, and the displacement of eastern tribes in the Iroquois wars. Despite these varied factors Midewiwin maintained the traditional forms of shamanic activity. The shamanic society developed a mythic lore whose dramatic recitation was extolled as a healing ritual. This healing privilege was presented, in a traditional man-

Looking into a Midewiwin lodge during a ceremony at Lac Courte Oreille, Wisconsin, in 1899. The Mide officers are moving past the child-candidate, who is held in his mother's arms. A child could be initiated into the Mide Society during a ritual ceremony to cure illness. Note the degree pole on the right, which designated the level of midewiwin being performed. The piled blankets served as payment for the ritual. Courtesy of the Smithsonian Institution National Anthropological Archives.

ner, as arising from contact with the manitou spirits. The midewiwin ceremony was authorized as the reenactment of the mythic gathering of manitou who created the primal midewiwin. The obligation exacted of the initiate also followed a traditional pattern. A substantial fee was paid to the manitou and distributed through their ritual representatives, the Mide Society shamans. This sacrificial act was required to ensure the powerful presence of the manitou.

Although the Mide shaman did not need a traditional dream validation, the rights and duties he adopted accorded him the traditional shamanic status. Despite this lack of dream authorization, the Mide shaman asserted the ultimate value of the tribal ethos, namely, the aggressive personal pursuit of manitou power. Thus, the central focus of Midewiwin's rights and duties was to initiate contact and identify with the "multileveled world of power." By maintaining this continuity with the traditional shamanistic practices, the Mide Society was accorded its special shamanic status. The novel feature of the society was that the dream-validated shaman shared equal status with ceremonially initiated patients. As one researcher observed:

> The never-cured doctor [the dream-validated shaman] meets on common ground with the non-doctoring cured one [the midewiwin-sanctioned shaman] inasmuch as both have had contact with the same supernaturals: the patient in being cured with supernatural power, and the doctor in getting hold of this power to use for the patient. During the ceremony in which he serves as a doctor, a mide [includes both patient and shaman] is identified with the supernaturals since he can use their power.[53]

The status of Mide shamans thus follows a similar pattern to that of the traditional Ojibway shamans. The "never-cured doctor" is the dream-validated shaman who uses Midewiwin to further his own pursuit of shamanistic power. Such individual shamans were those called by the generic status term "old man" to indicate their venerable contact with manitou.

The "non-doctoring cured one" also asserts his individual status as a society member. It is important, however, to distinguish the accomplished Mide Society shaman and the midewiwin-initiated patient. The status of Midewiwin is accorded to both, but their understanding of the society lore is very different.[54] Yet, by gathering the required fee, the Mide Society initiate enters into relation with the institutional lore of Midewiwin. His social position is improved, his physical well-being is healed, and his religious needs are satisfied.

The investigation of status among Ojibway shamans provides a significant insight into the tribal sanction accorded those shamans. Although status and sanction are more or less reciprocal concepts, the phenomenon of status provides a means of verifying the manner in which the tribe gives sanction. For status has an authoritative character based on certain rights and duties, while sanction entails no formal ceremonial act among the Ojibway. Thus the investigation of status accentuates those aspects of Ojibway shamanism that are of singular importance to the tribal ethos.

The unique characteristics that distinguish the Ojibway from other North American tribes have been summarized in the phrase "aggressive individualism." Consideration of the tribal ethos from economic, social, and political perspectives suggests how the Ojibway shaman is sanctioned by the tribe because of his or her special embodiment of that ethos.

The Ojibway shaman both forms and is formed by the tribal ethos. The shaman's pursuit of power is derived from traditional tribal values, while at the same time his or her rituals dramatize and thus develop the tribal ethos. The shaman serves as a unique catalyst for other tribal members in their pursuit of individual power.

The special status of the shaman in the tribe arises from his personal experience of the highest value in the Ojibway world, namely, contact with the numinous regions. The shaman's function is repeatedly described as the ability to transmit power; through dream experience he structures a healing contact with the manitou. Such ability to communicate with the "other world" in rituals is acknowledged in the status terms that are conferred on the shaman by the tribe. Thus he gradually acquires an unassailable personality that is simultaneously feared and respected. The aggressive pursuit of spirit power may bring the shaman some financial success and political influence, but even more important is the social status given to one who communes with the manitou.

In presenting the tribal sanction of the shaman by means of dreams, healing, and status, an effort has been made to demonstrate the Ojibway shaman's close connection with the tribal ethos. Individual shamans, as they gradually become heroic personalities to the tribe, cease to pursue the powerful spirits and begin to identify themselves as a manitou.[55] They see themselves as having compassion on their patients just as the manitou had compassion on them as fasting visionaries. Likewise, the patients make lasting commitments to their shamans just as the visionaries pledge themselves to their guardian spirits. Finally these shamans come to expect from their patients the respect that is due a manitou personality. The temptation that arises from this embodiment of manitou power can lead to either beneficial or harmful practices.

The egotistical temptations of shamans are constantly condemned by the Ojibway as sorcery. Ojibway mythology even warns of the *Windigo* sickness that may overtake such a self-aggrandizing shaman.[56] Nonetheless, the fear and respect accorded the shaman arise from the recognition of his or her power, regardless of how it is used.

The ritual by which the Ojibway shamans evoke their special powers is discussed in the following chapter. The ritual arises from the shaman's contact with the cosmic powers and his ability to relay that contact in a form that is readily appreciated by the tribe. Both the cosmological milieu and the tribal sanction are significant considerations that prepare us for understanding this ritual.

6

RITUAL REENACTMENT

THE Ojibway shaman's ritual is an expression of his initiation experience into the world of sacred power. Although there are collective types among Ojibway shamans, such as the *nanandawi, tcisaki,* or *wabeno,* each shaman is distinguished by the manner in which he or she initially experiences and later evokes personal power. In contrast to such a personal vision experience, the midewiwin initiate experiences a society vision. Yet even the midewiwin ceremony varies among Ojibway bands because of renewals and alterations that are prompted by the personal dreams of midewiwin officers.[1]

In their rituals Ojibway shamans use the unique cosmological images and gestures that were revealed to them during their initiating dreams or visions. Moreover, the reenactment of these revelations, which were personally communicated to them by the manitou, is the basis of their public performances. Thus each ritual is a unique reenactment that mediates between the society of which the shaman is a member and the sacred world which he or she has personally experienced.

Ritual reenactment is the ceremonial means by which the Ojibway shaman mediates between the personalistic powers of the mythic world and the tribal ethic of aggressive individualism. Reenactment, in this sense, is a multivalent term, the initiating dream or vision of the individual shaman is the basis of a symbolic ritual that fuses the tribal ethos with the tribal world view. Both the shaman and the ritual dramatize the beliefs of Ojibway society.

The shaman helps interpret tribal activity within the cosmology while functioning as a centering personality for the tribe. The development of such religious expertise depends upon proper shamanic initiation and subsequent elaboration of the ritual.

The Shaman's Call

A striking example of both a shamanic initiation and the resulting formation of a healing ritual is the story of Sky Woman.[2] This Ojibway woman lived during the early twentieth century in the forested regions of southern Ontario. Born into a family that was disturbed by violent parental disagreements, Sky Woman fled from this chaotic situation at nine years of age and wandered aimlessly in the northern woods until a search party found her. Among Sky Woman's rescuers was an old woman who was able to extend to her an affection and concern that the girl faithfully returned. Gradually Sky Woman adopted the old woman as her grandmother, finding in her the stability that she had missed in her own home. It was after many years together that the following incident occurred:

In the fall they went to Swampy River. They used to hunt and fish there every fall, and they stayed until the lakes froze. . . . While they were there her grandmother got sick, so sick that she thought she would not live. So Sky Woman sent word by someone who was passing by to tell the people that her grandmother was sick and might not live . . . so that people would know how they were. She never slept, watching over her grandmother. One time she fell asleep and dreamed of the time she had been lost. She dreamed that someone gave her a rattle and other things they use when they doctor, and spoke to her saying, "Try this on your grandmother. She might get better." So when she woke she made a little rattle, and started to *nananda wiat* (cure by sucking). When she finished, the old woman seemed to be brighter. That night she started again on *manitou kazo* (talking supernatural, or invoking supernatural) and cure by sucking. Before she was through she heard somebody outside. It was her father and mother and some people coming to see how they were. She did not stop with her *manito kazo*, but kept right on until she finished. Her father and mother made their wigwam close by, and about four days after, her grandmother got better and was up and around, so then from that people knew that she was a sucking doctor and she was wanted from one place to another to doctor the sick.[3]

Sky Woman's initiation into the *nanandawi* shaman's cure ostensibly occurred in response to the crisis of her grandmother's illness. Her dream validation, however, recalled her early youth, when she wandered lost and alone in the forest. At that time the manitou seemingly had pitied her, singling her out as a potential shaman, but it was not until many years later, during her grandmother's sickness, that her shamanic initiation was confirmed by her sacred dream. Sky Woman's shamanic call thus can be said to have had both a gradual and a spontaneous dimension.

The gradual aspect of her shamanic initiation began in the period of her youthful wandering, when, in tribal terms, she was "empty" of personal power. She had been at a proper age to fast for a vision to fill her spiritual void,[4] but her vision fast was not encouraged in her chaotic household, and, after running away, she wandered through the woods in a pitiable state. During this time she was a liminal person, having neither tribal status nor a manitou dream. Then, while lost, she had a memorable experience: "She dreamed that she was in a place where there were a lot of people, and she was very happy and had nice things to eat. . . . Here she was blessed so she could *nanandawi i we* (cure by sucking)."[5] The conferring of manitou power without her awareness was not unusual in the Ojibway world.[6] When Sky Woman later developed her own shamanic ritual, her childhood experience and dream provided her with a special sensitivity to the manitou.

The spontaneous dream initiation of Sky Woman came

An eighteenth-century drawing of an Ojibway shaman calling the manitou. The professional shamanic vocations perhaps developed from the example of such isolated meda, *or family, shamans. Note the pipe for communication with spirit power, the bowl for mixing herbs, and the rattle for "talking manitou."* Courtesy of the Smithsonian Institution National Anthropological Archives.

in response to the crisis of her grandmother's illness. Her dream, however, followed a traditional pattern. The manitou appeared in the dream and, pitying her, imparted the special shamanic powers of the *nanandawi*, by means of cosmological symbols peculiar to that shamanic vocation. The symbols that Sky Woman used in her ritual reenactment were all evocative of the mythic world of personalistic power. Her ritual established the bond of identification that had been given to her by the manitou during her pitiable experience as a lost child. Her reenactment also harkened back to her shamanic initiation, which her grandmother's sickness had spontaneously evoked. The identification with manitou among Ojibway shamans appears to result from an experience of deprivation that draws out power from the individual and from the earth. This sacrificial aspect of the deprivation state seems to be a cardinal aspect of the Ojibway shaman's formation.

Ritual Activity

Once given the manitou's aid, Sky Woman had the confidence to direct her power to the situation over which she had had no previous control, namely, her grandmother's illness. She summoned up the symbolic songs, gestures, and sucking practices that had been bestowed in her dream validation. Sky Woman's skillful orchestration of those powers suggests a magical quality in her cure. Indeed, as Bronislaw Malinowski observed, magical techniques help create a mood of confidence in which ritual practices can be effective:

Magic supplies primitive man with a number of ready-made ritual acts and beliefs, with a definite mental and practical technique which serves to bridge over the dangerous gaps in every important pursuit or critical situation. It enables man to carry out with confidence his important tasks, to maintain his poise and his mental integrity in fits of anger, in the throes of hate, of unrequited love, of despair and anxiety.[7]

Magic, for Malinowski, was the means by which practical remedies could be brought to bear even in extremely distressing situations. His understanding of magic, however, does not adequately take into account the ethos and world view in which the shamanic techniques function. Since he reduces shamanic magic to practical techniques, he does not explain the underlying tribal belief system that makes the shaman effective. While magical practices in the Ojibway context can be seen as aggressive individualistic acts, they reflect a belief system that is ongoing and not invoked only in crisis situations. Thus the shamanic ritual is more than magical techniques; it expresses a world view of personalistic contact with sacred power that is accessible for healing.

Sky Woman's ritual activity, for example, was a courageous response to a crisis. The repetitive songs, gestures, and sucking cures, however, were more than magical techniques to alleviate a difficult situation. Rather they were the actions of an individual aggressively evoking unique personalistic powers in which she trusted. By assuming the heroic qualities of a shaman, Sky Woman aspired to the highest authority for the power needed to heal. Her shamanic vocation was not simply dependent on the development of certain magical techniques; it was based on her sacrificial identification, which mediated sacred power to individuals and to the tribe as a whole.

The Ojibway cosmology of personalistic power portrayed phenomenal reality as a field of interpenetrating forces, with which the power personality could communicate. Thus the Ojibway world view encouraged a style of life in which the individual aggressively aspired to be a power personality, namely, a shaman. In Sky Woman's case the aspiration to shamanize was largely latent until her manitou dream. After that dream she performed her own ritual, which recreated her initial communication, thereby summoning her manitou patron for the power to heal.

The various actions that she performed in her ritual

were a reenactment of her initiating dream. Thus the rattle, the talking with supernaturals *(manitou kazo)*, and the sucking cure *(nananda wiat)* were given her as a pledge by her manitou patron. By performing those actions, she brought the manitou into the presence of her ailing grandmother. The determination with which she carried out those actions suggests the extent of her commitment to her grandmother as well as the dogged persistence of an individual Ojibway in pursuing power. Sky Woman's confidence centered on the ritual that she had been taught in her dream.

Generally the manner in which an Ojibway shamanic ritual develops depends upon renewed encounters with the symbols of the initiating dream. An early nineteenth-century Ojibway shaman, Chingawouk, described the intricate task of developing a shamanic ritual and emphasized the revelatory quality of dreams in fostering a shamanic vocation:

> What a young man sees and experiences during these dreams and fasts, is adopted by him as a truth, and it becomes a principle to regulate his future life. He relies for success on these revelations. If he has been much favored in his fasts, and the people believe that he has the art of looking into futurity, the path is open to the highest honors. The [shaman] begins to try his power in secret, with only one assistant, whose testimony is necessary should he succeed. As he goes on, he puts down the figures of his dreams or revelations, by symbols, on bark or other material 'til a whole winter is sometimes past in pursuing the subject and he thus has a record of his principal revelations.[8]

As described by Chingawouk, shamans have several formative dreams and visions which amplify the initial manitou call. The interpretation of these dreams requires a reflective period, which may be considered a gradual call. The withdrawal into solitude is sacrifice that prepares the shaman for the coalescence of his or her ritual identity with the manitou. The ceremony that the shaman eventually performs is the concrescence of his initiating experiences, whose reenactment by means of particular symbols mediates between the shaman and his personal power. The ritual thus gives meaning to the call, the sacrificial period of seclusion, and the later situations in which healing is needed. Each reenactment is a unique summons of power and an open display by recitation of the shaman's relationship with power that can transform a difficult situation.

Public recitation of the shaman's dream was problematic in the Ojibway world because there was a prohibition against open revelation of a sacred dream. It was feared that the dream's power would thus be dissipated, even though the shaman was required to recite the dream experience to evoke the manitou presence for healing, divining, and other shamanistic practices. The shaman often resolved this dilemma by narrating the dream in a hurried manner. Yet the purpose of the narration was not only the evocation of manitou power but also the edification of his patient. The following passage describes an Ojibway shaman's ritual that drew on certain symbols from his dreams. Although the audience might not be able to understand the full implications of the dream, they would recognize certain symbols, such as Thunderbird, his principal manitou patron:

She [the patient] spread blankets and tobacco before [the shaman], in payment of his forthcoming services. This fee is his exclusive property. He smoked the tobacco in offering to his supernatural patron, the Thunderbird. This offering is both toll and invocation. It is toll because the smoking sends to the [manitou] the spirit of the payment received by the doctor. It is invocation because it bespeaks the supernatural.

When he finished smoking, he asked Mrs. Wilson for water in which he put a hollow bone. The bone was of a light weight, about two and a half inches long from the leg of some bird. He beat his rattle against his chest, on his back, from his side to his side, and commenced to "talk about his dream." This helped him to doctor because it rallied his supernatural; and from another viewpoint, its mysteries gave confidence to himself and to his awed client. "He talks so quickly . . . quick as anything . . . you can hardly understand." The mumbling is his privilege, for to speak intelligibly would give his dream away.

After he said his dream, he started rattling and singing. He said he was singing to his dream . . . that the Thunderbird could see everything in the ground . . . that everything is scared of the Thunderbird.[9]

After this invocation the shaman began to perform the shamanic techniques appropriate to a *nanandawi* curer.

This description of an Ojibway *nanandawi*'s ritual illustrates the reenactment theme. The bone, with which the shaman seemingly extracted the object causing the illness, would have been conferred on him in his initiating dream. Similarly, the manner of rattling and the "talk about his dream" *(manitou kazo)* were also imparted in vision. Thus this shaman's ritual was a lively reenactment of words, gestures, and object manipulations bestowed on him by his manitou. The hurried recitation preserved the secrecy of his more specific dream images, but the shaman openly mentioned the primary symbol of his dream, namely Thunderbird. By open invocation of the Thunderbird he simultaneously contacted his manitou patron and aroused in the patient a confidence in his ability to mediate a healing energy. The Thunderbird symbol focused both the shaman and the patient in the belief that supernatural power could be brought to bear on the illness. For the shaman, having undergone his own traumatic initiating experiences, recapitulated his sacrificial identity with power, thereby mediating the healing manitou presence.

Such a therapeutic metamorphosis is operative in all Ojibway shamanic rituals. Just as the shamanic personality experiences a new identity by receiving the manitou dream, so also is the patient expected to receive a transformative power from the shaman. The shaman reenacts his initiating experience to presence this transforming power. The symbolic chants and gestures that he directs towards the patient

Medicine sticks and tobacco tray at a midewiwin at Lac Courte Oreille, Wisconsin, in 1899. The red and green sticks were presented to participants to summon them to the midewiwin ceremony. The tobacco tray held the tobacco that was smoked as an invocative offering to summon the manitou. Courtesy of the Smithsonian Institution National Anthropological Archives.

are intended to reverse the intruding sickness by applying a stronger "medicine." For example, the Ojibway shaman Chiahba chanted the following during his healing rituals: "What is this I put in your body? Snake skins I put in your body."[10] Since his vision of Snake manitou had given Chiahba power, he ritually called on its power to combat a patient's sickness.

All forms of Ojibway shamanic activity have a healing potential because of their evocation of manitou power. The *wabeno* shamans chant their initiating dreams and manipulate fire to attempt a reversal of an existing situation. Likewise, the *tcisaki*s recall their special dreams to summon the Master-manitou (Mistabeo) and other spirits to the conjuring lodge. The most complex reenactment ritual among the Ojibway, however, is midewiwin. In this ceremony the patient is not only cured physically but also receives a new identity through the healing.

As discussed in Chapter 4, midewiwin is an initiation rite that was bestowed on Nanabozho, the first patient. Traditionally midewiwin is intended to expose the patient-candidate to the manitou energies evoked by reenactment of the mythic midewiwin. This ritual reenactment is performed by a recitation of the ceremony's origin legends.[11] In midewiwin the individual dream-validated shamans set aside their special shamanistic abilities to portray the assembled manitou of the mythic ceremony. The patient-candidate recreates the role of the Cosmic Person, Nanabozho, who ritually died and was revived by the healing rite. The thaumaturgy of midewiwin redramatizes the Cosmic Person's death and rebirth and thus establishes the initiate's interconnectedness with the personalistic power of the universe.[12]

The pattern of *reenactment* can be used to interpret the cosmological symbols in the midewiwin ritual. Reenactment is the means by which the initiating vision of the Midewiwin lore is formed by the assembled shamans into a symbolic ritual. The effect of the ritual is to authenticate the tribe's cosmology and to affirm their assertive ethos.

Midewiwin draws extensively from the mythology of Nanabozho and the cosmological origin stories. Furthermore, the Ojibway world view is symbolically expressed in the ritual lodge, stone, and tree. The lodge in which midewiwin is performed *(midewigan)* symbolically reproduces the entire universe. Its four walls represented the cardinal directions, the open roof exposes the participants to the celestial regions, and the bare floor symbolizes the mystic earth below our own flat-earth.[13] The mide stone inside the lodge near the eastern entrance represents the enduring presence of manitou. Finally, each midewiwin lodge has one or more posts that portray the cosmic tree breaking through the many layers of power.[14]

The complete midewiwin ceremony covers eight periods, or *mide days,* that extend over varying lengths of time

Interior of the midewiwin lodge at Elbow Lake, White Earth Reservation, Minnesota, in 1909. The quilt flap at the main east entrance has been lifted revealing the chief mide officer seated behind the mide drum. Along both sides of the open lodge are the assembled mide participants. Courtesy of the Smithsonian Institution National Anthropological Archives.

determined by the midewiwin officer. During each of these periods the ceremony dramatizes the tribe's cosmology by relating a portion of the origin story, in accordance with the degree, or level, of midewiwin being performed. Midewiwin tradition is variously recorded as having four or eight degrees. The generally accepted view is that the first four are earth degrees, while the final four are sky degrees. Local variations in midewiwin practice account for the dif-

Exterior view of the midewiwin lodge at Elbow Lake, White Earth Reservation, Minnesota, in 1909. Cedar boughs line the lower four feet of the 80-by-20-foot lodge, which was made of overlapping lodge-pole pine. The ritual processional movement follows the east-west orientation. Courtesy of the Smithsonian Institution National Anthropological Archives.

ferent numbers of degrees.[15] Occasionally a shaman undergoes all eight midewiwin degrees, over an extended period
of time, although the final stages are considered psycho-
logically dangerous because of the awesome power that is
contacted.[16] Those midewiwin shamans who can bear the
financial strain and the psychic effort involved in the eight
degrees are feared for their shamanistic abilities and respected for their inner identification with the manitou.

During each of the eight mide days in one midewiwin
performance a section of the total cosmological drama is
reenacted. Each midewiwin degree repeats each mide day
but with a gradual elaboration of the cosmological narrative. As the degrees increase, the number of ritual officers
also increases. The specialized herbal lore and the drama-
tized ritual activity are also intensified with each progress-
ing degree of midewiwin. Basically, however, the higher
levels of midewiwin still reenact the same origin story.
Because of this repetition a consideration of the third mide
day provides a model for understanding the reenactment
theme involved in all of midewiwin.

On the morning of the third ceremonial day the chief
midewiwin shaman and the other officers join the patient-
candidate for a purifying sweat. The purpose of this ritual
purification is to cleanse themselves before meeting the
manitou. The sweat lodge can be interpreted within the
context of the Ojibway response to the human condition.
In it the midewiwin officers seek to transform their inherent weakness before they assume the role of a manitou.
They also endure this challenging sudorific for the patient,
who does not join them in this sweat lodge.[17]

Before the ritual purification begins, an elaborate dance
is held that recreates the path that Bear manitou followed
when he brought the midewiwin ceremony onto the present earth. The dance is called "eluding the manitou," and
it recreates the circuitous route that Bear took to escape
the Evil Manitou who sought to destroy the midewiwin
power.[18] The dance, repeated in each midewiwin cere-

Midewiwin sweathouse frame, Lac Courte Oreille, Wisconsin, 1899. The stones under the frame were heated and sprinkled with water from bunches of tied grass. Midewiwin candidates often receive instructions in Midewiwin lore during the sweat baths that purify and prepare him for the midewiwin ceremony. Courtesy of the Smithsonian Institution National Anthropological Archives.

mony, follows a symbolic path that winds around the poles of the sweat lodge. By retracing the tortuous route of Bear, the midewiwin officer, called *naganid*, purges the sweat lodge of all evil. These two ritual actions, namely the dance and the sweat itself, exemplify the reenactment motif in Ojibway shamanism. The prayerful dance and the purifying sweat evoke established cosmological symbols for reassuring aid in this world of conflicting forces. Just as the individual tribesperson exposes his weakness to the manitou while on the vision fast, so also the midewiwin officers purify their inherent weakness in the sweat lodge to prepare for the manitou presence. Similarly, the circuitous dance that reenacts the mythic travels of Bear is a symbolic means of harmonizing the forces of the cosmology with the tensions inherent in the tribal ethos.[19] Landes observed, "The ritual of 'eluding the manitou' also exposed life as a hard conflict of ethical forces, the midewiwin being a refuge from evil and defeat."[20] Through the dance the sweat lodge and, by extension, the midewiwin ceremony, transforms the oppressive forces of life.

While the midewiwin ritual reenacts the drama of cosmic struggles, it also recapitulates the Ojibway history. It was on midewiwin birchbark scrolls that the society's shamans kept a careful record of the westward migration of the consolidating tribal villages.[21] The tribal ethos was also celebrated in the great midewiwin shaman's thaumaturgy. For the Mide Society's "old men" not only narrated the stories of the assembled cosmic manitou but also told the story of the tribe's heroic migration by means of a pictographic chart. Thus narrated myth and oral history were fused in the midewiwin ritual, just as the individual practices of the Ojibway shaman ritually joined his or her personal mythic experience with the needs of the patient.

The interpretation of the midewiwin ritual as shamanic reenactment helps explain why its formation was so central to Ojibway tribal consolidation. Midewiwin joined together the essential belief in manitou spirits and the growing awareness of tribal formation in multi-clan villages during the westward migration. As Selwyn Dewdney has explained, "the Midewiwin was a device for reenacting ritualistically the agent's original mission [the mission of the patient-candidate, who symbolized Nanabozho and Bear] at the same time re-creating, in the four lodges of the Master scrolls, not only the agent's original initiation, but the major stopping-places on the westward movements of the ancestral Ojibway."[22]

In that passage Dewdney underscored the function of the midewiwin shaman's birchbark scrolls as mnemonic devices to aid in presenting the reenactment drama that occurs during midewiwin. The collective response of the tribal shamans to the transitional crisis of the colonial period was to structure a shamanic ritual, midewiwin. In this traditional shamanic healing ritual the tribe's aggressive migration westward is mythologized so that its reenactment communicates the cosmic powers.

In considering the Ojibway shaman's ritual in terms of its reenactment theme, a special emphasis is placed on the experience that initiated the shaman into his or her vocation. This first encounter with the other world of the personalistic powers links the shaman-initiate to the tribal cosmology and reveals his particular symbols of reenactment. In addition, the shaman's ritual has a clear connection with the Ojibway ethos of aggressive individualism, because every Ojibway shaman's ritual is intended to alleviate a tribesperson's distress through healing or divining. The shaman recalls his or her initial experience of manitou presence to invoke that transformative relationship for the patient's healing or to divine specific information.

The Ojibway shaman's ritual provides insight into both the self-awareness of these individuals and their traditional life-style. Indeed, the shamanic wisdom that is forged into a ritual celebration interlaces the individual shaman's vision, the communal ethos, and the tribal cosmology. Shamanic rituals, especially midewiwin, show the formative reflex that religious beliefs have on individual action and the consequent effect that tribal behavior has on the belief system. Within the shamanic ritual the trance state can be seen as a mediation between the Ojibway world view and ethos. The shaman becomes the mediator of special power by means of this trance experience.

7

TRANCE EXPERIENCE

THE Ojibway shaman's ritual depends on a special mode of trance communication with the spirit world. As the shamanic ritual evolves from the shaman's initiating experience, the formative encounter with the manitou provides the central symbols with which the shaman dramatically reenacts his vocational call. The psychic evocation and apprehension of the manitou during each shamanic performance is what is called *trance*. The objective of this chapter will be to elucidate the function and significance of the trance state in Ojibway shamanism.

In Chapter 5 the Ojibway shaman's healing and divining practices were analyzed as stages of invocation, practice of the healing craft, creation of a therapeutic field, and diagnosis of the underlying cause. In each of those stages the shaman's trance functions in a different capacity. The invocation, for instance, summons the manitou presence. The practice of the healing craft proceeds according to trance instructions. A therapeutic field is conveyed to the patient by means of the trance experience. The final diagnosis is a personal communication from the spirits. Thus what is broadly identified as the trance state is actually a coalescence of psychic-spiritual techniques that are interrelated throughout the shaman's ritual and are not wholly independent entities. Together they can be interpreted as a gestalt whose function depends on the particular shamanic practice.

While trance has different uses in specific shamanic practices, its significance is largely determined by the cultural context. A particular methodological approach, moreover, can significantly alter the interpretation of trance dynamics. For example, the interpretations of shamanistic reverie using the insights of medical psychology have varied extensively.[1] Schools of "medical materialism" have reduced shamanistic phenomena to manifestations of aberrant behavior originating from a pathological state.[2] On the other hand, some anthropological studies have idealized the shaman and uncritically accepted the more aberrant manifestations of shamanism.[3] These efforts to understand the shaman's psychic techniques have often been vitiated by the limits of the methodological approach used. Many studies have not situated the shamanistic trance in a larger hermeneutical context, what William James has expressed as "the way it works on the whole."[4] Our approach does not begin with a predetermined epistemology but rather with the tribal perspective. Although the analytical tools of contemporary psychology are available for later interpretation, the initial understanding should be developed as much as possible from within the tribal context.

The Ojibway tradition recognizes the trance techniques of their tribal shamans as gratuitous gifts that are bestowed on these personalities in a dream or vision.[5] The authorizing manitou dream, for example, is a significant experience of lasting import in the tribal understanding.[6] The shaman's reevocation of his sacred dream enables him to enter again into that experience of the liminal world. Having opened the threshold from the human world to the manitou spheres, the Ojibway shaman withdraws to develop his meditative techniques. The shaman is acknowledged as marginal to his society not because of his departure from a social norm but because he is now intimately associated with the manitou.[7] His perception of reality is now informed by his meditative posture, which draws him to the manitou. He is required to develop the resiliency that can endure the rigor of shamanic practice. He must also practice restraint so as not to be psychically overwhelmed by the manitou. Finally, the shaman must creatively channel the power that he is given if he is to obtain the approval of his tribe.

The shamanic trance techniques presented in the following pages are validated both by the personal dream experience of the shaman and by the tribal belief that such a dream can be a divine revelation.[8] The significance of the trance state is in this tribal understanding of dreams as a visionary mode. Shamanic trance can be interpreted as the concentrated effort of the shaman to enter into an intense visionary experience. In the Ojibway world this visionary experience is a contact with and reevocation of the archetypal symbols of his initiating dream. The contact with these symbols activates unique constellations of psychic energies for the shaman.

The following examples of Ojibway shamanic trance experience are drawn from the older shamanistic vocations, such as the *nanandawi,* the *wabeno,* the *tcisaki,* and the ceremonies of the Mide Society. Although the styles and status of Ojibway shamanic expressions have changed through the centuries, the traditional tribal sanction of the dream-validated trance state has persisted.[9]

Nanandawi

Among the Ojibway the tube-sucking shaman receives his doctoring abilities in a dream of the Thunderbird manitou or another spirit symbolically related to the Thunderbird.[10] Having been hired by a family to treat one of its members, the *nanandawi* invokes his manitou patron to locate the illness. In the early eighteenth century the French military commandant Antoine de la Mothe Cadillac observed, "They give out that it is a guardian spirit . . . who reveals to them and teaches them how and by what means the poison and spell have been cast upon the man who is sick."[11] Often the sucking shaman heightened the ritual drama by requesting that the patient's room be darkened so that his prognostic meditation might "see" more clearly.[12] Because

A nanandawi *shaman, sketched by Harold MacDonald in 1890 for Walter James Hoffman's study of the Minnesota Midewiwin. The na-nandawi, or tube-sucking, shaman pursued an ancient shamanic vocation among the Ojibway. These shamans and other specialists formed the core officers of the Mide Society.* Courtesy of the Smithsonian Institution National Anthropological Archives.

the entry into shamanic trance is dependent upon the shaman's personal power dream, various techniques are used. The following description by Cadillac is of a frenetic dream reenactment:

The part he [the *nanandawi*] plays is certainly humble to all appearance, and those who watch his performance can only imagine that he is possessed by a demon while he is doing his juggling. Those who stand around beat drums and strike on cooking pots and strips of bark with small sticks, and this continues as long as the illness lasts. . . . At intervals the surgeon dances, chants, makes hideous grimaces, rolls his eyes and casts them down, turns up his nose, thrusts forward his jaws and dislocates the lower jaw; his neck now stretches and now shortens; his lungs expand and his stomach swells; his fingers, hands and arms are extended and withdrawn; he spits blood from his mouth and makes it issue from his nose and ears, and he tears and pierces his skin; and, as I have already said, all these things and many others are done chanting and dancing.[13]

While Cadillac interpreted this *nanandawi's* ritual as an instance of demonic possession, his description still illustrates the psychophysiological exertion that the shaman may use to pass into the trance state. Of particular interest for interpreting these tumultuous psychic techniques are the drumming of the audience and the shaman's chanting. For the shaman to pass into the liminal state that the tribe recognizes as the dream evocation, an intensely concentrated mood has to be maintained. In Cadillac's example the drumming seems to have provided the percussive repetition that enabled the shaman to effect the transition into the trance state.[14] Along with this rhythmic drumming the shaman chanted his vision songs to activate the cosmological symbols of his initiating dream. By sustaining this rhythmic meditation, the shaman perceived the object intrusion causing the illness and proceeded to suck the affected part of the patient.

The sucking shaman's ability to maintain his perception in the ritual furor suggests that he was not wholly possessed by the trance experience. A certain restraint enabled him to direct his psychic energies toward the patient. Thus shamans engaged in healing practices direct the psychic forces that they ritually invoke. These acts of perception, restraint, and direction by Ojibway shamans prevent too close an identification of their trances with possession. Certain conditions associated with possession are evident, such as the shaman's actions as a medium, the shaman's depersonalization, and some intrusive spirit-illness. Yet the major characteristic of external intrusion by a spirit is absent in the Ojibway shaman.[15] The tribe speaks of the *nanandawi* not as possessed but as in contact with the manitou. This contact is not a total absorption by the spirit but rather the evocation of an established relationship between the reality of the manitou-dream and the shaman-dreamer.

Each Ojibway shaman's method of communication with the manitou patron is unique and is related to a personal dream experience. Thus in the example of the *nanandawi* shaman, Sky Woman, first given in Chapter 6, the communication of the healing energies substantially differed from Cadillac's description of a *nanandawi* trance above:

One time she [Sky Woman] fell asleep and dreamed of the time she had been lost. She dreamed that someone gave her a rattle and other things they use when they doctor, and spoke to her saying, "Try this on your grandmother. She might get better." So when she woke she made a little rattle, and started to *nananda wiat* [cure by sucking]. When she finished, the old woman seemed to be brighter. That night she started again on *manitou kazo* [talking supernatural or invoking supernatural] and cure by sucking.[16]

The importance of this example is its mention of the Ojibway term for the *nanandawi*'s trance state, namely *manitou kazo*, "talking supernatural." The pacific manner in which Sky Woman sustained the shamanic art manifested her personal style of *manitou kazo*. Her tranquil approach stemmed directly from her first manitou dream when she was lost in the woods: "All that time she dreamed that she was in a place where there were a lot of people, and she was very happy and had nice things to eat. . . . Here she was blessed so she could *nanandawi i we* (cure by sucking.)"[17] Later the manitou dream that Sky Woman received during her grandmother's illness activated the latent energies of her initiating dream. Thus, by chanting her *manitou kazo*, she recreated the reassuring mood of the manitou dreams.

The Ojibway believed that a person who performed shamanistic activities had to have some kind of communication with the archetypal spirit world. For this, *manitou kazo* was the traditional means of invoking the manitou patron.[18] Sky woman used *manitou kazo*, moreover, to create the healing context in which her sucking cure could be effective. As a trance technique *manitou kazo* produced a prolonged mediation between the manitou and the patient. Sky Woman maintained this healing environment by reen-acting the guidance of her sacred dream, namely, chanting inspired songs, playing the seed rattle, and applying the sucking cure.

Although the shaman's relation to the source of healing power and the patient are often described as those of a medium, the passive qualities of a medium are not entirely comparable to those of the Ojibway *nanandawi.* Instead, the terms *enstatic* and *ecstatic* are useful in describing the Ojibway shaman's inspired state. *Ecstatic* describes that type of trance in which the shaman's consciousness is said to leave the body. *Enstatic* applies to that inspired state in which the contact with the sacred is decidedly interior and meditative. Unlike the ecstatic journey of some Siberian shamans, the trance of the Ojibway *nanandawi* actively transmits the power necessary for healing through a more enstatic mediation.

The enstatic trance technique of *manitou kazo* estab-lishes a special relationship between the patient and the manitou. The *nanandawi* moves in rhythmic meditation between his manitou, who reveals the cause and the cure of the illness, and the patient, who "marvels at the sha-man's art and cleverness, and . . . begins to think he is healed."[19]

Wabeno

The *wabeno* is an ancient shamanic personality that was formerly found among several Algonquian groups.[20] The *wabeno*'s shamanistic art is performed singly or in a so-ciety composed of both men and women. The Ojibway *wabeno* is first described in the *Jesuit Relations* as healing by means of fire manipulations and erotic dances.[21] Named by the French as "jugglers," these *wabeno* handled live coals and then rubbed their heated hands over the patient while chanting their vision songs. Another *wabeno* speciality is divining, which they accomplish by gazing into glowing coals until inspiration moves them to respond to questions.[22] In addition, the earlier *wabeno* held a healing ritual in which naked shamans danced around the ailing patient.[23] These *wabeno* practices were at times condemned by European observers, which often led to conflict between tribal shamans and the Christian missionaries.[24]

By exhibiting his pyrotechnics, the *wabeno* shaman evokes the hypnotic mystery of fire and the mood necessary for his passage into trance. Herbal preparations are used to protect *wabeno* from the burning coals that they handle. "By the use of plants he is alleged to be enabled to take up and handle with impunity red hot stones and burning brands, and without evincing the slightest discomfort it is said that he will bathe his hands in boiling water, or even boiling maple syrup."[25] These protective practices are openly known. The *wabeno*'s skill lies not merely in herbal preparations but also in the effect he or she creates on the patient to be healed, in his or her own movement into trance, and in the dramatic spectacle that the audience witnesses.

By means of sustained concentration on the glowing embers, the *wabeno* evokes his manitou patron. The patron who bestows the *wabeno* vocation is described as a fiery figure with radiant horns.[26] The whole complex of the *wabeno* ceremony, including the fire handling, naked dance, drumming, rattling, and chanting, is devoted to the frenzied encounter with this horned manitou. After summoning the manitou and passing into an altered psychic state, the *wabeno* conveys the fiery manitou's presence by rubbing the patient with his heated hands. The patient's confidence in the *wabeno*'s healing ability is amplified by the fire juggling, which appears to demonstrate the shaman's authentic contact with the spirit world. As Eliade has said, "Mastery over fire, insensibility to heat, and, hence the 'mystical heat' that renders both extreme cold and the temperature of burning coals supportable, is a magical-mystical virtue that . . . translates into sensible terms the fact that the shaman has passed beyond the human condition and already shares in the condition of 'spirits.'"[27]

Thus the Ojibway *wabeno* passes into the "other world" of manitou power by virtue of his pyrotechnics. His entrancing techniques using fire help create a mood in which the shaman's vision can structure a healing rite. For this overwhelming attraction between the manitou and the shaman does not usually deteriorate into spirit possession. Rather the power from the manitou world is directed into healing and divining rituals for the tribal community.

Like fire manipulation, the *wabeno* shaman's erotic dance mediates the healing energies given him or her in dream or vision. The release of erotic energies for healing derives from the Ojibway shaman's ability to evoke the trancelike qualities of the sexual act. The psychic technique of naked dancing practiced by the *wabeno* also harks back to the ithyphallic pictographs found throughout Ojibway territory.[28] These rock paintings and carvings depict the Ojibway understanding of the manitou force inherent in the male sex. More than mere graphic art, these images "render visible the hidden meanings in nature whose significance it has been the shaman's task to conjure up and capture on stone."[29] Just as Ojibway visionaries conjured up their power dreams to execute this phallic art, so also the *wabeno* shaman channels a vital healing force through his or her ritual naked dance.[30]

The major *wabeno* ceremonials are usually performed by a group of these shamans. In many respects the development of the *wabeno* shamanic groups paralleled the formation of the Mide Society. Both shamanic groups crystalized around archaic shamanistic vocations among the Algonquian and arose during the crisis years of the formation of the Ojibway as a tribe. Each ritualized a shamanistic experience and opened it to those tribesmembers who paid the stipulated fee and underwent the rite of passage. John Tanner, who lived among the Ojibway for nearly three decades, described some of the characteristics of the *wabeno* relation to the midewiwin:

At this time [1800], the Waw-be-no was fashionable among the Ojibbeways, but it has ever been considered by the older and more respectable men as a false and dangerous religion. The ceremonies of the Waw-be-no differ very essentially from those of the Metai [midewiwin], and are usually accompanied by much licentiousness and irregularity. The Ta-wa-e-gun used for a drum in this dance, differs from the Woin Ah-keek, or Meti-kwaw-keek, used in the Metai, it being made of a hoop of bent wood like a soldier's drum, while the latter is the portion of the trunk of a tree hollowed by fire, and having the skin tied over it. The She-zhe-gwun or rattle, differs also in its construction from that used in the Metai. In the Waw-be-no, men and women dance and sing together, and there is much juggling and playing with fire. The initiated take coals of fire, and red hot stones in their hands, and sometimes in their mouths. Sometimes they put a [gun] powder on the insides of their hands, first moistening them to make it stick; then by rubbing them with coals or a red hot stone, they make the powder burn.[31]

Although John Tanner decidedly favored the midewiwin *(Metai)* ceremonial, he acknowledged the inspirational frenzy of the *wabeno* shamans. The drum that he describes was used to create an entrancing atmosphere for the initiates. It was usually painted with the image of the horned manitou who was the focus of the *wabeno* trance experience.[32] The use and construction of the drum also indicate that the trance contact was initiated and maintained by its percussive power.

During the troubled times of the Ojibway migration and the subsequent Indian wars the tribe often participated in the spring and summer *wabeno* initiation ceremonies. The transitional crisis during the eighteenth and nineteenth centuries caused the Ojibway to turn to their heroic personalities, the shamans, for leadership. The *wabeno* cult

responded to the tribal need by structuring ancient shamanic trance techniques into a community experience of
the manitou presence. As such it may have been a safety
valve channeling repressed energies during this crisis period.[33] Thus the *wabeno* trance not only healed individual
patients but also revitalized individual participants.

The *wabeno* cult did not gain a lasting position in the
Ojibway tribe, partly because of its frenetic trance techniques. The cult did not have the wide appeal to the various Ojibway bands that the more mythologized midewiwin
did. It also focused too exclusively on the trance as an end
in itself. Spirit possession is not an acceptable shamanic
technique among the Ojibway. Their traditional shamans
do not cultivate trances that result in loss of personal control. Such loss of control because of spirit possession is
comparable to the most deadly illness conceived by the
Ojibway, namely *Windigo*.[34]

The following contemporary account of a *wabeno* shaman reflects the later, subdued practices of this cult. Although the *wabeno* techniques of fire manipulation and
frenzied dance are not mentioned, the trance experience
via dream evocation is still evident. The name of this female shaman is Eternal Man, emphasizing the androgy-
nous quality of her shamanic vocation. The recovery of
her youthful dream and its use in trance enabled her to
enter into the Ojibway shamanic world, which was predominantly male:

Eternal Man had received the visionary powers of a *wabeno*
but did not think of employing them until she was urged by her
husband. When her twin girls were about three years old, she was
very sick and nearly died. Her husband cured her by sucking
and said to her, "You will get better if you do the things which
you were taught the time you wandered around the woods without any food. If you promise to do them you will get better."
She said she would, for she remembered that she had dreamed
of these things when she was lost; she had heard someone singing these *wabeno* songs. So she dreamed of them and sang them,

and she got better. The songs sounded very nice. Her husband was also a *wabeno*. People from other places used to come to their *wabeno* dances, for she kept on learning more songs.[35]

Eternal Man's youthful vision had come to her during a time of travail, and consequently it remained dormant until the burden of illness revived her memory. By reenacting her shamanic call in a trance state, she activated the powers that were given to her in the earlier dream. This activation initiated *manitou kazo,* or "talking supernatural," and brought her new song experiences from her manitou.

Eternal Man's *wabeno* trance experience is remarkably similar to that of the *nanandawi* shaman Sky Woman. In effect, the contemporary *wabeno* vocation reasserts the more traditional shamanic trance. The *wabeno* practices had become suspect among the Ojibway bands because they had developed into cultic spirit-possession performances by both men and women. Changes during the nineteenth and twentieth centuries in the *wabeno* trance state reasserted both the norm of traditional shamanic activity and variations in accordance with the shift in Ojibway societal values.

Tcisaki

The *tcisaki* are the most prominent shamans among the Ojibway.[36] They are called diviners because they are able to conjure spirits during trance and elicit information from them. They perform their trance rituals in a conical lodge that shakes while the spirits are present. Thus the *tcisaki* ceremony is usually called "shaking tent." The *tcisaki*'s vocation requires dream validation by the master spirit of the conjuring lodge. In the dream the *tcisaki* receives the chants with which to invoke his familiar spirits.[37] This invocation is performed before the shaking-tent ceremony itself. During this preliminary prayer these shamans may purify themselves in a sweat lodge, make an offering to their personal manitou, or sit and smoke tobacco in a sacred manner. Regardless of which preparatory activity is performed, the *tcisaki* intones initiating chants to summon the spirits. Such a chant may be very elaborate, using symbols from the shaman's dreams, or it may be quite succinct, as in the expression, "Open the sky from the center."[38]

The short chant would be repeated in varying tones, rhythms, and speeds, depending on the inclination of the *tcisaki*. The purpose of the chant is to summon the manitou, not individually but in unison. The manitou with whom the *tcisaki* communicates are not all necessarily dream patrons, but the *tcisaki's* initiating dream opens up the possibility for trance communication with several manitou.[39]

The *tcisaki's* invocation is a psychic technique that aids the shaman in internalizing the manitou forces. The brief chant "Open the sky from the center" indicates both the cosmic orientation of the *tcisaki's* mediation and the concern for individual psychic centering. Before the *tcisaki* even enters his conjuring lodge, he has begun to enter the trance state. This internal meditation on the approaching manitou is sustained by the rhythmic staccato of the drum and the soft seed sound of the rattle. The *tcisaki* becomes focused on the tree that rises above the other poles of the conjuring lodge. This cosmic tree is a centering symbol by which the *tcisaki* expands the psychic sky and establishes the path through which the archetypal forces can enter the lodge.

The invocation also serves to identify the *tcisaki* shaman with his personal visionary power. This identification provides the shaman with a unique sense of confidence with which to meet the constellated manitou who appear at a shaking-tent ceremony. The trance experience of the *tcisaki* is the mutual gravitation of a shamanic power personality together with the many manitou summoned to the ritual. By evoking his own power-identification, the *tcisaki* establishes the psychic resonance needed to activate the archetypal energies with which he will communicate.

The symbols of an Ojibway shaman's invocation chant are often etched into birchbark. These records are kept as mnemonic devices to aid the shaman in the ritual activity, especially as his repertoire of dream songs expands. Such a pictograph record was recorded by W. J. Hoffman in 1891. Although such figures can be deciphered only by their owner, Hoffman was given a general interpretation of the record that he received, in addition to the accompanying chant.[40] Such a chant calls forth the shaman's special privileges, such as *tcisaki* divining, herbal gathering, and midewiwin healing. It reaffirms the shaman's personal power identity and induces the trance state necessary for the conjuring ceremony. The pictographs that Hoffman was shown are in fig. 2. The two main symbols in the chant are the otter and the *migis*-shell manitou. The otter is of primary importance in the Ojibway world, for he is believed to have brought midewiwin and to have led the tribe on its westward migration. The symbol of the *migis* shell parallels that of the otter, in that the southern Ojibway maintain that this luminous shell "led" the westward migration.[41]

In the first pictograph the shaman identifies himself with his spirit patron, Otter, as he enters the *tcisaki* lodge. The second pictograph shows Otter as the intermediary figure who gave life to the tribe through midewiwin. This life medicine, which the Otter dug up, was then spread over the earth in the form of sacred plants. The third pictograph describes this transformation of manitou power into herbal medicine by means of the *migis* shell. In the fourth pictograph the shaman is seen as the one who completes this transformation by digging up the herbal medicine. In this act he repeats the primordial action of the otter, thereby becoming a transformative intermediary figure himself. The fifth pictograph shows the otter responding to the shaman's identification and affirming the shaman's inner transformation.

The shaman pauses in his prayer to allow the spirit

Fig. 2. The *Tcisaki*'s Chant

1.

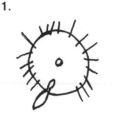

1. ***Me-we-yan, ha, ha, ha*** ("I go into the Jessakan to see the medicine"). The circle represents the *tcisaki*'s lodge, or *jessakan,* as viewed from above. The short lines denote the sacred character of the structure. The central ring or spot denotes the magic stone used by the shaman, who appears entering from the side in spirit form.

2.

2. ***Tschi-nun-don, he, he, he, he*** ("I was the one who dug up life"). The Otter manitou is emerging from the *midewigan,* which he received from Kitshi Manitou.

3.

3. ***Nika-ni we-do-ko-a, ha, ha*** ("The spirit put down medicine on earth to grow"). The sacred or magic lines descending to earth denote the supernatural origin of the *migis* shell, which is shown by the four small rings. The short lines at the bottom represent the ascending sprouts of magic plants.

4.

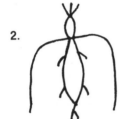

4. ***Te-ti-ba-tshi mut-a-wit, te, he, he*** ("I am the one that dug up the medicine"). The otter is shown emerging from the shaking tent. The shaman represents himself as "like unto Otter Manitou."

5.

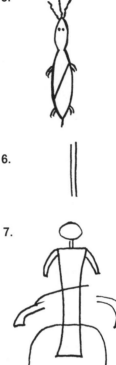

5. *Ki-wan-win-da ma-kwa-nan, na, ha* ("I answer my brother spirit"). The Otter Manitou responds to the invocation of the *tcisaki.* The diagonal line across the body signifies the "spirit character" of the animal.

6.

6. Rest or pause.

7.

7. *Wa-a-so-at wen-ti-na-man, ha, ha* ("The spirit has put life into my body"). The *tcisaki* is represented as being in the *midewigan* where Kitshi Manitou placed magic power in his body; the arms denote this act of putting the *migis* into his sides. The line across his body denotes a person to be possessed of supernatural power.

8.

8. *Ki-to na-bi-in, ne, he, he* ("This is what the medicine has given us"). The pictograph shows the *midewigan* and, on the upper line, the guardian manitou.

9.

9. *Ni-sha-we-ni-bi-ku, hu, hu, he* ("I took with two hands what was thrown down to us"). The *tcisaki* grasps life, i.e., the *migis,* to secure the mysterious power which he professes.

---

power to enter his body fully. In pictograph six he then acknowledges the presence of the supernatural power and relates it to the midewiwin. By situating his spirit power within the tradition of midewiwin (in pictographs six and seven), he sees his power in the traditional cosmic context symbolized by the midewiwin lodge. He thus consciously prevents a personalistic possession that could distort the power he has evoked. The final pictograph announces the intention of the shaman to bring together this power with traditional shamanistic knowledge for the ceremony he is about to perform.

As this birchbark record indicates, the essential elements of the *tcisaki* trance state are *identification* with the manitou patron, *transformation* into the power he represents, and *communication* with the power evoked. The shaman in his trance activates the archetypal symbols of the otter and the *migis* to create a mutual resonance between himself and the powers those symbols represent.

After sunset the *tcisaki* enters the shaking tent, which has been built earlier by his assistants in strict accord with the *tcisaki*'s dream authorization.[42] According to tribal tradition, the lodge begins to shake when the *tcisaki* enters it. The "winds" of the manitou presence are said to cause the structure to move. The mutual reciprocity of manitou and *tcisaki* is clearly demonstrated by this sign of spirit presence. A *tcisaki*'s trance may be stimulated by further drumming, but, when the lodge begins to move, the tribal audience knows that the spirits have arrived. Then the shaman ceases his drumming and crouches near the ground, responding to questions from the audience, who remain outside the lodge. The animated conversation is often in archaic expressions of the Ojibway language. Thus the *tcisaki* interprets the cryptic responses of the manitou.[43]

Two recurring characteristics of the *tcisaki*'s trance performance are the audible voices of the manitou and the appearance of light sparks within the shaking tent itself. These manifestations are usually explained as the products of the shaman's ventriloquism and hallucinations.[44] In any case, they are signs of the *tcisaki*'s trance state. Hearing voices and seeing bright lights are traditional signs of a visionary experience among the Ojibway. The *tcisaki*'s trance is part of this visionary mode linking individuals to significant cosmological symbols. The *tcisaki* shaman's identification with manitou power made him a religious personality capable of summoning a spiritual presence. The following passage expresses a former *tcisaki*'s belief in his shamanic role as a contact with the other world:

"I have become a Christian, I am old, I am sick, I cannot live much longer, and I can do no other than speak the truth. Believe me, I did not deceive you at that time. I did not move the lodge. It was shaken by the power of the spirits. Not did I speak with a double tongue. I only repeated to you what the spirits said to me. I heard their voices. The top of the lodge was filled with them, and before me the sky and the wide lands lay expanded. I could see a great distance around me, and believed I could recognize the most distant objects." The old dying *jossakid* [*tcisaki*] said this with such an expression of simple truth and firm conviction, that it seemed to me, at least, that he did not consider himself a deceiver, and believed in the efficacy of his magic arts and the reality of his visions.[45]

Despite his conversion to Christianity this shaman maintained his belief in the authenticity of the *tcisaki* trance ritual. He had entered sustained internal meditations in which he perceived voices coming from many spirits. It is clear that this *tcisaki* identified with the spirit world and was transformed into a visionary who saw into distant regions. It is, however, his role as communicator that is emphasized here, for he insists that he was only conveying the messages of the manitou. As another *tcisaki* expressed it, "I held communication with supernatural beings, or thinking minds or spirits which acted upon my mind or soul, and revealed to me such knowledge as I have described to you."[46]

This trance process, initiated by repetitive drumming

and chanting, activates archetypal symbols so that the shaman identifies with these manitou presences. This identification is intensified until the shaman experiences an internal transformation sustained by the rhythmic meditation. In this altered state he reestablishes a special mode of communication with the spirit world. This communication empowers him with knowledge appropriate for specific cases of healing and divining.

Midewiwin

The midewiwin ceremony draws extensively upon the psychic techniques of the earlier forms of Ojibway shamanism in its own ceremonial trance. These techniques are not private revelations, but are open to anyone who joins the Mide Society in a prescribed manner. Consequently, the trance states in midewiwin ceremony are both structured and spontaneous. In the structured trance the initiate is given the society's vision by means of the cosmological stories, sacred chants, shamanic tricks, and herbal lore. Through those esoteric teachings the candidate for a Midewiwin degree or the patient to be healed participates in the cosmic symbolism of the Ojibway origin stories. The Mide Society's mythological vision is given to the patient-candidate just as an individual dream or vision is given to a fasting visionary.[47] Along with this structured trance midewiwin ceremony uses a spontaneous mode of trance experience. During dramatic moments of this spontaneous trance the initiate is instructed by the society's shamans to be aware of the manitou strength that is being physically implanted in him. Both the structured and the spontaneous trance state are special means of communication with the spirit world that transmit a vital force.

Several different trance states are used during the eight periods, or mide days, of the society's ceremonial activity. The ones selected for discussion here illustrate the traditional Ojibway trance techniques. First, the structured recitation of midewiwin cosmologies and the presentation of esoteric lore create a context for trance participation by the initiate. Second, the midewiwin drum story not only continues the participatory trance but also induces a deeper trance by its percussive rhythm. Finally, the ritual event of *migis* shell shooting gives the patient-candidate a personal contact with manitou power.

During the eight mide days the chief ceremonial officer narrates a version of the society's cosmology to the candidate for a degree. Like the innovative sacred songs that are also given to the initiate by the midewiwin officers, these cosmological stories and songs are often repeated to confer a cumulative benefit on the patient candidate.[48] The value of the traditional cosmologies, as well as the innovative songs, is in their reenactment of the primordial creation of midewiwin. The patient is directed to respond to the midewiwin officer as if he or she is receiving a personal revelation of manitou. The narration of these cosmological stories and the chanting of vision songs is considered a "sacred talking." By audibly participating in these revelations, the initiate is brought into the presence of manitou power. Thus "sacred talking" is the midewiwin parallel to the solitary shaman's *manitou kazo.* Moreover, just as individual shamans hurry the narration of their personal dream, so also do some midewiwin shamans mumble their cosmological narrations or chant low and rapidly.[49]

The recitation of the cosmologies is also accompanied by the performance of special sleights of hand. These shamanic manipulations are an attempt by the midewiwin officer to induce the patient-candidate's participation in the mythic story presented to him or her. The following description is typical of the means by which such participation is effected. The midewiwin officers expose their magical objects to the candidate and explain their function. By so doing, they increase the sense of mystery surrounding the initiation ceremony and provide a context in which the trance can take place:

After an offering to Kitshi Manitou, with the pipe, they expose the articles contained in their Mide sacks and explain and expatiate upon the merits and properties of each of the magic objects. The candidate for the first time learns of the manner of preparing effigies, etc., with which to present to the incredulous ocular demonstration of the genuineness and divine origin of the Midewiwin or, as it is in this connection termed, religion.

Several methods are employed for the purpose, and the greater the power of the Mide the greater will appear the mystery connected with the exhibition. This may be performed whenever circumstances demand such proof, but the tests are made before the candidate with a twofold purpose: first, to impress him with the supernatural powers of the Mide [officers] themselves; and second, in an ocular manner, to ascertain if Kitshi Manitou is pleased with the contemplated ceremony and the initiation of the candidate.[50]

The shamanic tricks accompany the recitation of cosmological lore and enhance the atmosphere of sacred presence during the narration. Traditional tricks are causing beads to roll as if animated and making wooden dolls move unaided or a mide medicine sack *(midewayan)* speak. The success of the shamanic tricks indicates Kitshi Manitou's pleasure with the candidate's entrance into midewiwin. By means of such ritual activity the initiate enters into the reciprocal spirit that promotes the passage of healing energies.

A structured trance is also used to teach the herbal lore that is an integral part of midewiwin shamanism. The mide shaman Gagewin (Everlasting Mist) said: "The midewiwin is not so much to worship anything as to preserve the knowledge of herbs for use in prolonging life. The principle idea of the Midewiwin is that life is prolonged by right living, and by the use of herbs which were intended for this purpose by the mide manitou."[51] The patient-candidate is taught the accumulated plant medicine of the tribal shamans as he progresses through the degrees of midewiwin. This herbal lore is not a separate ceremony of midewiwin but woven into the narration of stories concerning the manitou, the songs that are continually chanted, and the manipulation of effigies.

Midewiwin's structured trance states induce various modes of perception. The initiate is taught consciously to participate in the repeated narration, the magical manipulation, and the herbal therapeutics. Trance participation during midewiwin is a means of instructing the candidate in shamanic lore, just as the individual shaman is taught when he withdraws into solitude to master his art. The initiate is urged to move toward the sources of the powers as he or she evokes their presence in his ritual trance.

The rhythm of the midewiwin ceremony is created by the drum, called *mitig wakik*.[52] Like all of the shamanic objects that are legitimized by vision, the ritual instruments used in midewiwin are sanctioned by the origin myth. The drum is celebrated in the origin myth as the means by which the manitou may be contacted. The midewiwin drum is a significant symbol of trance participation as the instrument for calling the manitou power. It also sets the rhythmic tempo in which the midewiwin shamans experientially induce the sustained meditation of the trance state.

The story of the mide drum involves Shell, the Earth manitou, and Bear, who is said to own midewiwin. In mythic lore Shell asked Bear to gather the manitou. Bear shook the mide rattle, but the sound was inadequate to assemble the spirits. So Bear went in search of a noisemaker:

He (Bear) left. When he returned (Shell asked) "Did you find him?" "I saw an old man, very old, almost of an age to die." "That will be the one. Go call him." Bear left. "I am calling you! That One (Shell) sitting there is who calls you!"

Then he (the oldster) came and he (Shell) spoke to him: "Will you not go and help the Indian with a voice?" (The oldster manitou answered) "Thank you. So that is what you want me to do. I will do it."

So he went to the center of the Earth. The manitou talked low to one another: "I don't believe the Indian can handle this

Midewiwin instruments and scrolls: from left to right, birchbark scrolls with incised pictographs indicating ceremonial songs, a round hand drum with striker, and a log drum partially filled with water used for midewiwin ceremonies. On top of the drum is a loon-shaped drumstick, and on the right are various rattles of tanned hide. Courtesy of the Smithsonian Institution National Anthropological Archives.

easily." The manitou guardians supposed that if the entire man turned into a drum, the result would be far too cumbersome for Indian strength. Then he (the old man) flew to pieces (by whirling clockwise a number of times, the number being that of the patient's grade.) Our Grandfather then took one piece (for the midewiwin drum).[53]

The midewiwin myth of the drum recapitulates the career of the ancient family shaman who "sounded the drum" to cure illness.[54] During midewiwin the patient-candidate undergoing the ceremonial cure becomes the archaic *meda* shaman. The patient-candidate, moreover, is analogous to the sacrificial oldster-manitou who "flew into pieces" at the earth's center to become the drum that calls the manitou. In effect, the midewiwin drum that is honored and respectfully handled during the ceremony symbolizes both the heroism of the patient-candidate who is "of an age to die" and the healing ability of the entranced shaman who calls the manitou power.

The drum is a multivalent symbol that draws together several seemingly unrelated entities. It is related to the cosmic symbolism of the Ojibway origin myth and to the particular symbolic requests of each midewiwin ceremony. Its rhythm calls the manitou down to the ceremony and disposes the celebrants to the sacrificial mode necessary for trance reenactment of the primordial midewiwin. As in so many shamanic rituals the rhythmic drum in midewiwin provides the steady pulsation that inspires and sustains the encounter with archetypal presences.

Perhaps the most impressive use of trance technique in midewiwin comes during the fifth-day public ceremony. On this day the mide officers "shoot" the patient with their medicine bundles, *midewayan*, which contain the sacred *migis* shells.[55] The killing of the patient reenacts both the primordial death of Nanabozho during the first midewiwin and the ceremonial death that initiates the patient-candidate into the sacred society of shamans. The significance of the action is as a spontaneous ritualized trance experience. At this midewiwin event the sick patient is expected to be cured, and the shaman-candidate initiated, by the infusion of manitou power in the form of *migis* shells.[56] The ritual death and revivification of the patient-candidate parallels the trance techniques of the solitary Ojibway visionary seeking shamanic powers. As in the fragmentation of the mide drum, the initiate undergoes the death experience to be rejuvenated as one able to communicate with the mysterious spirits.

The shooting ceremony takes place in the mide lodge, *midewigan*, which is built on the day of this public ceremony.[57] While the spectacular shell shooting is the major event of this mide day, some ritual hesitations customarily heighten the dramatic tension. First, when everyone is as-

Fig. 3. Midewiwin Chant During Ritual Placement of Shells

1.

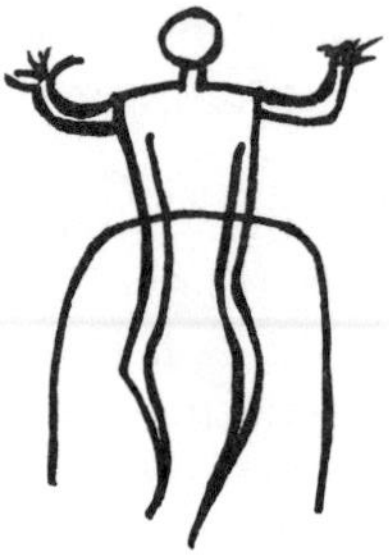

1. *We-nen-wi-wik ka-ni-an* ("The spirit has made sacred the place in which I live"). Establishing the cosmological context, the shamans look out from the midewiwin lodge and identify their location with certain power presences.

2.

2. *En-da-yan pi-ma-ti-su-i-un en-da-yan* ("The spirit gave the medicine which we receive"). In this pictograph the "sky regions" send down the manitou to the lower earth, where it appears in healing herbs.

3.

3. Pause. The pause is a ritual acknowledgement of the silent transformation for which the shamans pray.

4.

4. *Nin-nik-ka-ni man-i-tou* ("I too have taken the medicine he gave us"). The medicine power is shown as within the speaker's arm, that is, within his grasp.

5.

5. *Ke-kek-o-i-yan* ("I brought life to the people"). The shamans' symbolic identification with Thunderbird.

6.

6. *Be-mo-se ma-ko-yan* ("I have come to the medicine lodge also"). The shaman's symbolic identification with Bear manitou.

7.

7. *Ka-ka-mi-ni-ni-ta* ("We spirits are talking together"). The shamans speak intimately with the sacred power presences—*manitou kazo*.

8.

8. *O-ni-ni-shink-ni-yo* ("The *migis* is on my body"). The *migis*, symbolic of the transformative power, is shown being placed within the patient-candidate's body.

9.

9. *Ni man-i-tou ni-yan* ("The spirit has put away all my sickness"). The Mide Society shaman radiates the intensity of manitou presence, which forces out all intrusive illnesses.

Reproduced from Hoffman, "Midē'wiwin," pp. 218–19.

sembled in the *midewigan,* the chief midewiwin shaman begins to place *migis* shells on the prone body of the patient-candidate.[58] These placements are in accordance with an old shamanic understanding of the internalization of spirit presence.[59] Wherever the shells are placed, the manitou are believed to locate themselves in the physical body of the initiate. This is not, however, an intrusion of spirits that overwhelms the shaman's conscious mind. Rather, the shells placed during midewiwin encourage the spontaneous mode of trance by giving the shaman-initiate certain physical centers for meditation on power.

After the chief mide makes the shell placements, the assembled officers representing the manitou place their shells on the patient. During this ritual placement the mide officers teach the initiate the song in fig. 3.[60] Then, after the ritual dances and songs and recitation of the origin myth, a midewiwin officer, called the Bowman, strikes the drum saying, "Manitou, they are flying!"[61] Yet, even as the drama is heightened, there is another ritual hesitation. A previously killed dog is cooked and served in a public feast. This dog, which is laid across the western entrance, symbolizes Lion, the guardian of the midewiwin threshold.

After the meal the Bowman begins again to sing the sacred songs that are evocative of the midewiwin trance state. While singing, he takes up the medicine bundle of weasel skin that contains the *migis* shells symbolic of the strength that Kitshi Manitou has imparted to midewiwin. The following chant is sung by Bowman as he grasps the medicine skin:

> Here it is,
> The weasel skin.
> Through it I shoot the white shells.
>
> It never fails.
> The shell goes toward them
> And they fall.

Bear-paw Mide bag with cloth-and-bead wrap collected by Frances Densmore in 1929. This ritual object figured prominently in the public rite of the midewiwin ceremony. On that day Mide shamans ritually "shot" the migis *(cowrie) shell power at one another. This bear-paw medicine bundle is a traditionally sanctioned item of Midewiwin lore; yet the bead patterns represent personal dream and/or vision connections with the Thunderer manitou-spirit with a heart line and a wavy power line to the sun symbol of Kitshi Manitou, the Great Spirit.* Courtesy of the Smithsonian Institution National Anthropological Archives.

> My mide brother is searched.
> In his breast is found
> That which I seek to remove,
> A white shell.[62]

Then, slowly taking up his medicine sack and aiming it like a gun, Bowman "shoots" the patient, who is rehearsed to act as if he or she is physically affected by the medicine. After the patient collapses upon the ground, the other midewiwin members also point their *midewayan* skins and "shoot" the patient. It is at this moment that the patient-candidate emulates the trance state of the solitary visionary in the throes of spiritual encounter. The midewiwin initiate is filled with the symbolic presence of the manitou in *migis* form. Midewiwin tradition acknowledges that the *migis* shells do not actually travel from the medicine bundles to the patient-candidate. According to the midewiwin dogma, however, this ritual-reenactment guarantees, by the ceremony of "shooting," that the manitou empower the patient-candidate.[63] Upon the initiate's revival he regurgitates the *migis* shells previously "shot" into him. Then the patient and midewiwin members engage in open "shooting" of one another.

The "shooting" ceremony is the dramatic climax of the midewiwin trance. The individual tribesperson, in his pursuit of power, controls the archetypal symbols of the society vision. In the structured trance the candidate is inducted into the society's vision. In the spontaneous trance the patient receives his own vision experience with which to amplify his midewiwin vocation. By passing through this initiating experience, the candidate for a midewiwin degree receives a new power personality, and the patient receives new vitality.

The Ojibway shaman's trance is a highly individuated experience. Even during midewiwin ritual when the patient-candidate is guided into trance by the Mide Society's traditional vision, the initiate is encouraged to appropriate the vision as his own contact with power. Indeed, individual Mide Society shamans occasionally change the tradition on the basis of their own manitou revelations. Despite the differences in the Ojibway shamanic vocations, there are the characteristic modes of trance encounter between the shaman and his or her manitou that we have labeled identification, transformation, and communication. This three-fold trance process is summarized in the Ojibway term *manitou kazo,* "talking with supernaturals."

Identification is the stage of preparation in which the shaman ritually focuses his concentration upon the symbols given to him in his initiating experience. Regarding this intense identification while in the trance state, Paul Radin observes:

Among the Winnebago and Ojibwa, and I have reason to believe among other tribes, the efficacy of a blessing, of a ceremony, depended upon what the Indians called "concentrating your mind" upon the spirits. . . . It was believed that the relation between man and the spirits was established by this "concentration," and that no manner of care in ritualistic detail could take its place.[64]

Through this identification the shaman evokes the power presence of his personal manitou patron. With the development of the shaman's trance abilities this power presence becomes an abiding aspect of the shaman's psyche.

Transformation follows from the shaman's meditative evocation of the manitou and deepens the trance experience. For the shaman becomes the power he evokes. In this sense transformation is the distinguishing characteristic of the trance state and the shaman's means of acquiring healing power. As A. I. Hallowell says, "Metamorphosis to the Ojibwa mind is an earmark of power."[65] Having sacrificed his own personal identity, the shaman assumes the singular personality associated with his manitou patron.

Communication is the word we use for the Ojibway term *manitou kazo.* While our entire trance schema is actually the process of *manitou kazo,* communication accentuates the shaman's transmission of healing power in trance. Ruth Landes's description of the pipe-smoking invocation of a Mide Society shaman of the 1930s reflects an awareness of communication with the manitou: "When he smoked requests to his guardian, he used the collective term, implying that the aid of *all* Supernaturals was to be gained. He came to use his pleading and physical abasement like formal conjurings; results convinced him that his spirit guardian was now his creature."[66] This special communication with numinous energies leads us to an investigation of the manner in which the shaman develops as a religious personality.

8

STAGES IN THE FORMATION OF THE SHAMAN

BECAUSE of the shaman's unique capacity to experience the numinous forces pervading the universe, he or she is able to impart to the tribal audience that special vitality usually associated with a divine or transhuman mode of action. For the Ojibway this vitality resides primarily in their woodland environment and is expressed in the term *manitou.* Thus the Ojibway shamans guide their tribal peers into a world of power of which they are already cognizant. Through the shaman manitou power becomes present in a special way to the Ojibway community and enables the community to deal effectively with the awesome mysteries and terrifying urgencies of life.

As a religious personality the shaman has a fourfold function within the tribe. He or she is the focus of personal sacrifice, the source of trance experience, the leader of tribal ritual, and the instrument of healing and divining. As sacrificial personalities shamans maintain for the tribe a relationship with the manitou that is manifested in the inner death-rebirth experience. Because shamans are skilled in trance meditation, they become the messengers of the spirit world. As leaders of tribal ritual they evoke the sacred trance in which the tribe experiences numinous power. Finally, as healer and diviners they cure physical and psychic illnesses and relieve spiritual distress. Thus, multivalent instruments of renewal for both the patient and the tribe, they bring solace in time of need and strength in confronting the tragedies of life.

The Training of the Shaman

The shaman's formation classifies him or her as a religious personality. It is during this period that he or she develops the special qualities and skills needed to be spiritually effective. The formation is a gradual process filled with grave challenges and fraught with enormous difficulties. Despite the spontaneous nature of the initial contact with cosmic forces, the shaman-to-be passes through extensive periods of solitary reflection or training with elder shamans. He or she must overcome all manner of doubts and fears to master the sacred craft. Each shamanic vocation has unique nuances that can be investigated in terms of the stages of the shaman's formative process.

The stages of shamanic formation can be succinctly expressed as the *call from the spirits,* the *sickness or withdrawal from previous activities,* and the *emergence of the formed shaman.* Although the stages do not constitute an exhaustive model of shamanic formation, they are suggestive of the overarching phases of shamanic development. The stages are developmental patterns and cultural peculiarities that allow us to focus on the formation of the shaman as a religious personality. The following presentation of the Siberian shaman Kyzlasov and the Ojibway shaman Mis-quona-queb demonstrates those stages.

Call

Among the Sagay tribe of the Turkish region of Abakan in southwestern Siberia shamanic figures receive their vocational call in one of three ways: from the family-shaman spirits, by the will of a mountain spirit or from the spirit of some sickness.[1] Shaman Kyzlasov received his vocational call in the most traditional manner. He was made ill by the family spirits for many years, and then, during a particular dream, he was taken by the family spirits to the ancestral spirit. He described the dream as follows:

> I have been sick and I have been dreaming. In my dreams I had been taken to the ancestor and cut into pieces on a black table. They chopped me up and then threw me into the kettle and I was boiled. There were some men there: two black and two fair ones. Their chieftain was there too. He issued the orders concerning me. I saw all this. While the pieces of my body were boiled, they found a bone around the ribs, which had a hole in the middle. This was the excess bone. This brought about my becoming a shaman. Because, only those men can become shamans in whose body such a bone can be found. One looks across the hole of this bone and begins to see all, to know all and, that is when one becomes a shaman. . . . When I came to from this state, I woke up. This meant that my soul had returned. Then the shamans declared: "You are the sort of man who may become a shaman. You should become a shaman, you must begin to shamanize."[2]

The mythological location of the ancestral spirit among these Turkish Siberian tribes is at the center of the cosmic tree.[3] While Kyzlasov was sick and dreaming, he was led to that locus of cosmological power to be dismembered and reassembled with a new shamanic perception of reality. He witnessed the sacrificial death and rebirth through which he was called to his vocation. His new shamanic vision was identified with the "excess bone" across the opening of which he could look "to see all, to know all. . . ."

The shaman Mis-quona-queb (Red Cloud) was a central personality during the Ojibway migration westward. He was not only a *tcisaki,* naming visionary, and midewiwin shaman but also the most prominent war leader in southwest Ontario during the midnineteenth century.[4] His shamanic call came to him during his puberty fast for a vision:

> He came up to me where I lay. There was a light glowing all around him; it even looked as if the light shone right through his body. And his whole body was covered with hair from head to foot. I could not recognize the face because it was hidden behind the hair.

I was not going to speak to him because I was overwhelmed with surprise and fear. I never thought I would see anyone like that before me. It is very hard for me to describe what I saw.

When he first spoke to me his voice sounded like an echo from the sky above. I could not understand what he said, I was so afraid. . . . Then my fear vanished and I calmed down. He spoke words of greeting to me:

"Ke-koko-ta-chi-ken. Grandchild, be not afraid."

As he spoke he raised his arm in a friendly gesture. It was obvious he had not come to do me harm but teach me the things I had come there to learn. After a few moments he was so friendly my fears were gone. He spoke to me again:

"I know what you want without asking. I will help you as long as you live. Your future is clear and bright. If you follow my wisdom I will protect you from harm."[5]

Although the numinous presence of this glowing manitou covered with hair appeared to Mis-quona-queb as an awesome apparition, the traditional formula of greeting established the manitou's friendly intentions. At this shamanic call Mis-quona-queb was assured of his manitou's foreknowledge of his needs. This indication of divining abilities was confirmed when Mis-quona-queb later received the *tcisaki* vision from his manitou. It is significant that the manitou's wisdom is presented as an obligation to Mis-quona-queb. Thus the manitou establishes the relationship between the visionary and his future rights and duties.

The dream-calls of Kyzlasov and Mis-quona-queb initiated them into the powerful world of cosmic forces. Both shamans directly experienced this mysterious region because of the mediation of spirits. Kyzlasov was carried in a dream by the spirits of his clan to the cosmic tree, while Mis-quona-queb apprehended the manitou of a traditional cosmic personality. While the specific manner of the shamanic call was different, these encounters with the numinous forces that cause a personal transformation were similar. Kyzlasov's and Mis-quona-queb's shamanic call were alike in their experiential quality, in their cosmic centeredness, and in their capacity to direct the individual's life.

Sickness-Withdrawal

Two terms, *sickness* and *withdrawal,* are used to describe
the intermediate stage in the formation of a shaman. These
terms are used to convey the reactions of the shaman to
the numinous encounter. The sickness is a prolonged illness that may have both psychic and physical symptoms.
The withdrawal is a removal from social interaction because of the disequilibrium associated with the initial spiritual encounter. Both the sickness and the withdrawal reflect the enervating quality of this period of shamanic formation.

The Sagay shaman Kyzlasov was physically sick long
before his dismemberment in the presence of the ancestral
shaman. A similar shamanic sickness has been well documented throughout Siberia as a preliminary step to the
shamanic vocation.[6] Kyzlasov's illness, moreover, was described by his wife as the traditional manner of becoming
a shaman:

> How did he become a shaman? Sickness seized him when he
> was twenty-three years old and he became a shaman at the age
> of thirty. That was how he became a shaman, after the sickness,
> after the torture. He had been ill for seven years. While he was
> ailing, he had dreams: he was beaten up several times, some-
> times he was taken to strange places. He has been around quite
> a lot in his dreams and he had seen many things.[7]

Kyzlasov's sickness was more than an ordinary illness.
Although the tribe interprets any sickness as an extraordinary intrusion of some sort, such a shamanic affliction is
special. It is a forced preparation by which the spirits
limit the shaman's social interaction and turn him toward
inner psychic activity. The urgent nature of such a sickness
is acknowledged in the statements "You must take up shamanism so as not to suffer!" and "I became a shaman only

to escape illness.["8] Physical torment, infirmity, and even death plague the candidate who ignores the shamanic call.

Kyzlasov's preparation was not, however, limited to sickness. After his call he was expected to undergo extensive self-reflection and training with elder shamans. The stage of sickness-withdrawal was not part of a strict chronological sequence but simply one phase of the spiritual preparation of a shaman-to-be. Kyzlasov not only suffered the "shamanic sickness" but also underwent the trials stipulated by his particular shamanic community. Kyzlasov described, for example, his psychic journey to the "wealthy birch tree," where he carved his personal symbol as a sign of his vocation:

[Dioszegi inquired, "What happens after the shaman had been 'cut up'"?] First of all, he ordered food and drinks necessary for the initiation feast. As soon as the meat and the wine are ready, the shaman takes it to the ancestor. . . . When the shaman goes to the chief-shaman, that is, to the family ancestor, he has to cross the *ham sacraschan harazi* mountain along the way. On the top of that mountain there is a birch tree, its trunk resembles a six-sided log. The shamans carve their symbols into it, between the edges. Whoever places his marking, his *tamga,* upon it, then becomes a real shaman. It happens sometimes that a certain *tamga* "falls down," it disappears from the tree. Then its owner dies.[9]

The carving of the personal power symbol on the "wealthy birch tree" assures the Sagay shaman that he or she will have the health and prosperity needed to perform the exhausting shamanic ceremonies. The vision emblem, or *tamga,* identifies the shaman. The emblem's motif decorates the shaman's costume, is evoked in the shamanic ritual, and the shaman focuses on it in the shamanic trance. The solitary journey to the ancestor spirit symbolically celebrates the Sagay shaman's realization of the spiritual strength resulting from the sacrificial dismemberment.

Mis-quona-queb's sickness-withdrawal developed over an extended period. While the Ojibway do not speak of a

"shamanic sickness," the tribe does recommend an attitude of humility during the vision fast to obtain a manitou
blessing. Mis-quona-queb undertook this fast in an effort
to secure a teaching in his dreams.[10] His fasting paralleled
the sickness of Siberian shamans in that such a puberty
fast reduces the young visionary to an awareness of human
deprivation. Both the debilitation of the Siberian shaman
in his sickness and the fast of the Ojibway shaman are
sacrificial preparations for their vocations.

After his encounter with the manitou Mis-quona-queb
continued during this preparatory period to cultivate his
contacts with his manitou patron. Stories relate his mar-
velous experiences on the warpath against the Sioux. One
such story describes the resilience expected of a shamanic
personality. In the following brief passage the Ojibway
leader, Neta-mequan tests the shamanic power of the young
Mis-quona-queb:

> The council fire was set aflame early in the morning and
> Neta-mequan, the great leader of all the Ojibway tribes, came
> forth.
> Let us hear the advice of the Great Spirit before our war-
> riors set off on this venture. Let us hear from the divine pro-
> tector of the young Mis-quona-queb. Bury Mis-quona-queb in the
> sand, leaving only his face uncovered so that he may hear from
> the spirits.
> The wishes of head man Neta-mequan were carried out. It
> was a great honor for Mis-quona-queb to be asked to consult
> his spirits. He lay there under the sand for three days without
> food and drink and then he asked to be released; he had re-
> ceived a message from the spirit—the May-may-quay-shi.[11]

By proving himself in this trial Mis-quona-queb gradually
acquired tribal recognition of his unique powers. In Ojibway society, where virtually every person developed some
shamanistic technique, the more accomplished shamans
were required to train for long periods. Although there
is no record of Mis-quona-queb's withdrawal, the follow-

ing passage gives some idea of the extensive preparation of the Ojibway shaman:

The inner being in which the gift to heal reposed, had to be enlarged.

During the early years of his training, a young man or woman chosen for his special gifts, spent time in meditation and prayer. Alone in a secluded place, the young person sought a dream. At the same time he endeavoured to import his being to the plant and animal beings as he attempted to ingest their inner substances and make them part of himself.

In these retreats the medicine man or woman, it was hoped, would come to know himself and attain a high order of curative powers. Such retreats continued throughout the career of the medicine man. As the earth annually renews itself, so the medicine man had, each year, to withdraw into himself in order to maintain his powers.[12]

The period of withdrawal is used by the maturing Ojibway shaman to develop the enstatic reciprocity needed for communication with the manitou in the natural world. The shamanic call is gradually nurtured by this solitary reflection until the candidate resembles the power that he or she evokes. Indeed, throughout their lives Ojibway shamans undertake periodic retreats to commune with their manitou. Thus the solitary phase of withdrawal and renewal continues.

The shaman's dream encounter initiates him into the spirit world and profoundly affects his inner psychic harmony. Thus Kyzlasov spoke of a sickness that overwhelmed him. As he witnessed his physical dismemberment, his psyche was also radically fragmented. The reassembly of his bones and his body by the spirits marked the new identity that that sickness brought him. This sacrificial identity was gradually cultivated during the solitary period of recovery and withdrawal.

Ojibway shamans also develop their sacrificial personalities during their fasts for dreams and their subsequent retreats from the tribe. In solitude they reflect on their spirit encounters and nurture their maturing identity with the manitou in the use of plants and animals. Thus the former self is gradually and painstakingly transformed into an emerging spiritual personality.

Emergence

The term *emergence* describes the final stage of shamanic formation after the shaman's training is complete. Then the candidate comes out of the dark period of sickness and withdrawal like a plant arising from the soil. Having survived the call from the spirits and the subsequent illness, the shaman emerges as an integrated healer. Controlling the psychic trauma of the spirit call, he or she channels these energies into the shamanic art. Sergei M. Shirokogoroff has stated, "The shaman may begin his life career with a psychosis, but he cannot carry on his functions if he cannot master himself."[13] Through this struggle to overcome his or her own radical fragmentation, the shaman becomes capable of healing others ritually by bringing to the ritual a particular spiritual strength and psychic understanding to balance the destructive forces that threaten the tribe. Indeed, the shaman's formation is confirmed in the enactment of the trance ritual.

Vilmos Dioszegi gives a vivid description of a Siberian shaman's performance in his record of Kyzlasov's ceremonial chanting. Although he witnessed the chanting apart from a full-scale ritual, he acknowledges that it still had a profound impact on him. He is skeptical of the power that the shaman summoned from the spirit world, but he does not deny the impressive and "unforgettable" quality of the integrated shaman's performance:

This is just a simple demonstration. There is no devout congregation watching the shaman and truly fearing the invoked spirits. The playful reflections of the fire are missing, there is no flaming or glowing fire here, casting strange shadows upon the walls of the yurt, suggesting the presence of the assembling spirits. Nobody throws twigs or branches and weeds into the fire, so that their overpowering smoke might let the clouded eyes see all that the shaman is talking about. Kyzlasov has no drum, suggesting with its faster or slower, stronger or weaker beats, whether the mounted shaman gallops or ambles away. The ceremonial garb is lacking too, with its innumerable metal bells, straining the nerves with their tinking, jingling sound and whose several hundreds of coloured ribbons make the human likeness of the whirling shaman improbable with their fluttering. There is no dance, the movements of which help to represent and explain all the shaman wants to indicate and depict. And, last but not least, I have absolutely no faith in his spirits, which have been instilled in every Sagay from the cradle on. And still . . . it was an unforgettable experience.[14]

This unusual passage attests to the special abilities of the Sagay shaman Kyzlasov. Even without the supporting shamanic drama, Kyzlasov's chanting had a striking effect.

Overall, a Sagay ritual performance gives the impression of considerable control by the shaman. The shaman orchestrates his or her songs, dances, gestures, and costumes to reenact the shamanic call. Having summoned the spirits, he or she undertakes the ecstatic journey to heal, divine, or guide a soul. The mastery of a Sagay shaman over the initial sickness enables the shaman later to control the ritual activity.

Mis-quona-queb's emergence as a formed shaman was in conjunction with his selection as leader of the Lake of the Woods Ojibway band. He was required to demonstrate his shamanic skills as a herbal healer, naming visionary, and *tcisaki* before the elders would acknowledge his position as the major warrior of his people. Mis-quona-queb's naming ceremony required that he contact his spirits to obtain a name for a newborn child. Among the Ojibway this shamanic technique called for manitou authorization of the name, thus assuring the child a protective power. In the ceremony described here, the women joined Mis-quona-queb because the child was a girl:

During the early morning darkness, the guests filed into the wigwam. The mother held the baby in her arms while they waited for the light of a new day. Soon an elder declared there was light in the eastern sky. Then the mother handed her baby to Mis-quona-queb saying, "This my child I give you to name and to be her *O'gwi-me* [naming visionary]. As her *O'gwi-me* you must guide her in the future under the protection of the Great Spirit."

When the mother sat down, food was passed to all and the women filled their pipes with kini-kinuk [tobacco]. Smoke filled the air.

Mis-quona-queb, the O'gwi-me, holding the baby, spoke: "Take your pipes and smoke. Also take this food that has been placed before you as a covenant to the Great Spirit who brought us into being. Have faith and trust in your protectors."

"O, Great Spirit, protect this child whom I am about to give your name. I do not tremble or fear in carrying out my duty. In the many winters that follow, shine your light on her path so that she may see what lies in the forest beyond. I ask you to give her much happiness."

Still holding the baby, Mis-quona-queb began to chant. "Win-da-man-ke-towi. I name your soul."

Then talking to the baby, "Mis-quona-queb said, "You may have this name. Love it forever and ever. Pukanabik or Sitting Elsewhere is your name."

Then Mis-quona-queb kissed Pukanabik and passed her to the women who kissed her. When the women were finished, Mis-quona-queb gave a small boy [who was a living witness to the ceremony] a small carved bear totem to be placed on the child. The bear totem would be her clan. The naming ceremony was over.[15]

The simple dignity of the Ojibway naming ceremony hardly intimates the shaman's enduring struggle to develop his religious vocation. Yet the qualities of the shaman are everywhere evident. Mis-quona-queb openly exhibits his shamanic skill in determining the girl's name. Moreover, he gives of his acquired strength to support the frail child and accepts his duty as her spiritual guide. The naming shaman evokes the symbolism of the dawning sun to bestow the blessing of clear vision on the child. The whole ceremony manifests the inner strength and authority of the shaman. It is not surprising that the Ojibway require of their tribal war leaders the calm assurance that the shamanic naming technique requires.

The emergence of the tribal shaman into his community is a singular achievement both for the individual and for the society. The shaman, having accomplished the reassembly of his fragmented psyche, functions in an integrating capacity by healing, divining, and guiding. The tribal society, in turn, benefits from the presence of a religious personality who communicates with the sources of cosmic power.

Even this brief presentation of two shamans' progression through the stages of formation gives insight into the shaman's religious personality. The call demonstrates the highly experiential aspect of shamanic rituals, in which shamans bring themselves and their audiences to a direct perception of the vital forces that animate the natural world. Similarly, the process of sickness-withdrawal demonstrates the ongoing sacrifice by virtue of which shamans are able to make present the sacred spirits. This sacrificial quality has a variety of cultural expressions, but the ability of shamans to evoke the sacred presence by some type of sacrificial activity prevails as a universal characteristic of this religious figure. The final emergence of the integrated shaman highlights the singular psychic poise that shamans achieve because of their ability to balance the dynamic tensions that they experience within their own psyches. This inner balance, achieved through psychic struggle and with the aid of spirits, enables the shaman to channel both the destructive and the beneficial aspects of the cosmic forces.

9

THE SHAMAN AS A RELIGIOUS TYPE

FOR the shaman the psychic struggle for balance is essentially a religious experience characterized by the numinous call, the sacrificial identity that enables the shaman to contact power, the ritual act of mediating power, and the community's faith in the healing shaman. Those characteristic shamanic modes vary in different cultures and individuals. Yet it is possible to provide a context for understanding shamanic religiosity by situating it within the thematic patterns, such as cosmology, tribal sanction, ritual reenactment, and trance experience.

Standard expressions have been developed in the study of religions to describe particular religious types. Such a typology provides a context for interpretation of various spiritual paths. Not only do Western types, such as the prophet and the priest, inform our understanding of the religious personality but also Asian types, such as the yogi and the sage. The religious types to be discussed here are the prophet, priest, yogi, and sage. The differences among these religious personalities are more sharply delineated here than they may actually be in practice, where religious functions necessarily overlap. For example, the Ojibway midewiwin practitioner may more correctly be characterized as a shaman-priest than a shaman. The purpose here is not to relate the religious types to historical figures but simply to explain shamanism by distinguishing shamans from other religious types and their functions.

The Prophet

The term *prophet* is derived from the Greek word *prophetes* for the persons who narrated the cult legends at festivals.[1] This etymology highlights the primary characteristic of this religious type: the prophet is the one who speaks the divine revelation directly to the community. This mantic art effects change in the social and political order because the prophet's words carry the power of their divine source. Gerardus van der Leeuw expressed this by saying, "The word, the power-word, is equally a deed."[2] A poet who experienced the inspired word was originally considered to be filled with a god.[3] Prophets, however, are not exclusively poets, though they may use poetic forms.[4] Rather, they are religious figures whose words issue directly from the divine source of power.

The prophet's encounter with the revelatory word was expressed in a unique manner by the Hebrew prophetic figures. The richness and diversity of these prophets provide many examples of the characteristics of this religious personality. Generally, the Hebrew prophets experienced the revelatory word in two ways. The experience was either structured or spontaneous. The "structured" prophets gathered in communities and used various ecstatic techniques, such as music, dance, and fasting, to encounter the divine word.[5] The "spontaneous" prophets were more individuated and experienced the word without relying on techniques to induce prophetic rapture.[6]

The structured prophetic schools are first described in the Old Testament in relation to the prophet Samuel.[7] In the following passage Samuel sends Saul into a prophetic community to experience their unique form of rapture:

Then when you [Saul] reach the Hill of God, where the Philistine governor resides, you will meet a company of prophets coming down from the hill-shrine, led by lute, harp, fife, and drum, and filled with prophetic rapture. Then the spirit of the Lord will suddenly take possession of you, and you too will be rapt like a prophet and become another man.[8]

Thus the structured prophetic schools emphasized the experience of divine rapture, in which the "spirit of the

Lord" took possession of the prophets, or *nabi*. Such a rapturous trance is an important characteristic of this kind of prophet and marks him or her as a distinct spiritual personality. The immediacy with which the prophet experiences the divine word gives him or her an urgency in proclaiming the revelation. The early prophetic schools, however, tended to institutionalize the rapturous experience. From the eighth to the sixth centuries before Christ the structured prophets of Israel and Judah were often described as constrained by traditional techniques.[9]

The spontaneous prophetic figure is chosen from among a people to deliver a message from their God. These prophets are characterized by the immediacy of their contacts with the divine word, and that contact often leads to agitated behavior and an unconstrained freedom of expression. The better-known prophetic figures of the Old Testament were spontaneous prophets. Each received his call in a unique manner, but in each case the revelatory word, the message that was to be delivered, took precedence over ecstasy or prophetic rapture. Isaiah, for example, after his awesome vision of the Lord, responded in the following manner: "Then I heard the Lord saying, 'Whom shall I send? Who will go for me?' and I answered, 'Here am I; send me.' He said, 'Go and tell this people.'"[10] Likewise Jeremiah reveals in the following passage that his childish fears were set aside and the "word of the Lord" put on his lips:

> But the Lord said, "Do not call yourself a child; for you shall go to whatever people I send you and say whatever I tell you to say. . . ." Then the Lord stretched out his hand and touched my mouth, and said to me, "I put my words into your mouth. This day I give you authority over nations and over kingdoms, to pull down and to uproot, to destroy and to demolish, to build and to plant."[11]

Thus the prophetic vocation came suddenly and spontaneously to Isaiah and Jeremiah, bringing a singular revelation that conveyed the force of the one God of His chosen people. Although prophetic rapture was significant to the major prophets, they are rarely described as being in an ecstatic state when they deliver their special revelations.[12]

Nonetheless, the prophet's trance or rapture is significant in that it brings this religious type in contact with the divine word. The revelatory word, moreover, is not a vague premonition, but a clear message addressed again and again to specific historic events. When the spontaneous prophetic figure had fulfilled its religious function in the Israelite nation, it subsided as a dominant religious type in the Hebrew tradition. It continued to be a major force in Western religious traditions, however, because of certain distinguishing characteristics, namely, the relation to a personal, creative deity, the ancestral covenant, and the intrahistorical salvific process.

The numinous encounter with Yahweh is a major feature of the prophetic type. For the Hebrew prophet the revelatory word itself was symbolic of the personal creative deity who called him to his vocation. Although the Lord was believed to be the creator God who made the world, He was seen as transcendent to the natural order. The Hebrew prophets especially abhorred the identification of their deity with natural phenomena, as was characteristic of other neighboring tribes. Instead, they experienced Yahweh as absolute, transcendent, and monotheistic. Their deity informed their cosmology, and any manner of viewing the world was solely in terms of relatedness to the Lord.

The Hebraic prophet's relationship to the deity had been established by the tribal ancestors in the form of a covenant. The prophets fulfilled their religious vocations in the context of this sacred ancestral relation. Continually calling to the people with the revealed word, the prophets urged a return to the original, continuous covenant in order to restore the Lord's blessing. That covenant provided the prophet with his message of moral obligation.

The moral fervor of the prophetic type imposed restrictions on the people to refrain from syncretic practices that would sully the purity of their experience of God and their traditional relationship with Him. The prophets continually objected to the nature worship of neighboring cults, staunchly preserving the immediacy of their prophetic communication from the transcendent Lord. They were more than mere traditionalists, however, because they insisted on the inner, lived expression of the covenant relation over and above the performance of external rituals. This distinction appears in their prophetic utterances, especially in Samuel's words, "To obey is better than sacrifice."[13]

All this brings us to an understanding of a major characteristic of the prophetic personality, namely, his historical role. The prophet counsels the community in response to certain tensions of his time. He speaks a divine revelation that calls for individual reform to effect a communal transformation. Set in a specific historical context, the prophet's word asserts the salvation inherent in an ancestral covenant. The intrahistorical message gradually assumes a universal salvific dimension that is joined with the historical destiny of the people. Thus, in summary, the prophetic type is an instrument of the deity's revelatory word directed to specific historical ends.

There are profound sympathies between the prophetic and shamanic types. For both of these religious personalities the immediacy of the numinous experience evokes a new identity that finds its religious fulfillment in the social order. Both also have deeply personal contact with the source of sacred revelation, which can be experienced in trance. Yet, though their spiritual experiences are similar, the contexts in which they function and the roles that they perform in their societies are different.

Compared to the prophet, the shaman's symbol system does not arise in a highly traditional context. Instead, the shaman experiences a numinous revelation primarily in the natural world. The shamanic type does not announce

the revelatory message of a personal deity, but dramatizes his personal encounter with the numinous forces in
the natural world. The shaman's dramatic activity bespeaks
his intuitive and purposely vague apprehension of his personal power experience. His concept of deity is not clearly
developed in terms of a covenantal relationship, nor is his
spirit-patron expressed in transcendent, monotheistic terminology. Rather the shamanic figure addresses a transphenomenal presence that is all pervasive but singularly
manifest in a particular local hierophany.

The shaman's obligations arise from his personal encounter with the spirits rather than from a covenant with
a transcendent deity. Although the shamanic contact with
supernatural force may impose certain obligations of a
vocational nature, there is no moral mandate that im-
pinges on the shaman or the tribe because of this contact
with power. As received by the shaman, the power has no
moral charge; it can be used either for self-aggrandizement
or for altruistic purposes.

The shaman does not direct numinous energies into historical events but rather into transitional situations. He
or she does not develop a vision of historical destiny. The
shaman heals a sick person, divines the location of game
animals, or undertakes an ecstatic "journey" to satisfy the
community's immediate transitional needs. There is no
abiding covenant between the tribe and the spirits that
shamans promote in the pursuit of their religious vocation. Shamans heal by entering into the mysterious regions
of trance experience. They contact a timeless, ahistorical
power and channel it according to tribal needs. In summary, the tribal shaman experiences natural symbols as
revelatory of cosmic power and becomes the vehicle by
which this power is directed to healing ends.

The Priest

The word *priest* comes from the Greek *presbyteros*, which

is generally translated in the English New Testament as "elder."[14] It is "an ancient term for a sacral office," designating one who "may enter the presence of God."[15] The priest is the religious personage who is approved by the community to go into "the unapproachable domain of divine sanctity offering himself and his existence in sacrifice to God's incomprehensible dominion."[16]

The rise of the priestly type is usually associated with the formation of settled cultural centers that are characterized by well-articulated social and moral codes. The priest's sacerdotal function is related to the sacred center where ritual sacrifices are performed. The priest's particular role therefore can be described in political, ritual, and educational terms.

The political role of the priest was indispensable to the maintenance of the social order in archaic civilizations. Archaeological evidence from the Indus Valley cities indicates that a select group of people lived in the immediate vicinity of the central temple.[17] The official storage granaries were also near the temple. Thus there is an apparent connection between the economic and religious life of that civilization, which was managed by the priestly class. Likewise, the political power of the organized priesthoods in Mesopotamia is documented in the Book of Ezekial.[18] Indeed, the Mesopotamian king himself was ritually humiliated in an annual ceremony that was conducted by the high priest to remind the ruler of his subservience to the city god.[19] In Egypt the most celebrated priest was the pharaoh. As in the other archaic civilizations the Egyptian priesthood was organized in a hierarchy that was often hereditary. At the pinnacle was the pharaoh-priest, who embodied the divine presence:

The divine person of the pharaoh was too holy for direct approach. An ordinary mortal did not speak "to" the king; he spoke "in the presence" of the king. Various circumlocutions were employed to avoid direct reference to the king: "May thy majesty hear," instead of "majesty thou hear," and "one gave command," instead of "he gave command." One of these circumlocutions, per-aa, "the Great House," gave rise to our word "pharaoh."[20]

In the Hebrew tradition, from the period of the amphictyony to the building of the temple in Jerusalem, the priests acquired a growing political voice because of their association with the major centering symbols of the emerging Jewish people, such as the Ark of the Covenant.[21]

From these examples it is apparent that one of the significant characteristics of the priestly type is the particular role that priests play in the political and social order. This political dimension of the priest's role reflects the interweaving of the sacred and the profane in early civilizations. The priest fulfilled his political-religious role through various ritual ceremonies performed at the sacred centers of these cultures. In Babylonia, for example, the priests led the inhabitants of the city in a procession around the ziggurat. This ritual recreated the Babylonian cosmology and affirmed the existing political order.

The principal characteristic of the priestly type, however, is the performance of ritual sacrifice. In this sacerdotal capacity the priest thus takes an object from the profane world and makes it holy. Through special prayers and ritual actions the priest offers the object to the divine in the name of the entire community. Through the sacrifice the people are able to enter into communion with their deity. Whether the sacrifice is human (as in the Mayan world) or animal (as in the Hindu Brahmin tradition), the priest performs the ritual offering.

In leading the community sacrifice, the priest mediates between the people and the transcendent deity. The ritual is a clear expression of the deity's transcendent nature, which is often symbolized in the divine names or by a pantheon of gods and goddesses. Although the priest mediates with the deity, he need not have personal experience of the divine reality. Instead, the pronunciation of the divine name and the correct performance of the ritual sacrifice take precedence over direct experience.

Priesthoods tend to become both concerned with ritualistic detail and removed from the sphere of popular knowledge into rationalized theology. In this respect the priest's religious role has a distinctly educational aspect. For priests teach the religious science that is the core of learning in archaic civilizations. The concern for ritual perfection leads to advances in various fields, such as linguistics, architectural design, and the social sciences. As teacher of the sacred knowledge the priest performs a unique educational-religious role.

Recognizing the fullness of the priestly function and its paradigmatic quality as a traditional religious type, the author of the Epistle to the Hebrews described the Christ event in priestly terms: "Therefore He had to be made like His brethren in every respect, so that He might become a merciful and faithful high priest in the service of God, to make expiation for the sins of the people."[22] Thus, in summary, the priest functions as the representative of the believers in the sacrifice that produces communion with the divine in a traditional, ritualistic setting.

While the priest and the shaman are both ritualists concerned with the transmission of traditional power, there is a certain tension between the two in the performance of their characteristic roles. For the shaman promotes the direct experience of the numinous spirits, while the priest identifies the divine presence in a traditional text or situates it in an established sacred center. The priest promotes a religious science or theology in opposition to the shaman's predominantly intuitive explication of numinous reality. Despite those fundamental differences, however, there are marked similarities, as well as other contrasts of a religious nature, between these two religious types, because the shamans also have political, ritual, and educational functions.

The shaman's ability to experience directly the numinous presence and convey healing power often puts him or her in a dominant political position in traditional tribal societies. Unlike the priest, the shaman derives political-religious force not from working in concert with similar religious types but in an individual capacity. Those shamanic societies that wield considerable social influence do so because of the tribe's respect or fear of the society's individual members.

Like priests, shamans revere sacred space as it is revealed in the encounter with divine presence, but they do not function exclusively in one holy place. Rather they acknowledge that numinous forces reside in a variety of spirits in different localities. The sacred place is determined subjectively by the individual shaman, who thus identifies the numinous presence for the purposes of tribal ritual activity. Unlike the priest, the shaman's communication with the divine is not by means of preestablished ritual prayers or sacrifices. Shamans create their own unique modes of addressing the "Great Spirit" and their spirit helpers. Although they often draw on tribal shamanic lore or tradition, their methods are more frequently spontaneous and symbolically associated with the natural world.

The shaman's evocation of spirit power in his or her ritual is different from the priest's. Shamans do not transform any ritual object in order to promote a communion with the divine. Instead, they transform themselves by evoking their guardian spirits in trance and applying their spirits' power presence to a particular situation. While the belief of the patient and the audience in the shaman's abilities plays a significant part in the ritual, the ritual is not expressly a communal experience as much as an effort to induce a heightened visionary encounter.

The intense experience of the shaman is directed toward a personal, familiar power. The transcendent deity of the priest is not unknown among shamanic types. For example, the Ojibway speak in a traditional manner of the sun as Gicimanitou, a vague and distant force, though few Ojibway shamans have Gicimanitou as their patron spirit.[23] Yet the multiplicity of spirits in the shamanic consciousness is not as articulated as the litanies of divine names or the pantheons of the archaic civilizations.

The shaman's familiar spirit has decidedly cosmic qualities, and the shaman assumes those characteristics as a Cosmic Person related to the universal forces. The priest does not necessarily become the Cosmic Person himself but instead performs the Cosmic Sacrifice. It is for that reason that the priest's ritual must be free of human error. The cosmological context of the priestly figure is a well-established universe that is traditionally known and ritually accessible through sacrifice. In contrast, the shamanic cosmology may be more intimately known, though only to the shaman, because of his or her personal trance "journeys" or other vision revelations.

Shamans do not teach religious science or theology in the same way that priests convey sacred knowledge. They are guides through the numinous regions and at times performers of rites of passage. They develop symbolic expressions to describe their passages through the mystical regions, and they relate this information to the members of their tribe in ritual narrations. The religious science of the priest is a more rational mode of learning, whereby the priest educates to achieve intellectual awareness of the transcendent deity.

In conclusion, the most significant distinction between the priest and the shaman is that the priest is one who performs a traditional sacrifice based upon an acknowledged scripture or ritual formula, while the shaman is more spontaneous and less bound by tradition. Relying not on a verbal scripture or established theology, the shaman creates a personal, symbolic mode of sacrifice. The sacrificial element in shamanism is not a part of a preestablished rite as it is in priestly traditions. The ritual arises from the shaman himself. Thus the shaman personalizes the sacrificial experience, whereas the priest establishes it as an institutional act.

The Yogi

The yogi performs an ascetic discipline, *yoga*, that produces a state of quiescence apart from the temporal world. The word *yogi* is derived from *yoga*, whose origin is questionable but generally traced to the Sanskrit root term *yuj* meaning "to join or unite."[24] According to Sankhya philosophy, the yogi discovers the eternal, transphenomenal self, *purusha*, by deliberately suppressing the phenomenal self, *prakriti*.

There is evidence that yogis existed in the archaic civilization of the Indus Valley prior to the arrival of the Aryan/Vedic peoples.[25] Although the early Vedic writings of India do not describe yogic practices among the Aryans, the Rig Veda does mention pre-Aryan tribal figures, or *muni*, who were silent and solitary and possessed great magical powers.[26] By the Upanishadic period the pre-Aryan yogic techniques apparently had penetrated the Vedic religious ethos of sacrificial knowledge. Yogic practices became part of the "higher knowledge" that was taught by the sacred teacher, or *guru*. The *Brihad Aranyaka* states: "Now the man who does not desire—He who is without desire, who is freed from desire, whose breath is satisfied, whose desire is the soul—his breaths do not depart. Being very Brahman, he goes to Brahman."[27] Here the term *Brahman* is a metaphor for the deepest self, which is strikingly similar to the interior meditative goal of the yogi.

Although the personality of the yogi has been adapted by several religious traditions, it receives its fullest expression in the Hindu world, especially in the *Yoga Sutras*, which were compiled by Patanjali, probably during the early centuries of the Christian era. Patanjali arranged 194 aphoristic statements that guide the yogic personality in his quest for liberation. In these condensed expressions are found the basic characteristics of yoga, including the yogic cosmology, the concept of the Absolute, the state of yogic liberation, and yogic techniques.

The goal of the yogi is the suppression of all mental states so that the spirit abides in its own essence.[28] Yogic practice is based on the Sankhya cosmology, which interprets all reality in terms of spirit (purusha) and matter (prakriti).[29] For the yogi all phenomenal reality is to be transcended by means of an intense meditative effort until the deepest self, purusha, is liberated from its entrapment in both physical and mental gradations of matter, or prakriti. Having suppressed the world of prakriti by means of the yogic stages of enstatic meditation, the yogi attains the pure consciousness of purusha.

The nature of purusha is absolute quiescence. Although trapped in the phenomenal world, this absolute spirit is undisturbed and isolated from matter, time, and change. While purusha is the absolute reality for the yogi, Patanjali included the doctrine of *Ishvara,* or the Lord, upon whom the yogi could rely as a personal deity. Yogic devotional practices connected with the *Bhagavad Gita* developed the understanding of Purusha as the higher manifestation of Ishvara and of Prakriti as his lower nature. Patanjali recommends that the yogi develop a profound relation with the Lord. He writes, "God is the One unique Personality, untouched by desire, affliction, action or its result."[30] Again he says, "In Him lies the seed of omniscience."[31] Thus Patanjali establishes the concept of Ishvara as the supreme model upon which the yogi can concentrate and from whom the yogi can learn inner wisdom: "He is the master of even the ancient masters, being beyond the limits of time."[32] Yet Patanjali does not ultimately recommend the way of devotion that would bring the yogi to depend on the Supreme Lord. Rather, the highest state of yogic discipline is without support of any kind of images or symbols. In this "seedless contemplation" the yogi becomes totally liberated. Purusha then illumines the yogi's knowing; no mental processes disturb him. He is isolated in *kaivalya*, the state of yogic liberation.

Liberation *(moksha)* from the oppressive cycle of the human condition is a pan-Indian religious doctrine. The yogi pursues this religious ideal through complete extinction *(nirodha)* of all mental states that are bound to the phenomenal order. This extinction of mental processes also applies to those higher states of awareness that strive to comprehend reality: "Once the yogi is convinced that Self and intellect are two, he masters the qualities, masters their results, knows everything."[33] Isolated then from the limitations of the phenomenal order, the yogi rests in the equilibrium of his deepest self: "The dissolution of Qualities in their source, when nothing remains to be achieved, is liberation; the revelation of the power of Self, the foundation of the beauty of Self."[34] The realization of this ontological purity and identification with the cosmic quality of purusha, is the end-goal of an interior process of yogic techniques.

The eight stages of yogic techniques, as presented in the *Yoga Sutras,* guide the yogi into the illumined trance state of *samadhi.* Led by a knowledgeable teacher, the yogi disciplines himself in restraint, observance, posture, regulation of breath, abstraction (of the senses), concentration, meditation, and trance, or samadhi. The major techniques of the yogi, namely breath control *(pranayana),* posture *(asana),* and concentration *(ekagrata),* are the means used to discipline the ordinary mind and turn it towards a higher consciousness. By means of this psychic process the yogi undergoes the death experience in the phenomenal realm to be reborn into the blissful state of *kaivalya.* Thus the yogi's techniques constitute an initiation experience, which culminates in the suprapsychic trance (samadhi). This trance transcends the ritual, disciplined activity and emphasizes the predominantly dualistic nature of the yogic quest.

In the final quietude of samadhi-trance the yogi realizes the relationship between mind *(buddhi)* and purusha. No longer committed to the mental process itself: the mind functions as a mirror of the deepest self: "When mind's activity is controlled, illumination results, mind reflects the nature of either the seer, the seen, or the seeing, as pure crystal reflects the color of whatever is placed on it."[35] In summary, the yogic personality is an instrument for the expression of absolute quiescience. Having undergone the death-rebirth initiation in a psychic capacity, the yogi restructures his epistemological perspective and is released from the constraints of phenomenal reality.

When comparing the yogi and the shaman, it is clear that certain magical powers are common to both. Yet there are pronounced differences between the two religious types. Among the legendary "powers" of both the yogi and the shaman are magical flight, inner heat, and the ecstatic meditation.[36] For the yogi, however, these attributes are usually later Tantric developments that synthesize local shamanic techniques with Hindu and yogic religious practices. The differences between the yogi and the shaman can be clearly seen in their respective notions of cosmology, deity, the activation of spiritual energy, and psychic techniques.

The shaman's cosmology does not have the same dualistic emphasis as that of the yogi. Rather, the shamanic world view arises from a particular tribal cosmology that stresses the interpenetration of transphenomenal power into the temporal world. The shaman does not aspire to an isolated state within the transphenomenal realm. Instead he establishes a ritual means of contacting the numinous regions and transmitting sacred energies into the human order. Thus the shaman does not recover the alienated part of the universe in his person, but he becomes related to the cosmic levels in a personal manner.

The difference between the yogi and the shaman with regard to the notion of deity is striking. The shaman relies on a multiplicity of spirits. In some yogic traditions the yogi meditates on a divine lord, while in others there is no personal deity on which to concentrate. Not only does the shaman rely on the spirits initially to call him to his vocation but also he ritually identifies himself with his spirit patron. Thus the milieu in which the shamanic personality functions is not characterized by a quiescent, cosmic principle, or Absolute Lord, but by a multiplicity of personalistic spirits. The shaman's goal of transmitting healing power, moreover, is dependent upon his relationship to those numinous presences.

The shaman activates his special relation to his familiar spirits in the ritual that reenacts his initial call. Unlike the yogi, who isolates himself and abides in his own deeper essence (purusha), the shaman actively involves himself in the phenomenal order. By reenacting the initial shattering experience that led him to his religious vocation, the shaman transmits healing power for a patient's benefit. The yogi, on the other hand, commits himself to disciplined activity so that he may shatter his experience of the temporal world and be liberated into the serene realm of the deepest self.

The shamanic techniques also differ from those of the yogi. The principal difference is that the shaman symbolically images the transphenomenal power to evoke the ritual transmission of healing power. The yogi does not image forth the purusha in ritual but actually extinguishes those psychic states connected with symbol making. The yogi's psychic meditation is a disciplined suppression, while the shaman's psychic meditation is a ritual evocation.

The ritual techniques that bring the shaman into the trance state may be enstatic, as they are among some American Indian tribes, or ecstatic, as they are among some Siberian tribes. The yogi does not use ecstatic trance techniques to enter kaivalya, or the state of liberation. Even the yogi's enstatic meditation leading to samadhi differs from that of the shaman in that the yogi is attempting to merge into the quiescent state, whereas the shaman concentrates his or her inner resources to evoke his guardian spirit.

The difference in the ritual activity is most apparent when the yogi's quiet sitting is compared to the shaman's dramatic dancing, rhythmic drumming, and repetitive chanting. The shaman's ritual arises out of his or her spontaneous relationship with a personal spirit helper, while the yogi consciously conforms to established spiritual techniques taught him by a guru, or teacher. In summary, the shaman's psychic techniques contact forces that are identified in the tribal cosmology. This shamanic contact is not usually an absorption into cosmic power but rather the transmission of this vitality into the shaman's community. Thus the shaman is not directed towards self-integration but undergoes an integrating process to channel sacred energies into the tribe.

Sage

The sage is a person with a rich humanist and intratemporal orientation, as well as a sense of the all-pervasive numinous presence. As a religious type the sage is found in the humanist philosophical traditions of China and Greece. Because of the special realization of the sage personality in China, we will be dealing here principally with the Chinese sage tradition.

In China the sage became the ideal personality of the Confucian tradition. Confucianism uses the term *sage* to describe the legendary culture heroes and emperors whose achievements produced the conditions from which early civilization arose. Confucius creatively transformed the traditional understanding of the sage personality into the *chun-tzu*, or gentleman-scholar. According to Confucius, the sage's life vision permanently impresses the people.[37] Indeed, Confucius is himself the Chinese sage par excellence, the "Supreme Sage and Teacher," according to his traditional title.[38] Thus the sage personality is a religious figure of paramount significance in the East Asian world and, as such, is important to the larger human community.

In the Confucian cosmology there is an interrelation between the cosmic forces of Heaven, Earth, and Human. The interaction of these realities becomes the special characteristic of the Confucian tradition. The sage personality fulfills the potential for cosmic relatedness within the human order by cultivating sincerity *(ch'eng)*. In the Confucian tradition sincerity underlies the most authentic life possible, namely that of the sage personality. Sincerity completes the sage's own ethical responsibilities and enables him or her to aid all reality in the realization of its own integrity. As the *Doctrine of the Mean (Chung-yung)* expresses it: "Sincerity is the Way of Heaven; the attainment of sincerity is the Way of man. He who possesses sincerity achieves what is right without effort, understands without thinking, and naturally and easily is centered in the Way. He is a sage."[39] The *Doctrine of the Mean* further explicates the sage as a religious personality by identifying his creative integrity as equal with Heaven and Earth. In this manner the sage demonstrates that the authentic actions of the human being can assist in the transformation of the entire cosmic order:

Only he who possesses absolute sincerity can give full development to his nature. Able to give full development to his own nature, he can give full development to the nature of other men. Able to give full development to the nature of men, he can give full development to the nature of all beings, he can assist in the transforming and nourishing powers of Heaven and earth. Capable of assisting the transforming and nourishing powers of Heaven and earth, he may, with Heaven and earth, form a triad.[40]

The Confucian sage realizes that human existence is not isolated either from the activity of the earth or from the metaphysical events of the cosmos. The performance of the most ordinary *(yung)* human actions becomes for the sage personality the means for "transforming and nourishing" all beings that he encounters. In this manner the sage's religious activity is central *(chung)* to the interaction of Heaven and Earth.

By harmonizing his actions with his natural sincerity, the sage becomes attuned to the moral order in the universe. For the sage existence is ultimately grounded in the coalescence of self-harmony with this moral law at the center of all reality. The sense of divine personality and religious intimacy with that personality is not generally articulated by the sage. Recognizing the potential harmony with Heaven in moral rectification, the sage chooses to emphasize more immediate human values. Yet the sage does not overlook the numinous presence of Heaven. Confucius remarked:

"I wish I did not have to speak at all." Tzu Kung said: "But if you did not speak, Sir, what should we disciples pass on to others?" Confucius said: "Look at Heaven there. Does it speak? The four seasons run their course and all things are produced. Does Heaven speak?"[41]

Acknowledging the numinous manifestation in cyclic processes, the sage represents a way of seeing into the seasons of the earth, into the reciprocal relations between humans, and into the significance of ritual.

The sage activates human energy by cultivating a special mode of sympathetic relationship with phenomenal reality. This sensitivity marks him as one who participates in the inner dynamics of reality and thus is able to establish a reciprocity with all things. This particular vision of the inner, feeling dimension helps to arouse in others a self-reflection that reveals their own deepest humanity. Shao Yung expresses the sage's special activation of human energies by the image of "reflecting":

A mirror reflects because it does not obscure the corporeal form of things. But water (with its purity) does even better because it reveals the universal character of the corporeal form of things as they really are. And the sage does still better because he reflects the universal character of the feeling of all things. The sage can do so because he views things as they view themselves; that is, not subjectively but from the viewpoint of things. Since he is able to do this, how can there be anything between him and things?[42]

By reflecting on things as they view themselves, the sage mirrors the inner principle *(li)* of reality. He is able to cultivate this awareness in himself and in others by certain practical techniques.

The techniques of the sage are meditation, ritual, and education. The sage's meditation is an interior discipline that harmonizes the interior life with exterior actions. This meditation, which is performed while sitting quietly, is designed to concentrate the mind and to balance the demands of an active life. As Chu Hsi observed:

To be serious does not mean to sit still like a blockhead, with the ear hearing nothing, the eye seeing nothing, and the mind thinking of nothing. . . . It is merely to be apprehensive and careful. . . . In this way both body and mind will be collected and concentrated as if one is apprehensive of something. If one can always be like this, his dispositions will naturally be changed.[43]

The meditative technique is used for the sage's intellectual pursuits, "investigation of things," and for his or her altruistic activities, which the sage characterizes as "treating the people as if they were wounded."

The sage's sympathetic relation with others is identified in the term *humanity (jen)*, which is the primary Confucian virtue. The sage's activity finds fullest expression in his or her involvement in the human community. For the sage is the exemplar of ritualized relationships that promote the highest ideals of humanity.

The sage cultivates the "common root" that brings human beings into affective relations with Earth and Heaven.

This experience of reciprocity is ritualized by the sage in the five communities, namely: the universal cosmic community, the political community, the friendship community, the family community, and the individual as a community in himself.[44] These five areas of relationship provide a comprehensive life ritual that fosters the authentic human mode within the temporal order.

Teaching is perhaps the most significant characteristic of the sage personality, for it is in education that sages impart to others their articulated ideas and their comprehensive life-style. They attempt to transcend pedagogic techniques and instill in their students a feeling for their own innate humanity. As is written in the *Analects:*

Confucius said: "Shen! My teaching contains one principle that runs through it all." "Yes," replied Tseng Tzu. When Confucius had left the room the disciples asked: "What did he mean?" Tseng Tzu replied: "Our Master's teaching is simply this: loyalty and reciprocity."[45]

Thus the sage is a unique religious personality, in that his or her harmonization of inner integrity with social responsibility is not expressed in exclusively spiritual terms. Indeed, sages experience the numinous by entering into the dynamics of the universe in their daily actions. Their orientation leads them away from a preoccupation with other worldly concerns to problems in the social and political spheres. Most importantly, sages seek to rectify the moral order that is frequently in danger of being lost by the human community. For them moral rectification is the Way that reestablishes the basic harmony between Heaven, Earth, and Human. As one scholar interprets the sage personality in the Neo-Confucian context:

Whatever the mode of intellectuality, moral endeavor, social engagement or religious practice which prevailed in a given period . . . for the Neo-Confucian the conception of the sage remained crucial as the expression of man in his fullness, embracing as wide a range of human experience as possible, and actively integrating it into a holistic view of life at one with the Way.[46]

There is a special relationship between the Confucian sage and the shamanic personality. It is likely that the Confucian sense of active responsibility to the community *(ju)* is directly related to the earlier shamanic ideals of the Shang dynasty and the Chu state.[47] Sufficient evidence is not yet available to fully substantiate this historical claim, but similarities in the religious types support the hypothesis. For the involvement of both the sage and the shaman in social action is based on a belief that their practices will effect a harmony between the orders of reality. The Confucian sage rectifies the inner principle of things to harmonize Heaven, Earth, and Human. The shaman ritually journeys in a trance state or undertakes intense concentration to mediate healing energies that will correct physical or psychic imbalances. Both the sage and the shaman act to recover an integral harmony that is essential to life. The similarities between the two, however, were significantly altered by the sage's commitment to the more complex social and cultural order in Chinese civilization.

The shamanic cosmology, which deals with the interpenetration of a variety of spirit presences, is different from the sage's cosmological context. For the sage the orders of Heaven, Earth, and Human are mutually complementary realities. The three form a universe that communes in all its aspects. The shamanic world view, however, posits a distinct numinous region that is the source of spirit power. The shaman communicates in trance with that realm, which, although separate from the phenomenal order, manifests itself in spirit presences in the natural world. The shaman's spirit guardians are personalistic powers that place no specifically moral mandate on the shaman. The shaman's trance is different from the sage's communion with the inner principle *(li)*, which demands moral rectification. The shaman does not activate a moral principle common to all reality but rather evokes the sustaining energies of the spirit world.

A shaman's activation of sacred energies by the ritual reenactment of the initiating spirit call also distinguishes him or her from the sage. The sage's ritualization of relationships constitutes a religious mode that transforms the secular into the sacred. The shaman's ritual, however, represents a dramatic break in ordinary events that communicates transphenomenal power.

The relations of the sage and the shaman to cosmic reality are parallel. The sage educates people towards a realization of their place in the cosmic order, and the shaman evokes cosmic powers for his ritual performance. Yet these two religious types are differentiated by their techniques and goals.

Shamanic techniques, such as gazing at burning coals, sucking with an animal bone, or dancing according to a vision revelation, are not intended to promote the integrity of the individual or to reassert morality in the social order. Rather, the shaman's religious activity is directed toward alleviating immediate distress. The shaman's drama is intended to activate archetypal presences in the psyche and thereby convey an efficacious energy. The sage's rituals and teaching mirror ultimate principles in order to provide a rational, moral guide for human behavior. Thus the goals of the shaman are different from those of the sage. The sage manifests in his own authentic behavior the integrity of the cosmos. Consequently, he or she guides the social order by means of personal meditative reflections and the example of his or her own life. The shaman's goals, on the other hand, are more specific, such as ensuring a successful hunt, curing illness, and promoting long life.

The shaman is a sacrificial personality who experiences an intimate relationship with cosmic power that he or she is able to mediate through a trance state. The shaman's

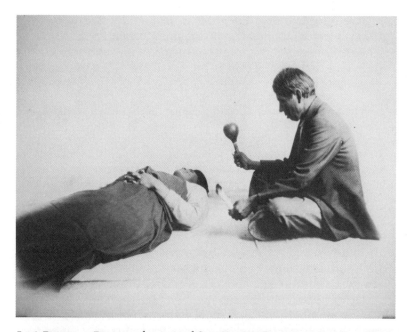

José Panco, a Papago shaman of San Xavier Reservation, circa 1920.
He is shown here invoking his spirit power with the rattle and deer
tail. The rhythmic quality of the shaman's chanting, along with the
movement of the rattle and the deer tail, engender the shamanic
trance and subsequent transfer of healing power to the patient. Courtesy of the Smithsonian Institution National Anthropological Archives.

healing power arises from an understanding of his or her
earliest sacrificial encounters. Visions and dreams help
the shaman to interpret the psychic or physical dismemberment experienced earlier. This early "sickness" is not
simply a pathological phase; it is an initiation into the
shaman's role as the sacrificial healer of the tribe. The
shamanic formation is a precarious passage to inner stability. Often the contact with the spirits overwhelms the
shaman's psyche and results in destructive, egotistical behavior. Such aberrations are not infrequent, but they are
discouraged by tribal traditions that guard against sorcery.

The integration of the shaman frequently is a passage through terror and isolation before inner balance is achieved. The early formation is often characterized by extreme solitude and suffering. Yet it is here that the shaman's inner wisdom is born:

> A real shaman does not jump about the floor and do tricks, nor does he seek by the aid of darkness, by putting out the lamps, to make the minds of his neighbors uneasy. For myself, I do not think I know much, but I do not think that wisdom or knowledge about things that are hidden can be sought in this manner. True wisdom is only to be found far away from people, out in the great solitude, and is not found in play but only through suffering. Solitude and suffering open the human mind, and therefore a shaman must seek his wisdom there.[48]

In that passage a Caribou Eskimo shaman acknowledges that suffering and solitude are something to be actively sought by a future shaman, not avoided. Although a "death" crisis may fragment the shaman psychically and physically, and dismemberment is frought with potential chaos, it is by passing through that sacrificial state that the shaman achieves his or her own inner balance and hence the creative power to heal. As Mircea Eliade says:

> The total crisis of the future shaman, sometimes leading to complete disintegration of the personality and to madness, can be valued not only as an initiatory death but also as a symbolic return to the precosmogonic Chaos, to the amorphous and indescribable state that precedes any cosmogony. Now, as we know, for archaic and traditional cultures, a symbolic return to Chaos is equivalent to preparing a new Creation. It follows that we may interpret the psychic Chaos of the future shaman as a sign that the profane man is being "dissolved" and a new personality being prepared for birth.[49]

Fragmented and dismembered, the shaman is then remade in the image of a spirit power. Often the shaman finds a new identity in an animal form, taking possession of the animal to acquire its natural strength and rhythms. Thus the shamanic masks that are used in healing ceremonies are frequently of animal figures to make present the numinous strength of the spirit patron.

Through constant communication with their particular spirit powers, shamans are able to call on healing energies both for themselves and for their tribe. Their ability to use spirit power marks them either as authentic or as ineffectual. Although their task is difficult, genuine shamans are inspired by an understanding of their sacrificial role. The Russian ethnographer Sieroszcewski vividly described that role, citing the personal confrontation of the shaman with the spirits and extolling the shaman's courage as the source of creative shamanic energies:

The duties undertaken by the shaman are not easy; the struggle which he has to carry on is dangerous. There exist traditions about shamans who were carried away still living from the earth to the sky, about others killed by spirits or struck down at their first meeting with the powers whom they dared to call upon. The shaman who decides to carry on this struggle has not only material gain in view but the alleviation of the griefs of his fellow men; the shaman who has the vocation, the faith and the conviction, who undertakes his duty with ecstasy and negligence of personal danger, inspired by the high ideals of sacrifice, such a wizard always exerts an enormous influence over his audience. After having seen once or twice such a real shaman, I understood the distinction that the natives drew between the "Great," the "Middling" and the "Mocking" or deceitful Shamans.[50]

Most characteristics of the shamanic religious personality follow from the shaman's fourfold function as the focus of personal sacrifice, the source of trance meditation, the leader of tribal ritual, and the instrument of healing and divining. For example, as the focus of personal sacrifice the shaman structures for the audience an experiential contact with cosmic energies. The distinctive aspect of the shaman's sacrificial personality is his or her struggle with the sacred energy that controls and sustains the universe. The capacity to undergo deprivation and eventually forge an identity with power is what makes the shaman effective as a healer and unique as a religious figure. The shaman is one who cultivates the art of balancing the creative and dissipative energies of human life in relation to the natural world.

As the source of trance meditation the shaman passes among the human, natural, and mythic worlds described in tribal cosmologies. In order to act as the mediator between the human community and the natural and spirit worlds, the shaman develops many trance techniques. The shaman uses not only ecstatic journeys to the heavenly regions but also intense meditative states and complete spirit possession to relay requests to his or her guardian spirits. The continued use of various altered states of consciousness by shamanic personalities ensures their capacity to deal with any phenomenal occurrence by contacting transphenomenal power.

While the shaman is not the sole leader of ritual activity, he or she does function as the ceremonial guide in encounters with the spirit world. The shaman journeys for the community into those mysterious regions toward which the tribal group is oriented. As the leader of tribal ritual he or she dramatizes a personal encounter with the spirits and symbolizes it by images from the natural world. Thus the shaman can be characterized as a dramatic seer whose rituals foster the tribe's religious ethos by expressing their reverence for natural phenomena.

As the instrument of healing and divining the shaman demonstrates a continued commitment to the phenomenal order. Without this commitment the more esoteric aspects of shamanistic ritual activity would remain ineffective. For a shaman sees his or her healing capacity as analogous to that of nature, which sustains all of life. Without this direct experiential link to the earth some shamans remain merely esoteric personalities who are not grounded in the realities of tribal needs. Thus, although the spirits may single out shamanic personalities, the tribe enables them to function by endorsing their rituals and confirming their commitment to the phenomenal order.

Shamans are important religious personalities because of their unique ability to give symbolic meaning to the forces that animate the cosmology. Often identifying themselves with primordial earth processes, they establish for their tribes a particular religious consciousness which they continually reassert during difficult transitional times. This religious consciousness is marked by a symbol system drawn from the archetypal earth images that are a valuable resource in shamanic healing.

Thus the experience of resonance with the natural world distinguishes the shaman as a religious type from the prophet, priest, yogi, and sage. Perceiving the vital link between earth processes and human life is not simply a technique of magic or manipulation. It is rather a method of experiencing the constellations of energy in the natural world and channeling those forces into the tribal community. The shaman provides the means for a sacred interpretation of tribal life. Through the shaman the tribe is able to develop a symbolic understanding of the intimate association between the human group and earth processes in hunting and agriculture.

The shaman's particular capacity to evoke resonance with the natural world appears again as a need for our own time. The shamanic consciousness of abiding earth energies can apparently be nurtured even within the contemporary technological milieu. It is a paradox that we in the twentieth century have inherited both the capacity for technological domination of the earth and a comprehensive understanding of the earth's evolutionary history. There arises a challenge to bridge the gap between these different perspectives on the modern world by developing a religious consciousness that is aware of our psychic-physical roots in the earth itself. There is a need not for manipulation but for communion with earth processes. The shamanic consciousness has preserved the capacity for evocation rather than domination. The sympathetic relation of the shaman to his environment is an invaluable corrective in times when we apparently have lost this primordial mode of religious perception.

An interpretation of the abiding shamanic component in the human psyche is also necessary in an age of spiritual groping. Just as the shaman was prey to aberrant behavior, so also are contemporary shamanic developments subject to certain destructive forces. The study of the shamanic experience becomes indispensable in interpreting current religious movements. With the sudden increase of purely charismatic and fundamentalist groups both inside and outside of the institutional religions, an appreciation of the experiential quality of shamanism is necessary. Also, because of the ecological recognition of human interaction with the natural environment, the profound beauty and meaning of many shamanic symbols is being rediscovered.

This enduring shamanic component in the human psyche enables us to see the natural world and to experience its internal mystery in a unique way. Ancient as the stirrings of the imagination in paleolithic cave art, the shamanic mystery has remained a vital source of energy throughout human history. Indeed, the invocation of the shamanic mode of consciousness gives rise to an awareness of the patterns of meaning inherent in the earth. As the Ojibway shaman chants:

> It will resound
> Clearly
> The sky
> When I come
> Making a sound.[51]

NOTES

Chapter 1. Introduction

1. While this power presence is articulated in a variety of expressions, a comprehensive statement on this religious experience is found in Gerardus van der Leeuw, *Religion in Essence and Manifestation,* pp. 23-28.

2. Rudolf Otto, *The Idea of the Holy,* trans. John Harvey (London: Oxford University Press, 1923).

3. *Oxford Dictionary of English Etymology,* ed. C. T. Onions (Oxford: Clarendon, 1966), s.v. "numen," p. 617.

4. Otto, *The Idea of the Holy,* p. 26. Also Robert R. Marret uses "awe" in *The Threshold of Religion,* 4th ed. (London: Methuen, 1929).

5. J. R. Swanton, "Social Conditions, Beliefs and Linguistic Relations of the Tlingit Indians," *Twenty-sixth Annual Report of the Bureau of American Ethnology,* pp. 451-52.

6. For "hierophany" see Mircea Eliade, *Cosmos and History,* trans. Willard Trask (New York: Harper and Bros., 1959), p. 4; for "wholly other," see Otto, *The Idea of the Holy,* pp. 25-30.

7. Alice Fletcher, *Peabody Museum Report* (1868-69): 276, quoted in Christopher Dawson, *Progress and Religion,* pp. 84-85.

8. Van der Leeuw, *Religion in Essence and Manifestation* 1:33.

9. Ibid., 1:83-84. The articulation of this personal experience of power is culturally determined, but the spirits are distinctly personalistic and not indiscriminate, impersonal power; see Paul Radin, "Religion of the North American Indians," *Journal of American Folklore* 27 (1914): 335-73.

10. R. H. Codrington, *The Melanesians* (1891), p. 118, quoted in Van der Leeuw, *Religion in Essence and Manifestation* 1:24.

11. J. N. B. Hewitt, "Orenda," in Frederick Webb Hodge, ed., *Handbook of American Indians;* and "Orenda and a Definition of Religion," *American Anthropologist,* n.s., 4:33-46.

12. Alice Fletcher, "Wakonda," in Hodge, ed., *Handbook of American Indians;* Sword Finger, One-Star, and Tyon, "Oglala Metaphysics,"

in Barbara and Dennis Tedlock, eds., *Teachings from the American Earth*, pp. 205–218.

13. Clark Wissler, *The American Indian* (3rd ed., Gloucester, Mass.: P. Smith, 1957), p. 192.

14. J. R. Swanton, "Social Conditions, Beliefs and Linguistic Relations of the Tlingit Indians," pp. 451–52.

15. Ruth Landes, *Ojibwa Religion and the Midewiwin*, p. 22; and William Jones, "The Algonkian Manitu," *Journal of American Folklore* 18:183–90.

16. Because of the special nature of the Ojibway term *manitou*, it appears in its original form in this work. In this regard we follow the procedure of earlier researchers on the Ojibway, such as William Jones, A. I. Hallowell, and Ruth Landes. The metaphors of power, energy, and force are used interchangeably with the term *manitou*. Also manitou is not altered to form the plural; rather, the same form is used for both singular and plural. An effort has been made to ensure that the context in which manitou is used will clarify the number intended. Also see Mary B. Black, "Ojibwa Power Belief System," in *The Anthropology of Power*, ed. Raymond D. Fogelson and Richard N. Adams, pp. 141–51.

17. Van der Leeuw, *Religion in Essence and Manifestation*, 1:83–90.

18. Motoori Norinaga, in Wm. Theodore de Bary, ed., *Sources of Japanese Tradition* (New York: Columbia University Press, 1964), pp. 21–22.

19. Langdon Warner, *The Enduring Art of Japan* (New York: Grove Press, 1952), p. 18.

20. Ibid., p. 17.

21. Lev Iakovlevich Shternberg, "Divine election in primitive religion (including material on different tribes of N.E. Asia and America)," in *Congrès international des americanistes: Compte-Rendu de la XXIe session, 2ème partie* (held at Göteborg, Switzerland, in 1924).

22. John Lame Deer and Richard Erdoes, *Lame Deer, Seeker of Visions* (New York: Simon and Schuster, 1972), pp. 145–46.

23. Sergei M. Shirokogoroff, *The Psychomental Complex of the Tungus*, pp. 350–51.

24. W. P. Fairchild, "Shamanism in Japan," *Folklore Studies* 21 (1962): 1–122; also Hori Ichiro, *Folk Religion in Japan* (Chicago: University of Chicago Press, 1968), especially chapter 5, "Japanese Shamanism."

25. Quoted in Dawson, *Progress and Religion*, p. 81.

26. This term is used in the manner of Arnold van Gennep, *The Rites of Passage* (London: Routledge and Kegan Paul, 1960), and Victor Turner, *The Ritual Process*.

27. Turner, *The Ritual Process*, pp. 116–17.

28. Mircea Eliade, *Shamanism: Archaic Techniques of Ecstasy*, p. xiii.

29. Ibid., pp. 4 and 495.

30. M. A. Czaplicka, *Aboriginal Siberia*, p. 144.

31. Ibid., p. 197.

32. Berthold Laufer, "Origin of the Word 'Shaman,'" *American Anthropologist* 19 (1917): 362-63.

33. Ibid., p. 364.

34. Mircea Eliade, *Shamanism*, p. 495; Julius Nemeth, "Über den Ursprung des Wortes *Saman* und einige Bemerkungen zur Turkisch-Mongolischen Lautgeschichte," in *Keleti Szemle* 14 (1913-14): 240-49; and Berthold Laufer, "Origin of the Word Shaman," pp. 361-71; for Dorji Banzarov, see M. A. Czaplicka, *Aboriginal Siberia*, p. 191.

35. S. M. Shirokogoroff, *The Psychomental Complex of the Tungus*, p. 282.

36. Weston La Barre, *The Ghost Dance: The Origins of Religion*, p. 352.

37. These early Russian sources are detailed in the extensive bibliography by A. A. Popov, *Tavgytzy: Materialy po ethnografi avamskilch i vedeyevskikh tavgytzev* (Moscow and Leningrad: Akademia Nauk Soyuza Sovetskikh Sotzralesticheskikh Respublik Ethnografi, 1936), 1:5.

38. Franz Boas's earlier work with the Northwest Coast tribes of North America led the expedition to concentrate on Alaskan and Siberian peoples. The terms *Neo-* and *Paleo-Siberian* are from Czaplicka, *Aboriginal Siberia*, which was written in 1914, after the expedition, from which the author drew extensive materials.

39. Waldemar G. Bogoras, "The Chukchee," especially pp. 441ff.; also Waldemar Jochelson, *The Koryak*, pp. 416ff.; also, Jochelson, *The Yukaghir and the Yukaghirized Tungus*, pp. 30-38.

40. Robert Lowie, *Primitive Religion;* Paul Radin, *Primitive Religion: Its Nature and Origin;* and Radin, "Religion of the North American Indians," *Journal of American Folklore* 27 (1914): 335-73.

41. Horst Kirchner, "Ein archaeologischer Beitrag zur Urgeschichte des Schamanismus," *Anthropos* 47 (1952): 244-86.

42. Andreas Lommel, *Shamanism: The Beginnings of Art.*

43. Gustav Rank, "Shamanism as a Research Subject," in Edsman, ed., *Studies in Shamanism*, p. 21.

44. Franz Boas, ed., *General Anthropology* (New York: D. C. Heath and Co., 1938), p. 673.

45. N. D. Mironov and S. M. Shirokogoroff, "Sramana-Shaman: Etymology of the Word 'Shaman,'" *Journal of the Royal Asiatic Society, North American Branch* 55:105-130.

46. Vilmos Dioszegi, *Tracing Shamans in Siberia*, p. 38; for Anisimov, see "The Origins of the Shamanistic Rite," in *Studies in Siberian Shamanism*, ed. Henry Michael, pp. 84-124; for Zelenin, see Gustav Rank, "Shamanism as a Research Subject," in *Studies in Shamanism*,

ed. Edsman, pp. 17-19.

47. Dioszegi, *Tracing Shamans in Siberia*, pp. 10-11.

48. Ake Ohlmarks, "Arktischer Schamanismus und altnordischer Seider," *Archiv für Religionswissenschsft* 36 (1939), 1:171-80; Ohlmarks's thesis is presented in Eliade, *Shamanism*, p. 24.

49. J. L. Maddox, *The Medicine Man: A Sociological Study of the Character and Evolution of Shamanism*; L. L. Leh, "The Shaman in Aboriginal American Society," *University of Colorado Studies* 20 (1934); W. T. Corlett, *The Medicine Man of the American Indian* (Springfield, Ill.: C. C. Thomas, 1935).

50. Mircea Eliade, *Shamanism*; also see Mircea Eliade, "Shamanism," in *Forgotten Religions*, pp. 299-308.

51. Eliade, *Shamanism*, p. 504.

52. Ibid., p. 12.

53. I. M. Lewis, *Ecstatic Religion: An Anthropological Study of Spirit Possession and Shamanism*.

54. C. G. Jung, "The Complications of American Psychology," *Collected Works* 10:502-514; *Psychology and Religion*, in *Collected Works*, vol. 11, especially pp. 227n., 274, 294; *Alchemical Studies*, in *Collected Works* 13:303-341.

55. Hans Findeisen, "Das Schamanentum als spiritistische Religion," *Ethnos* 25, nos. 3 & 4 (1960): 192-213; and E. Stiglmayr, "Schamanismus, eine spiritistische Religion?," *Ethnos* 27 (1962): 40-48.

56. Ake Hultkrantz, "Spirit Lodge, A North American Shamanistic Seance," in *Studies in Shamanism*, ed. Carl-Martin Edsman, pp. 32-68; also, Hultkrantz, "Book reviews: 'Anthropological Approaches to Religion,'" *History of Religions* 9 (1970): 337-52.

57. See Wayne Proudfoot, "Religion and Reduction," in *Essays in Honor of James A. Martin, Jr., Union Seminary Quarterly Review* 27 (1981-82): 13-25.

58. Joachim Wach, *The Comparative Study of Religion* (New York: Columbia University Press, 1958), p. 24.

59. Karl Rahner and Herbert Vorgrimler, *Theological Dictionary* (New York: Herder and Herder, 1968), p. 456.

60. See Henry Warren, *Buddhism* (New York: Atheneum, 1974), p. 47.

61. Frederick W. Mote, *Intellectual Foundations of China* (New York: Alfred A. Knopf, 1971), p. 30.

62. Irving I. Zaretsky and Mark P. Leone, *Religious Movements in Contemporary America*, 1977.

63. Anthony Wallace, *Culture and Personality* (New York: Random House, 1970), p. 188.

64. Victor W. Turner, *The Ritual Process*, pp. 128-29.

65. Raymond H. Prince, "Cocoon Work: An Interpretation of the

Concern of Contemporary Youth with the Mystical," in *Religious Movements in Contemporary America*, ed. Zaretsky and Leone, pp. 255-71.

66. Mircea Eliade, *Sacred and Profane*, trans. Willard Trask (New York: Harcourt, Brace, 1959).

67. Lame Deer and Erdoes, *Lame Deer, Seeker of Visions*, p. 153.

Chapter 2. Siberian Shamanism

1. Van der Leeuw, *Religion in Essence and Manifestation* 1:195.

2. For contributions from American Indians see Barbara and Dennis Tedlock, eds., *Teachings from the American Earth;* Walter H. Capps, ed., *Seeing with a Native Eye* (New York: Harper and Row, 1976); and Joseph Epes Brown, *The Sacred Pipe: Black Elk's Account of the Seven Rites of the Oglala Siox* (Norman: University of Oklahoma Press, 1953).

3. The generalized description of Siberia here is taken from the interesting work *Aboriginal Siberia*, by M. A. Czaplicka, pp. 1-22; and M. G. Levin, *Ethnic Origins of the Peoples of Northeastern Asia*, p. 41.

4. Levin, *Ethnic Origins of the Peoples of Northeastern Asia*, p. 41.

5. A. P. Okladnikov, *Yakutia: Before its Incorporation into the Russian State,* p. 163; also A. F. Anisimov, "Cosmological Concepts of the Peoples of the North," in Henry N. Michaels, ed., *Studies in Siberian Shamanism*, p. 180.

6. Karl J. Narr, "Barenzeremoniell und Schamanismus in der Alteren Steinzeit Europas," *Saeculum* 10, no. 3 (1959): 233-72; and Hans Findeisen, "Der Adler als Kulturbringer im nordasiatischen Raum und in der amerikanischen Arktis," *Zeitschrift für Ethnologie* 81 (1956):70-82; and Andreas Lommel, *Shamanism: The Beginnings of Art*, pp. 127-33.

7. S. M. Shirokogoroff, *Social Organization of the Northern Tungus*, p. 364.

8. Okladnikov, *Yakutia*, p. 264ff.

9. Ibid., p. 268.

10. Okladnikov, *Yakutia*, p. 270.

11. Eliade, *Shamanism*, p. 272; also Adolf Friedrich, "Das Bewusstsein eines Naturvolkes Haushalt und Ursprung des Lebens," *Paideuma* 6, no. 2 (August, 1955): 52ff.

12. Wenceslas Sieroszewski, "Du chamanisme d'apres les croyances des Yakoutes," *Revue de l'histoire des religions* 46 (1902): 322.

13. Ibid., p. 625; and Czaplicka, *Aboriginal Siberia*, p. 213.

14. Shirokogoroff, *Psychomental Complex of the Tungus*, p. 296.

15. Ernst Cassirer, *The Philosophy of Symbolic Forms* 2:260.

16. V. M. Mikhailvoskii, "Shamanism in Siberia and European Russia,

Being the Second Part of *Shamanstvo, Journal of the Royal Anthropological Institute* 24 (1894): 63.

17. Ibid., p. 87.

18. Anisimov, "Cosmological Concepts of the Peoples of the North," p. 112.

19. Czaplicka, *Aboriginal Siberia*, p. 185.

20. Ibid., p. 186.

21. Uno Harva (Holmberg), "The Shaman Costume and Its Significance," *Annales universitas fennicae aboenis*, Series B, 1(1923): 2.

22. Eliade, *Shamanism*, p. 147.

23. Ibid., p. 146; also, Czaplicka, *Aboriginal Siberia*, pp. 204 and 218.

24. Mikhailovskii, "Shamanism in Siberia and European Russia," p. 138.

25. Vilmos Dioszegi, *Tracing Shamans in Siberia*. His work, researched in the 1950s, gives a good indication of the enduring quality of Siberian shamanism. See also Sevyan Vainshtein, *Nomads of South Siberia: The Pastoral Economies of Tuva* and "Shamanism of the Touvinians," *VII International Congress of Anthropological and Ethnological Sciences* (Moscow: Nauka, 1964), for discussions of more contemporary expressions of Siberian shamanism.

26. Dioszegi, *Tracing Shamans in Siberia*, p. 62.

27. Ibid., p. 58.

28. Ibid., pp. 73–76. Also see Czaplicka, *Aboriginal Siberia*, p. 270, for the importance of the drum among Siberian tribes.

29. Dioszegi, *Tracing Shamans in Siberia*, p. 74.

30. Ibid., p. 75.

31. Otto, *The Idea of the Holy*, p. 144.

32. Rodney Needham, "Percussion and Transition," in *Reader in Comparative Religion*, ed. William Lessa and Evon Vogt (New York: Harper and Row, 1958), pp. 305–306.

33. Claude Lévi-Strauss, *Structural Anthropology*, p. 175.

34. Sieroszewski, "Du chamanisme," p. 641; also Czaplicka, *Aboriginal Siberia*, p. 234.

35. Sieroszewski, "Du chamanisme," p. 642; also Czaplicka, *Aboriginal Siberia*, p. 235.

36. Sieroszewski, "Du chamanisme," p. 643; also Czaplicka, *Aboriginal Siberia*, p. 237.

37. Sieroszewski, "Du chamanisme," p. 644; also Czaplicka, *Aboriginal Siberia*, p. 237.

38. See Forrest E. Clements, *Primitive Concepts of Disease*, pp. 189, 212–13, 216; also, the link of primal healing to current medical practices, see Guido Manjo, *The Healing Hand* (Cambridge, Mass.: Harvard University Press, 1975).

Chapter 3. Ojibway Shamanism and Its Historical Background

1. Alfred L. Kroeber, "Cultural and Natural Areas of Native North America," *University of California Publications in Anthropology and Ethnology* 38 (1939): 35–36.

2. J. V. Wright, "A Regional Examination of Ojibway Culture History," *Anthropologica*, n.s., 7 (1965): 189–227; also, Charles A. Bishop, *The Northern Ojibwa and the Fur Trade: An Historical and Ecological Study*.

3. The Ojibway reservations in Michigan are Ontonagon, L'Anse, Bay Mills, Beaver Island, Hog Island, and Isabella. In Wisconsin the reservations are Lac du Flambeau, Lac Courte Oreilles, Saint Croix, Mole Lake (or Sokoogan Community), Bad River, Mille Lac, Red Cliff, and Lac Vieux Desert. In Minnesota the reservations are Red Lake, Fond du Lac, Deer Creek, Vermillion, Leech, White Earth, Grant Portage, Mille Lacs, and Nett Lake. In North Dakota the Turtle Mountain reservation is predominantly Ojibway. See William C. Sturtevant, ed., *Handbook of North American Indians*, vol. 15, *Northeast*, pp. 743–71.

4. The Canadian reserves are too numerous to list. See Sturtevant, ed., *Handbook of North American Indians*, vol. 6, *Subarctic*. Regarding the expansion of the Plains Ojibway into Montana, I have been told by Minnesota Ojibway that there are significant numbers of Ojibway at Rocky Boy reservation.

5. Reuben Gold Thwaites, *The Jesuit Relations and Allied Documents* 18:229–30.

6. See Bishop, *The Northern Ojibway and the Fur Trade*, p. 17 n. 1.

7. See William Warren, *History of the Ojibway Nation*, pp. 256–59.

8. Thwaites, *Jesuit Relations* 18:230.

9. Herbert Spinden, "First Peopling of America as a Chronological Problem," in *Early Man*, ed. George Grant McCurdy (New York: Lippincott, 1937), pp. 105–14.

10. F. Field and E. Prostov, "Results of Soviet Investigation in Siberia," *American Anthropologist* 44 (1942):403.

11. James B. Griffin, "Northeast Woodlands Area," in *Prehistoric Man in the New World*, ed. Jesse D. Jennings and Edward Norbeck, pp. 223–77; also, George E. Hyde, *Indians of the Woodlands*, pp. 3–16.

12. Wright, "A Regional Examination of Ojibway Culture History," p. 217.

13. Warren, *History of the Ojibway Nation*, p. 56.

14. For Woodland culture traits see Alfred Kroeber, *Cultural and*

Natural Areas of Native North America, rev. ed. (Berkeley: California University Press, 1947); also, Harold E. Driver, *Indians of North America* (Chicago: University of Chicago Press, 1970).

15. See A. I. Hallowell, "Bear Ceremonialism in the Northern Hemisphere," *American Anthropologist,* n.s., 28 (1926): 135ff.; Goldmund Hatt, *Asiatic Influence in American Folklore;* also Clark Wissler, *The American Indian* (New York: Douglas C. McMurtrie, 1917); and M. G. Levin, *Ethnic Origins of the Peoples of Northeast Asia.*

16. Hatt, *Asiatic Influence in American Folklore,* pp. 10-11 and 106-110.

17. Wissler, *The American Indian,* pp. 9-14.

18. Hallowell, "Bear Ceremonialism in the Northern Hemisphere," pp. 153-63.

19. J. V. Wright, "A Regional Examination of Ojibway Culture," p. 217.

20. Warren, *History of the Ojibway Nation,* pp. 79-80; see also Calvin Martin, *Keepers of the Game,* pp. 84-93, for a provocative discussion of migration myth.

21. Warren, *History of the Ojibway Nation,* pp. 89-90.

22. Sturtevant, *Handbook of North American Indians* 8:743.

23. Joan M. Vastokas and Romas K. Vastokas, *Sacred Art of Algonkians,* pp. 57-59; and A. P. Okladnikov, *Yakutia: Before its Incorporation into the Russian State,* pp. 160-63.

24. Jordan Paper, "The Meaning of the 't'ao-t'ieh,'" *History of Religions* 18, no. 1 (1978): 18-41.

25. A. I. Hallowell, "Ojibwa Ontology, Behavior and World View," in *Teachings from the American Earth,* ed. Barbara and Dennis Tedlock, pp. 149-50; also, Richard J. Preston, *Cree Narrative: Expressing the Personal Meaning of Events,* app. 1, pp. 288-94.

26. Warren, *History of the Ojibway Nation,* pp. 43-53.

27. Ibid., pp. 44-45.

28. Paul Radin, "Some Aspects of Puberty Fasting among the Ojibwa," pp. 69-78.

29. Victor Barnouw, *Wisconsin Chippewa Myths and Tales,* p. 8.

30. Radin, "Some Aspects of Puberty Fasting," p. 77.

31. George Copway, *The Life, History and Travels of Kah-Ge-Ga-Gah-Bowh* (Philadelphia: Lippincott, Giambo, 1847), quoted in Elemire Zolla, *The Writer and the Shaman* (New York: Harcourt Brace Jovanovich, 1973), p. 239.

32. Hallowell, "Ojibwa Ontology, Behavior and World View," pp. 149-53.

33. Paul Radin, "Religion of the North American Indians, pp. 349-50; and Preston, *Cree Narrative,* especially pp. 171-234, for this closely related tribe's understanding of human-manitou relationship.

34. Robert Lowie, *Primitive Religion*, pp. 14–18.

35. Ruth Landes, *The Ojibwa Woman*, p. 133.

36. For Ojibway shamanic techniques, see Ruth Landes, *Ojibwa Sociology*, p. 123; *Ojibwa Religion and the Midewiwin*, pp. 47, 51; and *The Ojibwa Woman*, p. 134.

37. W. J. Hoffman, "The Midē'wiwin or 'Grand Medicine Society' of the Ojibwa," p. 157.

38. Hultkrantz, "Spirit Lodge, a North American Shamanistic Seance," pp. 60–61.

39. Landes, *Ojibwa Sociology*, pp. 120–21.

40. Hoffman, "The Midē'wiwin," pp. 156–57.

41. Frank Speck, "Penobscot Shamanism," pp. 240–48; also, Adrian Tanner, *Bringing Home Animals*, pp. 136–52.

42. While the *meda*, or family shaman, is generally absent in research on Ojibway shamanism, a clear description of this shamanic vocation is found in Edward James, ed., *Narrative of John Tanner's Thirty Years of Indian Captivity*, pp. 30–40.

43. It should be noted that the form *Midewin* is in some areas the more acceptable designation of the medicine society.

44. Landes, *Ojibwa Religion*, pp. 71–72.

45. Ibid., pp. 3–4; and Basil Johnston, *Ojibway Heritage*, p. 84.

46. Landes, *Ojibwa Religion*, pp. 95–96.

47. Ibid., p. 54.

48. Ibid., pp. 76–77; also Hoffman, "The Midē'wiwin," pp. 163ff.

49. For detailed discussion of *Dzibai* midewiwin, see W. J. Hoffman, "The Menomini Indians," pp. 3–328.

50. Landes, *Ojibwa Religion*, p. 190.

51. Ibid., pp. 203–204; also Hoffman, "Menomini Indians," p. 254, for a similar talk at a *Dzibai* midewiwin.

52. Harold Hickerson, "Notes on the Post-Contact Origin of the Midewiwin," pp. 404–423.

53. Frank Speck, "Penobscot Shamanism," p. 274; also Alfred Goldsworthy Bailey, *The Conflict of European and Eastern Algonkian Cultures*, pp. 126–47.

54. Harold Hickerson, *The Southwestern Chippewa: An Ethnohistorical Study*, pp. 65–72, and Calvin Martin, *Keepers of the Game*, pp. 69–109.

Chapter 4. Cosmology

1. See A. I. Hallowell, "Ojibwa Ontology and World View" and *The Role of Conjuring in Saulteaux Society*.

2. Hallowell, "Ojibwa Ontology," p. 215; also, Frances Densmore,

Chippewa Customs, pp. 97–103.

3. Although separate birchbark scrolls are used to record the origin stories and migration accounts, our joining of the two is based on Hoffman, "The Midē′wiwin," pp. 174ff., and Warren, *History of the Ojibway Nation,* pp. 79–94.

4. A. I. Hallowell, *Culture and Experience,* chap. 5.

5. While this statement may appear as an oversimplification of the diversity in Midewiwin cosmologies, it accentuates the creation theme inherent in every origin story and migration account. For a discussion of the origin tales see Selwyn Dewdney, *The Sacred Scrolls of the Southern Ojibway,* pp. 40–56.

6. John Tanner describes such a ritual relationship in James, ed., *Thirty Years Indian Captivity,* pp. 164–65. Also see Adrian Tanner, *Bringing Home Animals,* pp. 108–135.

7. Basil Johnston, *Ojibway Heritage,* p. 15.

8. Bernard Coleman, *Ojibwa Myths and Legends,* p. 87.

9. See Hallowell, "Ojibwa Ontology," pp. 217ff. For Bishop R. R. Baraga's helpful comments on Ojibway grammar and the animate verb, see his *A Theoretical and Practical Grammar of the Otchipwe Language,* pp. 14–15.

10. Victor Barnouw, *Wisconsin Chippewa Myths,* p. 41. Barnouw uses *manido* (singular) and *manidog* (plural) in this quotation and the quotation referred to in n. 29.

11. Henry Schoolcraft, *Information Respecting the History, Condition and Prospects of the Indian Tribes of the United States* 1:413–14.

12. Dewdney, *Sacred Scrolls of the Southern Ojibway,* pp. 115–30; also, Landes, *Ojibwa Sociology,* pp. 133–60.

13. Landes, *Ojibwa Religion,* p. 104.

14. Dewdney, in *Sacred Scrolls,* p. 155, speaks of the Sacred Pole in midewiwin as *Kitchi chisigong* (literally, *Kitchi,* or *Gici,* meaning "great"; *chisig,* meaning *tcisaki,* or "conjurer"; and *ong,* meaning "place of"), "the place of the Great Tcisaki."

15. The manner of performing the *tcisaki* ceremony varied extensively. For eyewitness accounts that demonstrate both the variations and the similarities in cosmic symbolism, see J. G. Kohl, *Kitchi-Gami Wanderings Around Lake Superior;* also, Hallowell, *The Role of Conjuring,* especially chap. 7; and James Redsky, *Great Leader of the Ojibway: Mis-quona-queb,* pp. 26, 37, 62, 114–16; and A. K. Black, "Shaking the Wigwam," *Beaver,* December, 1934, Outfit 265, pp. 13–34.

16. See also fig. 4 in Hoffman, "The Midē′wiwin."

17. Landes, *Ojibwa Religion,* p. 103.

18. The introductory pages of Jean Herbert's *Shinto: At the Fountainhead of Japan* (New York: Stein & Day, 1967) are helpful in understanding such multivalent concepts as *manitou, kami,* and *wakan.*

19. For *manitou kazo* see Chapter 7 below.

20. Antoine Denis Raudot, "Memoir Concerning the Different Indian Nations of North America" in *Relation par lettres de l'Amérique Septentrionale*, as quoted in W. Vernon Kinietz, *The Indians of the Western Great Lakes*, p. 305.

21. Landes, *Ojibwa Religion*, pp. 98–99.

22. Ibid., p. 109.

23. Ibid., p. 45.

24. Warren, *History of the Ojibway*, p. 27.

25. See Paul Radin, *The Trickster*; also, MacLinscott Ricketts, "The Structure and Religious Significance of the Trickster-Transformer-Culture Hero in the Mythology of the North American Indians," Ph.D. diss., University of Chicago, 1964.

26. The assertive characteristics of the trickster are developed in MacLinscott Ricketts, "The North American Indian Trickster," pp. 327–50.

27. Radin, *The Trickster*, p. 22.

28. For the Nanabozho tales see William Jones, *Ojibwa Texts*, ed. Truman Michelson, Publications of the American Ethnological Society, vol. 7, pts. 1 and 2 (Leyden: E. J. Brill, 1917); also, Truman Michelson, "Ojibwa Tales," pp. 249ff.; and Barnouw, *Wisconsin Chippewa Myths and Tales*, pp. 13–93; and Bernard Coleman, *Ojibway Myths*, pp. 55–100.

29. Barnouw, *Wisconsin Chippewa Myths and Tales*, p. 41.

30. Ibid., pp. 44–45.

31. See C. G. Jung, "On the Psychology of the Trickster Figure," in *The Trickster*, ed. Paul Radin, pp. 195–211.

32. See Daniel G. Brinton, *Myths of the New World*, 3d ed. (Philadelphia: David McKay, 1896), p. 194.

33. See James Teit, *Traditions of the Thompson River Indians* (New York: Houghton Mifflin, 1898), pp. 4–10, for Franz Boas's introduction.

34. John Fischer and Christopher Vecsey, "The Ojibwa Creation Myth: An Analysis of Its Structure and Content," a paper delivered at the American Academy of Religion conference at Northwestern University in 1975.

35. Landes, *Ojibwa Religion*, pp. 21–22. Preston, *Cree Narrative*, p. 294, n. 6, conjectures that the term "for fun" and by extension "play" indicates the absence of sorcery.

36. Hallowell, *The Role of Conjuring*, p. 59.

37. Landes, *Ojibwa Religion*, pp. 62–63.

38. Seymour Parker, "The Wiitiko Psychosis in the Context of Ojibwa Personality and Culture," *American Anthropologist* 62 (1960): 602–23.

39. Dewdney, *Sacred Scrolls*, p. 115.

40. Thomas Berry, "Cosmic Person," in *Riverdale Papers* (New York:

Riverdale Center for Religious Studies Press, 1975).

41. Barnouw, *Wisconsin Chippewa Myths and Tales*, p. 35.

42. Warren, *History*, p. 110.

43. Landes, *Ojibwa Religion*, pp. 114-15.

44. Hallowell, "Ojibwa Ontology," p. 228.

45. Hoffman, "The Midē'wiwin," pp. 185-86; and Warren, *History*, pp. 67 and 79.

46. Berry, "Cosmic Person," p. 17.

47. Landes, *Ojibwa Religion*, pp. 44-45 and 85-86.

Chapter 5. Tribal Sanction

1. Arthur O. Lovejoy used the concept of "unit ideas" to indicate conscious conceptual themes that have become largely "unconscious mental habits." It is in this sense that we characterize the tribal ethos as certain unit ideas that are consciously acted out yet are unconsciously motivated. Lovejoy's term is quoted in Robert Nisbet, *Sociology as an Art Form* (New York: Oxford University Press, 1976), p. 35.

2. See Clifford Geertz, *Islam Observed*, p. 97.

3. Ruth Landes, *Ojibwa Religion and the Midewiwin*, quotation on dust jacket.

4. The formation of the Ojibway into a tribe is the subject of an ongoing historical debate. See Ojibway bibliography under Hickerson, Bishop, Smith and H. Tanner.

5. For the "atomistic" argument see Ruth Landes, "The Ojibwa of Canada," in *Cooperation and Competition among Primitive Peoples*, ed. Margaret Mead (New York: McGraw Hill, 1937), p. 102; also Victor Barnouw, *Acculturation and Personality among the Wisconsin Chippewa*, pp. 15ff.; and A. I. Hallowell, *Culture and Experience*, pp. 7, 105, 120, and 147.

6. For the "corporate" argument see Harold Hickerson, *The Chippewa and Their Neighbors;* also, Charles Bishop, *The Northern Ojibway and the Fur Trade,* and J. V. Wright, "A Regional Examination of Ojibway Culture History," pp. 189-227.

7. Ruth Landes, *The Ojibwa Woman*, pp. 124-30.

8. See Ojibway bibliography, especially Truman Michelson for folktales and Schoolcraft, vol. 1, for the heroic personality.

9. Landes, *Ojibwa Woman*, p. 12.

10. The special treatment of bones is particularly evident among Subarctic peoples. For the Ojibway-Saulteaux, see Alanson Skinner, "Notes on the Eastern Cree and Northern Saulteaux," *Anthropological Papers of the American Museum of Natural History* 9, pt. 1 (1911): 68-76, 162-64; Victor Barnouw, *Wisconsin Chippewa Myths and Tales*, p. 55;

Adrian Tanner, *Bringing Home Animals*, pp. 170-81; and A. I Hallowell, "Bear Ceremonialism in the Northern Hemisphere," pp. 135-37.

11. Landes, *Ojibwa Religion*, pp. 25ff. See also the provocative thesis of Calvin Martin, *Keepers of the Game*, especially pp. 69-112, regarding hunter-animal relations and the historic fur trade.

12. Warren, *History of the Ojibway Nation*, p. 264; also, James ed., *Thirty Years Captivity of John Tanner*, p. 111.

13. James, *Thirty Years Captivity*, p. 111.

14. Warren, *History*, pp. 85-86.

15. Landes, *Ojibwa Sociology*, p. 3.

16. On the formation of the Midewiwin, see Harold Hickerson, "The Sociohistorical Significance of Two Chippewa Ceremonials," p. 74; for southern Ojibway clan organization and the Mide Society as social mechanisms of organization, see Landes, *Ojibwa Sociology*, p. 52.

17. See Fred Eggan, ed., "The Ojibwa and the Indians of the Great Lakes Region: The Role of Cross Cousin Marriage," in his *The American Indian* (Cambridge: Cambridge University Press, 1966) pp. 78-111.

18. See R. G. Thwaites, ed., *The Jesuit Relations and Allied Documents* 54:133.

19. Skinner, "Notes on the Eastern Cree and Northern Saulteaux," p. 150; Frank Speck, "The Family Hunting Band as the Basis of Algonkian Social Organization," pp. 249ff.; Landes, *Ojibwa Sociology*, pp. 89-95; and Tanner, *Bringing Home Animals*, pp. 182-202.

20. Peter Grant, "The Saulteaux Indians: About 1804," in *Les Bourgeois de la Compagnie du Nord-Ouest*, ed. L. R. Masson, 2:326-27.

21. Landes, *Ojibwa Sociology*, p. 144.

22. Ibid., pp. 5-6; and Paula Brown, "Changes in Ojibwa Social Control," pp. 57-70.

23. Landes, *Ojibwa Sociology*, pp. 115ff; *Ojibwa Woman*, p. 3; *Ojibwa Religion*, pp. 21-41; Barnouw, *Wisconsin Chippewa*, p. 8.

24. Antoine Denis Raudot, "Memoir Concerning the Different Indian Nations of North America," in *Relation par lettres de l'Amérique Septentrionale*, as quoted in W. Vernon Kinietz, *Indians of the Western Great Lakes*, pp. 351-52.

25. Gerald Vizenor, *Tribal Scenes and Ceremonies*, p. 170.

26. On personal interpretation of dreams, see James, ed., *Thirty Years Captivity*, pp. 32ff. and 180-84; also on Algonquian dream shamans and dream society, see Alanson Skinner, "Associations and Ceremonies of the Menomini Indians," *Anthropological Papers of the American Museum of Natural History* 13, pt. 2 (1915); and Frank Speck, "Penobscot Shamanism," p. 268.

27. Landes, *Ojibwa Religion*, p. 9.

28. Frances Densmore, *Chippewa Customs*, p. 78.

29. Landes, *Ojibwa Religion*, p. 40.

30. The Ojibway shamans, befitting their individualistic ethos, do not have a common shamanic costume. On the significance of Ojibway shamans' paraphernalia and dress, see Densmore, *Chippewa Customs*, pp. 44-46 and 79-80; also, Hoffman, "The Midē'wiwin," pp. 182-83 and 189-92.

31. Landes, *Ojibway Sociology*, pp. 120-21, and *Ojibwa Religion*, pp. 47ff.

32. Hoffman, "Midē'wiwin," pp. 156-57; also H. Schoolcraft, *Information*, vol. 1, pp. 366-67 and 399.

33. Hallowell, *Role of Conjuring*, pp. 22-24, and Preston, *Cree Narrative*, pp. 105-108.

34. Hoffman, "Midē'wiwin," p. 164; also Landes, *Ojibwa Sociology*, p. 128. More direct methods may be used to join the midewiwin society, such as request by purchase, but the dream sanction is considered most proper, as it ensures manitou approval of the candidate; see Selwyn Dewdney, *Sacred Scrolls*, pp. 87-88.

35. Landes, *Ojibwa Sociology*, p. 115.

36. Hallowell, "Myth, Culture and Personality," p. 551.

37. Landes, *Ojibwa Sociology*, p. 124.

38. Barnouw, *Wisconsin Chippewa*, p. 265-66.

39. The drum has a prominent place in Ojibway shamanism: see Hoffman, "Midē'wiwin," pp. 156ff.

40. Hallowell, *Role of Conjuring*, pp. 53ff.

41. Landes, *Ojibwa Sociology*, p. 122.

42. Hallowell, *Role of Conjuring*, pp. 44-47 and, especially, p. 50.

43. Ibid., pp. 74-75; also, Schoolcraft, *Information* 1:392.

44. Johnston, *Ojibway Heritage*, p. 15.

45. Munro S. Edmonson, *Status Terminology and the Social Structure of American Indians* (Seattle: University of Washington Press, 1973), p. 6.

46. See Frank Speck, "Penobscot Shamanism," pp. 243ff.; and Johnston, *Ojibway Heritage*, p. 34.

47. See Hoffman, "Midē'wiwin," p. 156; and Robert and Pat Ritzenthaler, *The Woodland Indians of the Western Great Lakes*, p. 101.

48. See Landes, *Ojibwa Sociology*, p. 120.

49. Johnston, *Ojibway Heritage*, p. 91; Hoffman, "Midē'wiwin," pp. 157ff.; and Hallowell, *Role of Conjuring*, p. 10, especially n. 7; and Landes, *Ojibwa Sociology*, pp. 121-22.

50. Landes, *Ojibwa Sociology*, pp. 30-31.

51. Ibid., p. 37.

52. Ibid., pp. 1-2.

53. Ibid., pp. 126-27.

54. See L. T. Lafleur, "On the Mide of the Ojibway," pp. 706-707.

55. Landes, *Ojibwa Religion*, pp. 45-46.

56. Seymour Parker, "The Wiitiko Psychosis in the Context of Ojibwa Personality and Culture," pp. 602-623; and Ruth Landes, "Personality of the Ojibwa," in *Character and Personality* 6 (1937): 51-60.

Chapter 6. Ritual Reenactment

1. See Landes, *Ojibwa Religion*, pp. 44ff., 56, 85, 87-88, 105, and 112; also, Victor Barnouw, "A Chippewa Mide Priest's Description of the Medicine Dance," pp. 77-97.

2. Landes, *Ojibwa Woman*, pp. 138ff.

3. Ibid., pp. 139-40.

4. This particular conception of the Ojibway ethos that children were "void" or "empty" of power is presented in Landes, *Ojibwa Woman*, pp. 3-10.

5. Ibid., p. 7.

6. Landes, *Ojibwa Sociology*, p. 116.

7. Bronislaw Malinowski, *Magic, Science and Religion*, p. 90.

8. Schoolcraft, *Information*, vol. 1, quoted in Vastokas, *Sacred Art of the Algonkians*, p. 44.

9. Landes, *Ojibwa Sociology*, p. 121.

10. James, ed., *Thirty Year Indian Captivity*, p. 376.

11. Landes, *Ojibway Religion*, pp. 72, 89-113; also Hoffman, "Midē' wiwin," pp. 162-87.

12. Shamanic initiation has been widely interpreted as a process of death and rebirth. See Mircea Eliade, *Shamanism*, pp. 33ff. What is important to elucidate, however, is the particular cultural context of this shamanic symbology of death and rebirth and the personalized expressions of the shaman in question.

13. W. J. Hoffman, "The Menomini Indians," p. 301, and "Midē'wi-win," pp. 207ff.; and Werner Müller, "Die Blaue Hütte," *Studies zur Kulturkunde* 12 (1954), pp. 19ff. and 80ff., and *Die Religionen der Waldlandindianer Nordamerikas* (Berlin, 1956), pp. 198ff.; and Landes, *Ojibwa Religion*, p. 184.

14. Landes, *Ojibwa Religion*, pp. 130 and 184; also, Joan M. and Romas K. Vastokas, "The Shamanic Tree of Life," pp. 139-48, and *Sacred Art*, p. 39; and Dewdney, *Sacred Scrolls*, p. 155, especially n. 25.

15. For four degrees, see Hoffman, "Midē'wiwin," p. 167; for eight degrees, see Landes, *Ojibwa Religion*, pp. 52ff.

16. Landes, *Ojibwa Religion*, p. 52.

17. Hoffman, "Midē'wiwin," p. 204, differs from the majority of descriptions of midewiwin ritual in saying that the patient joins the mide officers in the sweat lodge. Local variations could explain the difference,

or else Hoffman has confused a patient's personal preparatory sweat lodge for the ritual sweat lodge of third-day midewiwin ceremony.

18. Landes, *Ojibwa Religion,* p. 120.

19. The story of Bear's travels and its significance in Ojibway mythology are discussed in Dewdney, *Sacred Scrolls,* pp. 98–109; also James Redsky, *Great Leader of the Ojibway: Mis-quona-queb,* pp. 100–106.

20. Landes, *Ojibwa Religion,* p. 120.

21. For an extensive treatment of the midewiwin birchbark scrolls, see Hoffman, "Midē'wiwin," pp. 167–87. Also an extensive interpretation is available in Dewdney, *Sacred Scrolls.*

22. Dewdney, *Sacred Scrolls,* p. 54.

Chapter 7. Trance Experience

1. For a positive view of shamanic trance see Edwin H. Ackerknecht, "Psychopathology, Primitive Medicine and Primitive Culture," pp. 30–67; the negative view is presented in Weston La Barre, *The Ghost Dance,* pp. 299–321.

2. The classic example is Waldemar Bogoras, *The Chukchee.*

3. For example, A. P. Elkin, *Aboriginal Men of High Degree.*

4. William James, *Varieties of Religious Experience* (New York: Longmans, Green, 1925; Mentor Book, 1958), pp. 33–34.

5. Landes, *Ojibwa Sociology,* pp. 115ff.

6. The pseudoshaman or impostor in Ojibway understanding would be the person who practices shamanism without the proper dream validation. See Hallowell, *The Role of Conjuring,* p. 22; also Landes, *Ojibwa Religion,* pp. 36–37.

7. Landes, *Ojibwa Religion,* p. 9. For a consideration of the relation between trance, the invoked spirit, and a migratory society, see E. Bourguinon, "Cross-Cultural Perspective on the Religious Use of Altered States of Consciousness," in *Religious Movements in Contemporary America,* eds. Irving Zaretsky and Mark Leone, pp. 228–43.

8. Johnston, *Ojibway Heritage,* pp. 119–27; and Frances Densmore, *Chippewa Customs,* p. 79.

9. See Norval Morriseau, in *Legends of My People the Great Ojibway,* ed. Selwyn Dewdney (Toronto: Ryerson Press, 1965); also, Gerald Vizenor, *Tribal Scenes and Ceremonies,* especially p. 18.

10. Landes, *Ojibwa Religion,* pp. 47–48.

11. Antoine de la Mothe Cadillac. "Relation on the Indians." Edward Ayer Collection, Newberry Library, Chicago; also in Kinietz, *The Indians of the Western Great Lakes,* p. 305.

12. Densmore, *Chippewa Customs,* p. 46.

13. Cadillac, quoted in Kinietz, *Indians of the Western Great Lakes,*

pp. 305–306.

14. Rodney Needham, "Percussion and Transition," *Man* 2 (1967): 606–614; and Chapter 2 above under "The Shaman and the Tribe" and "The Numinous Encounter and Its Reenactment."

15. On spirit possession, see E. Bourguignon, "World Distribution and Patterns of Possession States," in *Trance and Possession States*, ed. Raymond Prince (Montreal: R. M. Bucke Memorial Society, 1968); also, I. M. Lewis, *Ecstatic States*, pp. 18–36.

16. Landes, *Ojibway Woman*, p. 139.

17. Ibid., p. 7.

18. Ibid., p. 74; also Schoolcraft, *Information* 5:436.

19. Cadillac, quoted in Kinietz, *Indians of the Western Great Lakes*, p. 306.

20. Schoolcraft, *Information* 1:319; also Speck, "Penobscot Shamanism," p. 254; and Robert E. and Pat Ritzenthaler, *The Woodland Indians of the Western Great Lakes*, p. 101.

21. Thwaites, *Jesuit Relations* 54:175–80.

22. Walter J. Hoffman, "Shamanistic Practices"; also Harlan I. Smith, "Certain Shamanistic Ceremonies among the Ojibwas," *American Antiquarian*, September, 1896.

23. For the *wabeno* naked dance, see Thwaites, *Jesuit Relations* 54:173–74.

24. For the conflict between Ojibway shamans and Christian missionaries, see Thwaites, *Jesuit Relations* 14:223 and 20:265.

25. Hoffman, "Midē'wiwin," p. 157.

26. Schoolcraft, *Information* 1:392.

27. Eliade, *Shamanism*, p. 325.

28. Selwyn Dewdney and K. E. Kidd, *Indian Rock Paintings of the Great Lakes*, and "Dating Rock Art in the Canadian Shield"; Vastokas, *Sacred Art of the Algonkians.*

29. Vastokas, *Sacred Art*, p. 141.

30. The *wabeno* is sometimes associated with other forms of love magic among the Ojibway; see Hoffman, "Midē'wiwin," pp. 275ff.; also Landes, *Ojibwa Religion*, p. 64; and James, ed., *Thirty Years Captivity*, pp. 181, 369–72.

31. James, *Thirty Years Captivity*, p. 122.

32. Hoffman, "Midē'wiwin," p. 223.

33. S. F. Nadel develops an interpretation of shamanism based on the safety-valve theory in "A Study of Shamanism in the Nuba Mountains," especially pp. 36–37.

34. See Raymond D. Fogelson, "Psychological Theories of *Windigo* 'Psychosis' and a Preliminary Application of a Models Approach," in *Context and Meaning in Cultural Anthropology*, ed. Melford E. Spiro (New York: Free Press, 1965), pp. 74–99.

35. Landes, *Ojibwa Woman*, p. 159.

36. Schoolcraft, *Information* 1:359 and 5:405; also Hallowell, *Role of Conjuring*, pp. 9–17; and Landes, *Ojibwa Sociology*, pp. 125–26.

37. Hallowell, *Role of Conjuring*, pp. 23ff.; and Landes, *Ojibwa Sociology*, pp. 121–22.

38. Hallowell, *Role of Conjuring*, p. 44.

39. On the complex of spirits that attend a shaking-tent ceremony, see Hallowell, *Role of Conjuring*, p. 24.

40. Hoffman, "Midē'wiwin," pp. 253–54.

41. The regional preferences for the otter versus the *migis*-shell symbol is set forth in Warren, *History of the Ojibway Nation*, pp. 77–89; also, Dewdney, *Sacred Scrolls*, pp. 53, 69, 71, and 78; and Hoffman, "Midē'wiwin," pp. 183ff.

42. Hallowell, *Role of Conjuring*, p. 24; Schoolcraft, *Information* 1:389; and Frances Densmore, *Menominee Music*, Bulletins of the Bureau of American Ethnology, no. 102 (Washington, D.C.: Government Printing Office, 1932), p. 102.

43. The unintelligibility of the language coming from the *tcisaki*'s lodge was observed in the seventeenth century by the French explorer Samuel de Champlain, who wrote, "These rogues . . . speak in a language unknown by the savages" (quoted in H. P. Biggar, ed., *Works of Samuel Champlain*, Publications of the Champlain Society, no. 10 (Toronto, 1932), pp. 85–86. The same phenomenon was also observed by the Jesuit missionary Le Jeune, quoted in Thwaites, *Jesuit Relations* 6:162 and 12:17. For a modern account see Hallowell, *Role of Conjuring*, p. 50.

44. Hallowell, *Conjuring*, pp. 45 and 50–51. For an extended interpretation of the *tcisaki* phenomena and related shamanistic seances, see also Richard Preston, *Cree Narrative*, pp. 25–197, and the interpretative discussion in Ake Hultkrantz, "Spirit Lodge: A North American Shamanistic Seance," pp. 32–68; for a parallel shamanic performance among the Dakota, see Richard Erdoes and John (Fire) Lame Deer, *Lame Deer, Seeker of Visions* (New York: Pocket Books, 1976), pp. 172–86.

45. Kohl, *Kitchi-Gami Wanderings*, p. 280.

46. Emma Hardinge, *History of Modern American Spiritualism* (New York: Wm. C. McClelland, 1870), pp. 286ff.

47. Landes, *Ojibwa Religion*, p. 115.

48. Hoffman, "Midē'wiwin," p. 164; and Landes, *Ojibwa Religion*, p. 103.

49. Landes, *Ojibwa Religion*, p. 87.

50. Hoffman, "Midē'wiwin," p. 204.

51. Densmore, *Chippewa Customs*, pp. 86–87; also, for an extensive listing of Midewiwin herbal therapeutics, see Hoffman, "Midē'wiwin,"

pp. 197-203. By the 1930s this shamanistic practice had reverted back to individuals other than Mide Society shamans; see Landes, *Ojibwa Religion*, p. 202.

52. Densmore, *Chippewa Customs*, pp. 95-96.

53. Landes, *Ojibwa Religion*, p. 101.

54. Speck, "Penobscot Shamanism," pp. 204-205; and Johnston, *Ojibway Heritage*, p. 84.

55. This ritual event described in Hoffman, "Midē'wiwin," pp. 217, 234-35, 248, 257, and 265; also Landes, *Ojibwa Religion*, pp. 138-67.

56. On *migis* shells, see Dewdney, *Sacred Scrolls*, pp. 71-72.

57. Hoffman, "Midē'wiwin," pp. 189ff., 224, 240, and 255ff.

58. On these shell placements, see Landes, *Ojibwa Religion*, pp. 139ff.

59. The manitou presence was located in the shaman's body; see Landes, *Ojibwa Religion*, pp. 38-41 and 170.

60. Hoffman, "Midē'wiwin," pp. 218ff.

61. Landes, *Ojibwa Religion*, p. 155.

62. Densmore, *Chippewa Customs*, p. 88.

63. See Landes, *Ojibwa Religion*, p. 138.

64. Radin, "Religion of the North American Indian," p. 367.

65. Hallowell, "Ojibwa Ontology," p. 163.

66. Landes, *Ojibwa Religion*, pp. 43-44.

Chapter 8. Stages in the Formation of a Shaman

1. Vilmos Dioszegi, *Tracing Shamans in Siberia*, p. 54.

2. Ibid., p. 62.

3. Eliade, *Shamanism*, pp. 69ff.

4. James Redsky, *Great Leader of the Ojibway*, p. 21.

5. Ibid., pp. 25-26.

6. The classic source is M. A. Czaplicka, *Aboriginal Siberia*, especially pt. 3; also, Lommel, *Shamanism: The Beginnings of Art*, chap. 1, and Eliade, *Shamanism*, pp. 25ff.

7. Dioszegi, *Tracing Shamans*, p. 58.

8. See Sieroszewski's account of the famous shaman Tiuspiut, trans. William G. Sumner in his "The Yakuts: Abridged from the Russian of Sieroszewski," *Journal of the Royal Anthropological Institute* 31 (1901): 65-110; also, Dioszegi, *Tracing Shamans*, p. 58.

9. Dioszegi, *Tracing Shamans*, pp. 65-66.

10. Redsky, *Mis-quona-queb*, p. 25.

11. Ibid., p. 30.

12. Johnston, *Ojibway Heritage*, p. 82.

13. Sergei M. Shirokogoroff, quoted in I. M. Lewis, *Ecstatic Religion*, p. 184.

14. Dioszegi, *Tracing Shamans*, p. 72.

15. Redsky, *Mis-quona-queb*, p. 39.

Chapter 9. The Shaman as a Religious Type

1. *Oxford Dictionary of English Etymology*, s.v. *prophecy*, p. 716; also, Karl Rahner and Herbert Vorgrimler, *Theological Dictionary*, pp. 383–84.

2. Gerardus van der Leeuw, *Religion in Essence and Manifestation* 1:224.

3. Plato presents this position in his *Apology and Phaedrus*; see Irwin Edman, ed., *The Works of Plato* (New York: Random House, 1928), pp. 65 and 310. See also II Samuel 23:2 and Psalm 40:3.

4. On the prophets' use of poetic forms, see Isaiah 5:1-6 and 23:16 and the funeral dirge in Amos 5:2.

5. See Yehezkel Kaufman, *The Religion of Israel* (New York: Schochen, 1972), pp. 96 and 275; also, Daniel Jeremy Silver, *A History of Judaism* (New York: Basic Books, 1974), especially pp. 88-89.

6. Kaufman, *The Religion of Israel*, pp. 348-49 and 354; Silver, *History of Judaism*, p. 94.

7. I Samuel 3:20. See W. F. Albright, *Archaeology and the Religion of Israel* (Baltimore: Johns Hopkins Press, 1942) and *Interpreting the Prophetic Tradition* (Cincinnati: Hebrew Union College Press, 1969).

8. *The New English Bible* (New York: Oxford University Press, 1971), p. 312; see I Samuel 10:5-6.

9. For a description of these "structured" prophetic schools, see II Kings 6:1, Amos 7:14, Isaiah 3:2, Micah 3:5, and Jeremiah 28:1 and 5:31.

10. Isaiah 6:8-9.

11. Jeremiah 1:7 and 10.

12. Silver, *History of Judaism*, p. 79.

13. I Samuel 15:22.

14. *Oxford Dictionary of English Etymology*, s.v. *priest*, p. 709.

15. Rahner and Vorgrimler, *Theological Dictionary*, p. 376.

16. Ibid., p. 376.

17. Sir John Marshall et al., *Mohenjo-daro and the Indus Civilization* (London: Routledge and Kegan Paul, 1931).

18. See Ezekial 40-68.

19. Henri Frankfort et al., *Before Philosophy* (New York: Penguin Paper, 1974), pp. 207-213.

20. John A. Wilson, "Egypt: The Function of the State," in Frankfort et al., *Before Philosophy*, pp. 84-85.

21. Kaufman, *The Religion of Israel*, pp. 238ff. and 301-304.

22. Epistle to the Hebrews 2:17.

23. Rev. Frederich Baraga, *Chippewa Indians,* pp. 33–42.

24. Sir Monier-Williams, *Sanskrit-English Dictionary* (Oxford: Oxford University Press, 1872), s.v. *yoga,* p. 476.

25. Pictured on seatite seals, the pre-Aryan figure is now generally accepted as yogic; see Marshall, *Mohenjo-daro and the Indus Civilization,* vol. 1, pp. 49ff. and 83–92.

26. See Rig Veda 10:136; also Atharva Veda 11:5,5 and 15:7,1.

27. Swami Prabhavananda and Frederich Manchester, *The Upanishads* (New York: Mentor Paperback, 1957), p. 109; also, Aimslee Embree, *Hindu Tradition* (New York: Modern Library, 1966), p. 63.

28. This statement derives from the first three aphorisms of Patanjali; see Bhagwan Shree Patanjali, *Aphorisms of Yoga,* trans. Shree Purshit Swami (London: Faber, 1973), p. 25.

29. For Shankhya thought, see Wm. Theodore de Bary, ed., *Sources of Indian Tradition* (New York: Columbia University Press, 1958), pp. 296–99; also, Sarvepalli Radhakrishna and Charles Moore, eds., *Indian Philosophy* (Princeton: Princeton University Press, 1957), pp. 424–52.

30. Patanjali, *Aphorisms of Yoga,* 1:24, p. 37.

31. Ibid., 1:25, p. 38.

32. Ibid., 1:26, p. 38.

33. Ibid., 3:49, p. 73.

34. Ibid., 4:34, p. 86.

35. Ibid., 1:41, p. 42.

36. See Mircea Eliade, *Yoga: Immortality and Freedom,* Bollingen Series, no. 66 (Princeton: Princeton University Press, 1969), pp. 318–41.

37. Wm. Theodore de Bary, ed., *Sources of Chinese Tradition* (New York: Columbia University Press, 1960), pp. 30ff., especially no. 18.

38. Ibid., p. 19.

39. Ibid., 20, *Doctrine of the Mean,* p. 120.

40. Ibid., 22, *Doctrine of the Mean,* pp. 120–21.

41. Ibid., 27:19, *Analects,* p. 30.

42. Ibid., Shao Yung's *Observation of Things,* p. 465.

43. Chu Hsi, quoted in Wing Tsit Chan, *A Source Book in Chinese Philosophy* (Princeton: Princeton University Press, 1973), p. 607.

44. Thomas Berry, "Affectivity in Classical Confucianism," in *Riverdale Papers III* (New York: Riverdale Center for Religious Research Press, 1975).

45. de Bary, *Sources of Chinese Tradition,* Analects 4:15, p. 25.

46. Wm. Theodore de Bary and Irene Bloom, eds. *Principle and Practicality* (New York: Columbia University Press, 1979), pp. 179–80.

47. Frederich W. Mote, *Intellectual Foundations of China* (New York: Knopf, 1971), p. 30.

48. Knud Rasmussen, "The Intellectual Culture of the Hudson Bay

Eskimos," pp. 54–55.

49. Mircea Eliade, *Rites and Symbols of Initiation* (New York: Harper Torchbook, 1958), p. 89.

50. From Sieroszewski's *Twelve Years Among the Yakuts,* as quoted in M. A. Czaplicka, *Aboriginal Siberia,* p. 173.

51. Gerald Vizenor, "The Sky Will Resound," *Summer in the Spring: Lyric Poems of the Ojibway,* p. 59.

BIBLIOGRAPHY

Siberian Shamanism

Anisimov, A. F. "Cosmological Concepts of the Peoples of the North." In *Studies in Siberian Shamanism*, edited by H. N. Michaels, pp. 157-229. Toronto: University of Toronto Press, 1963.

———. "The Shaman's Tent of the Evenks and the Origins of the Shamanic Rite." In *Studies in Siberian Shamanism*, edited by H. N. Michaels, pp. 84-123. Toronto: University of Toronto Press, 1963.

Balazs, Janos. "The Hungarian Shaman's Technique of Trance Induction." In *Popular Beliefs and Folklore Tradition in Siberia*, edited by Vilmos Dioszegi, pp. 387-405. General Publications Series, no. 57. Bloomington, Ind.: Indiana University Research Center, 1968.

Balzer, Marjorie Mandelstam. "Rituals of Gender Identity: Markers of Siberian Khanty Ethnicity, Status and Belief." *American Anthropologist* 83, no. 4 (1981): 850-67.

Bogoras, Waldemar. "The Folklore of Northeastern Asia, as Compared with That of Northwestern America." *American Anthropologist*, n.s., 4 (1902): 577-683.

———. *The Chukchee.* American Museum of Natural History Memoirs, no. 11. New York, 1904.

———. "The Shamanistic Call and the Period of Initiation in Northern Asia and Northern America." *Proceedings of the 23rd International Congress of Americanists.* New York, 1928.

Buddruss, Georg, and Adolph Friedrich, trans. *Schamanengeschichten aus Sibirien.* Munich: Planegg, 1955.

Chadwick, Norak. "Shamanism among the Tartars of Central Asia." *Journal of the Royal Anthropological Institute* 39 (1936): 75-112.

Chernetsov, V. N. "Concepts of the Soul among the Ob Ugrians." In *Studies in Siberian Shamanism,* edited by H. Michaels, pp. 3-45. Toronto: University of Toronto Press, 1963.

Czaplicka, M. A. *Aboriginal Siberia.* Oxford: Clarendon Press, 1914.

Dioszegi, Vilmos. "Die Überreste des Schamanismus in der ungarischer Volks-Kultur." *Acta Ethnographica* 7 (1958): 97-135.

———. "Bericht über eine Forschungsreise nach Südsibiren." *Sociologus,* n.s., 9 (1959): 60-66.

———. "Der Werdegange zum Schamanen bei den nordöstlichen sojoten." *Acta Ethnographica* 8 (1959): 269-91.

———. "Die Typen und interethnischen Beziehungen der Schamanentrommeln bei den Selkupen." *Acta Ethnographica* 9 (1960): 159-79.

———. "Problems of Mongolian Schamanism: Report of an Expedition Made in 1960 in Mongolia." *Acta Ethnographica* 10 (1961): 195-206.

———. "Tuva Shamanism: Intraethnic Differences and Intraethnic Analogies." *Acta Ethnographica* 11 (1962): 143-90.

———. "Denkmäler der samojedischen Kultur im Schamanismus der ostsajanischen Völker." *Acta Ethnographica* 12 (1963): 139-78.

———. *Tracing Shamans in Siberia.* New York: Humanities Press, 1968.

———. "The Origin of the Evenki Shamanic Instruments (Stick, Knout) of Transbaikalia." *Acta Ethnographica* 17 (1968): 265-311.

———. *Popular Beliefs and Folklore of the Siberian Peoples.* General Publications Series no. 57. Bloomington, Ind.: Indiana University Research Center, 1968.

Dixon, Roland. "Some Aspects of the American Shaman." *Journal of American Folklore* 21 (1908): 1-12.

Findeisen, Hans. *Schamenentum: Dargestellt am Beispiel Bessenheitspriester nord-eurasiatischer Völker.* Stuttgart: W. Kohlhammer Verlag, 1957.

———. "Oskar Peschels Thesen über Schamanismus im Lichte der neusten Forschung unter besonderer berücksichtigung Nordasiens. Ein Beitrag zur Geschichte der Religionswissenschaft." *Rundschau für Menschen und Menscheitskunde* 1 (1967): 44-67.

Galdi, L. "On some problems of versification in Samoyed Shamanistic songs." In *Popular Beliefs and Folklore Tradition
in Siberia*, edited by Vilmos Dioszegi, pp. 125-36. Bloomington, Ind.: Indiana University Research Center, 1968.

Grube, W. "Das Schamanentum bei den Golden." *Globus* 71
(1897): 89-93.

Hajdu, P. "The Classification of Samoyed Shamans." In *Popular
Beliefs and Folklore Tradition in Siberia*, edited by Vilmos
Dioszegi, pp. 147-73. Bloomington, Ind.: Indiana University
Research Center, 1968.

Harva, Uno (Holmberg). "The Shaman Costume and Its Significance." *Annales universitatis fennicae aboenis. Turku*, Ser.
B, vol. 1 (1922).

Hatt, Goldmund. *Asiatic Influences in American Folklore.* Copenhagen: Ejnar Munksgaard, 1949.

Hoffmann, Helmut. *Quellen zur Geschichte der tibetischen Bon-
Religion.* Wiesbaden, 1950.

———. *The Religions of Tibet.* New York, 1961.

———. *Symbolik der tibetischen Religionen und des Schamanismus.* Stuttgart: A. Hiersemann Verlag, 1967.

Jochelson, Waldemar. *The Koryak.* American Museum of Natural History Memoirs, no. 10. New York: 1905-1908.

———. *The Yukaghir and Yukaghirized Tungus.* American Museum of Natural History Memoirs, no. 13. New York: 1924-
26.

———. *The Yakut.* American Museum of Natural History Anthropological Papers, no. 33, pt. 2. New York: 1933.

Jucker, Ernst. *Nomaden, Eigenbrötler und Schamanen, neue
Erinnerungen aus Siberia Urwald und Steppe.* Bern: P. Haupt,
1955.

Karsten, Rafael. *The Religion of the Samek.* Leiden: E. J. Brill,
1955.

Krader, L. "Shamanistic Tradition of the Buryats (Siberia)." *Anthropos* 70 (1975): 105-44.

Lessing, F. D. "Calling the Soul: A Lamaist Ritual." In *Semitic
and Oriental Studies: A Volume Presented to Wm. Popper on
the Occasion of His Seventy-fifth Birthday*, edited by Walter
J. Fischel, pp. 263-84. University of California Publications
in Semitic, no. 11. 1951.

Levin, M. G. *Ethnic Origins of the Peoples of Northeastern*

Asia. Toronto: University of Toronto Press, 1963.

Li, An-Che. "Bon: The Magico-Religious Belief of the Tibetan-speaking Peoples." *Southwestern Journal of Anthropology* 1 (1948): 31-41.

Lindgren, E. F. "The Shaman Dress of the Dagurs, Solons and Numinchens in Northwest Manchuria." In *Svenska sallskapet for antropologi och geografi,* edited by Sven Hedin, pp. 365-78. Stockholm: Hyllningsskrift tillagnad, 1935.

Michael, Henry N., ed. *Studies in Siberian Shamanism.* Toronto: University of Toronto Press, 1963.

Mikhailovski, V. M. "Shamanism in Siberia and European Russia, Being the Second Part of *Shamanstvo.*" Translated by Oliver Wardrop. *Journal of the Royal Anthropological Institute* 24 (1894): 62-100 and 126-58.

Mironov, N. D., and S. M. Shirokogoroff. "Sramana-Shaman: Etymology of the word 'Shaman.'" *Journal of the Royal Asiatic Society* (North-China Branch, Shanghai) 55 (1924): 105-30.

Nachtigall, H. "Die erhöhte Bestattung in Nord- und Hochasien." *Anthropos* 48 (1953): 44-70.

————. "Die Kulturhistorische Wurzel der Schamanenskelettierung." *Zeitschrift für Ethnologie* (Berlin) 77 (1952): 188-97.

Nebesky-Wojkowitz, René de. *Oracles and Demons of Tibet.* The Hague: 1956; Graz, Austria: Akademische Druck u. Verlagsanstadt, 1975.

Nemeth, Julius. "Über den Ursprung des Wortes *Saman* und einige Bemerkungen zur türkisch-mongolischen Lautgeschichte." *Keleti Szemle* (Budapest) 14 (1913-14): 240-49.

Nioradze, Georg. *Der Schamanismus bei den sibirischen Völkern.* Stuttgart: Stescker und Schroder, 1925.

Ohnuki-Tierney, Emiko. "The Shamanism of the Ainu of the Northwest Coast of Southern Sakhalin." *Ethnology* 12 (1973): 15-30.

————. *Illness and Healing Among the Sakhalin Ainu: A Symbolic Interpretation.* Cambridge: Cambridge University Press, 1981.

Okladnikov, A. P. *Yakutia: Before its Incorporation into the Russian State.* Translated by Dr. and Mrs. S. P. Dunn. Montreal: McGill-Queens University Press, 1970.

Pallisten, N. "Die alte Religion der Mongolen und der Kultus Tschingis-Chans." *Numen* 3 (1956): 178-229.

Partanen, Jorma. "A Description of Buriat Shamanism." *Journal de la Société Finno-Ougrienne* 51 (1941–42).

Pilsudski, Bronislav. "Der Schamanismus bei den Ainu-Stämmen von Sachalin." *Globus* 95 (1909): 72–79.

Quinan, Clarence. "The American Medicine-Man and the Asiatic Shaman: A comparison." *Annals of medical history*, n.s., 10 (1938): 508–33.

Rintschen, A. R. "Schamanische Geister der Gebirge Dörben Ayula-yin Ejed in Ugraen Pantominem." *Acta Ethnographica* 6 (1958): 441–44.

Rock, Joseph F. "Contributions to the Shamanism of the Tibetan-Chinese Borderland." *Anthropos* 54 (1959): 796–818.

———. "Studies in Na-Khi Literature: I, The Birth and Origin of Dto-mba Shi-lo, the Founder of the Mo-so Shamanism According to Mo-so Manuscripts." *Art Asiae* (Leipzig) 7 (1937): 5–85.

Sandschejew, Garma. "Weltanschauung und Schamanismus der Alaren-Burjaten." Translated by R. Augustin. *Anthropos* 22 (1927): 576–613, 933–55; 23 (1928): 538–60, 967–86.

Schroder, Dominik. "Zur Religion der Tujen des Sininggebietes (KuKunor)." *Anthropos* 47 (1953): 849–81.

———. "Zur Struktur des Schamanismus." *Anthropos* 50 (1955): 849–81.

Shirokogoroff, Sergei M. "General Theory of Shamanism among the Tungus." *Journal of the Royal Asiatic Society* (North China Branch, Shanghai) 54 (1923): 246–49.

———. "What is Shamanism." *China Journal of Arts and Sciences* (1924): 275–79, 368–71.

———. *Social Organization of the Northern Tungus.* Shanghai: Commercial Press, 1929.

———. *The Psychomental Complex of the Tungus.* London: Kegan, Paul, Trench, Trubner and Co., 1935.

Shternberg, Lev Iakovlevich. "Divine Election in Primitive Religion." Paper delivered at the Congrès International des Americanistes, Göteburg, 1924. In *Congrès International des Americanistes, Compte-Rendu de la XXIème Session,* pt. 2. Reprint. Nendeln, Liechtenstein: Kraus-Thomson Organization Ltd., 1968.

Sieroszewski, Wenceslaus. "Du chamanisme d'après les croyances des Yakoutes." *Revue de l'histoire des religions* 46

(1902): 204-33, 299-338.

Stein, R. A. *Tibetan Civilization.* Stanford, Calif.: Stanford University Press, 1972.

Steida, L. "Das Schamanentum unter den Burjäten." *Globus* 52 (1887): 250-53.

Tucci, Giuseppe. *Tibetan Painted Scrolls.* New York: Weiser, 1961.

Vainshtein, Sevyan. *Nomads of South Siberia: The Pastoral Economies of Tuva.* Translated by Michael Colenso. Cambridge: Cambridge University Press, 1980.

Vajda, L. "Zur phaseologischen Stelling des Schamanismus." *Ural-altaische Jahrbucher* 31 (1959): 456-85.

Ojibway Shamanism

Bailey, Alfred Goldsworthy. *The Conflict of European and Eastern Algonquian Cultures.* 2d ed. Toronto: University of Toronto Press, 1969.

Balicki, Asen. "Note sur le midewiwin." *Anthropologica* 2 (1956): 165-217.

Baner, J. G. R. and J. L. Bellaire. *Kitch-iti-ki-pi.* Manistique, Mich., 1933.

Baraga, F. R. *A Theoretical and Practical Grammar of the Otchipwe Language.* Montreal: Beauchemin and Valois, 1978.

————. "Chippewa Indians (Being Bishop Baraga's Response to the Questions from Commissioner William Medill, 1847)." *Studia Slovenica* (New York and Washington, D.C.) 10 (1976).

————. *A Dictionary of the Otchipwe Language Explained in English.* Montreal: Beauchemin and Valois, 1880.

Barnouw, Victor. "The Phantasy World of a Chippewa Woman." *Psychiatry* 12 (1949): 67-76.

————. *Acculturation and Personality Among the Wisconsin Chippewa.* American Anthropological Association Memoir, no. 72. Menasha, Wis., 1950.

————. "Reminiscences of a Chippewa Mide Priest." *Wisconsin Archeologist* 35 (1954): 83-112.

————. "A Psychological Interpretation of a Chippewa Origin Legend." *Journal of American Folklore* 68 (1955): 73-86, 211-23, and 341-55.

————. "A Chippewa Mide Priest's Description of the Medicine

Dance." *Wisconsin Archeologist* 41 (1960): 77-97.
——. "Chippewa Social Atomism." *American Anthropologist* 63 (1961): 1006-1013.
——. *Wisconsin Chippewa Myths and Tales.* Madison: University of Wisconsin Press, 1977.
Bernard, M. "Religion and Magic Among the Cass Lake Ojibwa." *Primitive Man* 2 (1929): 52-55.
Bishop, Charles A. *The Northern Ojibwa and the Fur Trade: An Historical and Ecological Study.* Toronto: Holt, Rinehart and Winston of Canada, 1974.
Black, Mary B. "Ojibwa Power Belief System." In *The Anthropology of Power: Ethnographic Studies from Asia, Oceania and the New World,* edited by Raymond D. Fogelson and Richard N. Adams, pp. 141-51. New York: Academic Press, 1977.
Black, Mary Rose. "An Ethnoscience Investigation of Ojibwa Ontology and World View." *Dissertation Abstracts* 28 (1967-68).
Blair, Emma H. *The Indian Tribes of the Upper Mississippi Valley and the Region of the Great Lakes.* Cleveland: Arthur H. Clark Co., 1911-12.
Blessing, F. K. "An Exhibition of Mide Magic." *Minnesota Archaeologist* 20 (1956): 9-13.
Brown, Jennifer. "The Cure and Feeding of Windigos: A Critique." *American Anthropologist* 73 (1971): 20-22.
Brown, Paula. "Changes in Ojibwa Social Control." *American Anthropologist* 55 (1952): 57-70.
Cadzow, A. "Bark Records of the Bungi Midewiwin Society." *Indian Notes* 3 (1926): 123-34.
Callender, Charles. "Social Organization of the Central Algonkian Indians." *Publication* (Milwaukee Public Museum) 13 (1962): 1-140.
Carson, William. "Ojibwa Tales." *Journal of American Folklore* 30 (1917): 491-93.
Casagrande, Joseph B. "The Ojibwa's Psychic Universe." *Tomorrow* 4 (1956): 33-40.
Chamberlain, A. F. "Nanibozhu Amongst the Otchipue, Mississaguas and Other Algonkian Tribes." *Journal of American Folklore* 4 (1891): 193-215.
Chatfield, W. "The Midewiwin Songs of Fine-Day." *Museum News* (South Dakota University, Wm. H. Over Museum) 15,

no. 10: 368-79.

Coleman, Bernard. "The Religion of the Ojibwa of Northern Minnesota." *Primitive Man* (July, October, 1937): 1-2.

————, Ellen Frogner, and Estelle Eich. *Ojibwa Myths and Tales*. Minneapolis, Minn.: Ross and Haines, 1962.

Copway, George. *Traditional History and Characteristic Sketches of the Ojibway Nation*. Boston: Sanborn, Carter, Bazin and Co., 1850.

Cooper, John. "The Shaking Tent Rite among Plains and Forest Algonquians." *Primitive Man* 17 (1944): 60-84.

————. "The Northern Algonquian Supreme Being." *Primitive Man* 6 (1933): 41-112.

————. "The Cree Witiko Psychosis." *Primitive Man* 6 (1933): 20-24.

Culkin, W. E. *Chippewa Tribal Dances*. Minneapolis, Minn.: Ross and Haines, 1963.

Dailey, Robert. "The Midewiwin, Ontario's First Medical-Society." *Ontario History* 50 (1958): 133-38.

Densmore, Francis. "An Ojibway Prayer Ceremony." *American Anthropologist* 9 (1907): 443ff.

————. *Chippewa Music*. Reprint. Minneapolis: Ross and Haines, 1968.

————. *Chippewa Customs*. Reprint. Minneapolis: Ross and Haines, 1970.

Dewdney, Selwyn, and K. E. Kidd. *Indian Rock Paintings of the Great Lakes*. Toronto: University of Toronto Press, 1967.

Dewdney, Selwyn. "Dating Rock Art in the Canadian Shield." In *Art and Archaeology*, Royal Ontario Museum Occasional Paper, no. 24. Toronto, 1970.

————. *The Sacred Scrolls of the Southern Ojibway*. Toronto: University of Toronto, 1975.

Dixon, Roland. "The Mythology of the Central and Eastern Algonkian." *Journal of American Folklore* 22 (1909): 1-9.

Dorson, Richard M. *Bloodstoppers and Bearwalkers*. Cambridge, Mass.: Harvard University Press, 1952.

Dunning, R. W. *Social and Economic Changes Among the Northern Ojibwa*. Toronto: University of Toronto Press, 1959.

Eggan, Fred. *The American Indian*. Cambridge: Cambridge University Press, 1980.

Flannery, Regina. "The Shaking Tent Rite among the Montagnais of James Bay." *Primitive Man* 12 (1939): 11-16.

Gilfilian, Joseph A. "The Ojibways in Minnesota." *Minnesota Historical Collections* (1901): 55ff.

——. *Indian Tribes of the Upper Great Lakes Region.* Cleveland: Arthur H. Clark Co., 1911.

Grant, Peter. "The Sauteux Indians: About 1804." In *Les Bourgeois de la Compagnie du Nord-Ouest,* edited by L. R. Masson. Quebec: Côte et Cie, 1890.

Gregorich, Joseph. *The Apostle of the Chippewas: The Life Story of the Most Reverend Frederick Baraga.* Lemont, Ill.: Franciscan Fathers Press, 1932.

Hallowell, A. Irving. "Bear Ceremonialism in the Northern Hemisphere." *American Anthropologist* 28 (1926): 1-172.

——. "Some Empirical Aspects of the Northern Saulteur Religion." *American Anthropologist* 36 (1934): 389-404.

——. "The Passing of the Midewiwin in the Lake Winnipeg Region." *American Anthropologist* 38 (1936): 32-51.

——. *The Role of Conjuring in Saulteaux Society.* Philadelphia: University of Pennsylvania Press, 1942.

——. "Myth, Culture and Personality," *American Anthropologist* 49 (1947): 544-56.

——. *Culture and Experience.* Philadelphia: University of Pennsylvania, 1955.

——. "Ojibwa Ontology, Behavior and World View." In *Culture and History: Essays in Honor of Paul Radin,* edited by S. Diamond, pp. 207-44. New York: Columbia University Press, 1960.

Hickerson, Harold. "The Feast of the Dead among the 17th Century Algonkians of the Upper Great Lakes." *American Anthropologist* 62 (1960): 81-107.

——. *The Southwestern Chippewa: An Ethnohistorical Study.* American Anthropological Association Memoir, no. 92. Menasha, Wis.: 1962.

——. "The Sociohistorical Significance of Two Chippewa Ceremonials." *American Anthropologist* 65 (1963): 67-85.

——. "Notes on the Post-Contact Origin of the Midewiwin." *Ethnohistory* 9 (1962-63): 404-23.

——. "Some Implications of the Theory of the Particularity or 'Atomism' of Northern Algonkians." *Current Anthropology* 8 (1967): 313-43.

──── . *The Chippewa and Their Neighbors: A Study in Ethno-history.* New York: Holt, Rinehart and Winston, 1970.

Hoffman, Walter James. "Pictographs and the Ojibwa Religion." *American Anthropologist* 1 (1888): 209-31.

──── . "Shamanistic Practices." *University Medical Magazine,* Nov., 1890.

──── . "The Midē'wiwin or 'Grand Medicine Society' of the Ojibwa." In *Seventh Annual Report of the Bureau of American Ethnology,* pp. 143-300. Washington, D.C.: Government Printing Office, 1891.

──── . "The Menomini Indians." In *Fourteenth Annual Report of the Bureau of American Ethnology,* pp. 3-328. Washington, D.C.: Government Printing Office, 1896.

Howard, James H. "The Henry Davis Drum Rite: An Unusual Drum Religion Variant of the Minnesota Ojibwa." *Plains Anthropologist,* 1966.

James, Edward, ed. *Narrative of John Tanner's Thirty Years of Indian Captivity.* Reprint. Minneapolis, Minn.: Ross and Haines, 1956.

Jenness, Diamond. *The Ojibwa Indians of Parry Island, Their Social and Religious Life.* National Museum of Canada Anthropological Series, no. 17. Ottawa: 1935.

Johnston, Basil. *Ojibway Heritage.* New York: Columbia University Press, 1976.

Jones, William. "The Algonkin Manitu." *Journal of American Folklore* 18 (1905): 183-90.

Keesing, Felix. *The Menomini Indians of Wisconsin.* Memoirs of the American Philosophical Society. Philadelphia: 1939.

Kinietz, W. Vernon. *Chippewa Village. Bulletin* (Cranbrook Institute of Science) 25 (1947): 1-259.

──── . *The Indians of the Western Great Lakes (1615-1760).* Ann Arbor, Mich.: Ann Arbor Paperbacks, 1965.

Kohl, J. G. *Kitchi-Gami Wanderings Around Lake Superior.* Translated from 1860 German original by Lascelles Wraxall. Reprint. Minneapolis, Minn.: Ross and Haines, 1957.

Kurath, G. P. "Blackrobe and Shaman." *Michigan Academy of Science, Arts and Letters* 44 (1959): 209-15.

Lafleur, L. T. "On the Mide of the Ojibway." *American Anthropologist,* n.s., 42 (1940): 706-708.

Landes, Ruth. *Ojibwa Sociology.* Columbia University Contri-

butions to Anthropology, no. 29. New York: 1937.
———. "The Personality of the Ojibwa." *Character and Personality* 6 (1937): 51-60.
———. "The Abnormal Among the Ojibwa." *Journal of Abnormal and Social Psychology* 33 (1938): 14-33.
———. *The Ojibwa Woman.* Columbia University Contributions to Anthropology, no. 31. New York: 1938.
———. *Ojibwa Religion and the Midewiwin.* Madison, Wis.: University of Wisconsin Press, 1968.
———. *Mystic Lake Sioux.* Madison: University of Wisconsin Press, 1969.
———. *The Prairie Potawatomi: Tradition and Ritual in the Twentieth Century.* Madison: University of Wisconsin Press, 1970.
Martin, Calvin. *Keepers of the Game: Indian-Animal Relationships and the Fur Trade.* Berkeley: University of California Press, 1978.
Michelson, Truman. "Ojibwa Tales." *Journal of American Folklore* (April-June, 1911): 249ff.
Müller, Werner. "Die Blaue Hütte." *Studien zur Kulturkunde* 12 (1954): 1-145.
Murdock, George Peter. *Ethnographic Bibliography of North America.* 4th ed., revised by Timothy J. O'Leary. 5 vols. New Haven: Human Relations Area File Press, 1975.
Overholt, Thomas, and J. Baird Callicot. *Clothed-in-Fur and Other Tales: An Introduction to an Ojibwa World View.* Lanham, Md.: University Press of America, 1982.
Parker, Seymour. "The Wiitiko Psychoses in the Context of Ojibway Personality and Culture." *American Anthropologist* 62 (1960): 602-23.
Preston, Richard. *Cree Narrative: Expressing the Personal Meanings of Events.* National Museum of Man Mercury Series, no. 30. Ottawa: Canadian Ethnology Service.
Radin, Paul. "Some Aspects of Puberty Fasting among the Ojibwa." *Geological Survey of the Canadian Bureau of Mines* 2 (1914): 1-10.
———. "Religion of the North American Indians." *Journal of American Folklore* 27 (1914): 335-73.
———. *Crashing Thunder: The Autobiography of an American Indian.* University of California Publications in American Ar-

chaeology and Ethnology, no. 16, 1920. Reprint. New York: Dover, 1963.

———. *Primitive Religion: Its Nature and Origin.* Reprint. New York: Dover, 1957.

———. *The Road of Life and Death: A Ritual Drama of the American Indians.* Bollingen Series, no. 5. Princeton, N.J.: Princeton University Press, 1945.

———. *The Trickster: A Study in American Indian Mythology.* New York: Philosophical Library, 1956.

Redsky, James. *Great Leader of the Ojibway: Mis-quona-queb.* Toronto: McClelland and Stewart, 1972.

Reports of the Committee on Indian Health. Courtesy of Robert M. Sandeen, M.D., Chairman, Committee on Indian Health, Minnesota Academy of General Practice. Buffalo, Minn.: 1967-1970.

Ritzenhaler, Robert, and Pat Ritzenhaler. *The Woodland Indians of the Western Great Lakes.* Garden City, N.Y.: Doubleday, 1970.

Rogers, Edward S. "The Round Lake Ojibwa." In *Art and Archaeology,* Royal Ontario Museum Occasional Paper, no. 5. Toronto: University of Toronto Press, 1962.

Salzer, Robert J. "Bear-walking: A Shamanistic Phenomena Among the Potawatomi Indians in Wisconsin." *Wisconsin Archaeologist* 53 (1970): 110-46.

Schmerler, Henrietta. "Trickster Marries His Daughter." *Journal of American Folklore* 44 (1931): 196-207.

Schoolcraft, Henry. *Algic Researches.* 6 vols. New York: Harper and Brothers, 1839.

———. *Information Respecting the History Condition and Prospects of the Indian Tribes of the United States.* Philadelphia: Lippincott, Giambo and Co., 1853.

Skinner, Alanson. "Notes on the Eastern Cree and the Northern Saulteaux." *Anthropological Papers of the American Museum of Natural History,* no. 9, pt. 1 (1911).

———. "Plains-Ojibwa Tales." *Journal of American Folklore* 32 (1919): 280-305.

———. "Medicine Ceremony of the Menomini, Iowa and Wahpeton Dakota." *Indian Notes and Monographs* (Museum of the American Indian, Heye Foundation, N.Y.) 4 (1920).

Smith, James G. E. *Leadership Among the Southwestern Ojibwa.* Publications in Ethnology, no. 7. Ottawa, National Museums of Canada, 1973.

Speck, Frank. *Penobscot Shamanism.* Memoirs of the American Anthropological Association, no. 6. Menasha, Wis.: 1919.

————. "Myths and Folklore of the Timiskaming Algonquin and Timagami Ojibwa." Canada Department of Mines, Anthropological Series, Geological Survey, no. 71. Ottawa: 1915.

————. "The Family Hunting Band as the Basis of Algonkian Social Organization." *American Anthropologist* 17 (1915): 289-305.

Sturtevant, Wm. C., ed. *Handbook of North American Indians.* Vol. 6, *Subarctic,* and vol. 15, *Northeast.* Washington, D.C.: Smithsonian Institution, 1978.

Tanner, Adrian. *Bringing Home Animals.* New York: St. Martin's Press, 1979.

Tanner, Helen H. *The Ojibwas: A Critical Bibliography.* Published for the Newberry Library. Bloomington, Ind.: Indiana University Press, 1976.

Thwaites, Reuben Gold. *The Jesuit Relations and Allied Documents.* 73 volumes. 1896-1901. Reprint. New York: Pageant, 1959.

Vastokas, Joan M., and Romas K. Vastokas. *Sacred Art of the Algonkians.* Peterborough, Ont.: Mansard Press, 1973.

————. "The Shamanic Tree of Life." 30th anniversary issue of *Arts Canada* (Toronto, Canada), Dec., 1973-Jan., 1974.

Vizenor, Gerald. *Summer in the Spring.* Minneapolis, Minn.: Nodin Press, 1965.

————. *Tribal Scenes and Ceremonies.* Minneapolis: Nodin Press, 1976.

Warren, William Whipple. *History of the Ojibway Nation.* 1885. Minneapolis, Minn.: Ross and Haines, 1970.

Wright, J. V. "A Regional Examination of Ojibway Culture History." *Anthropologica* 7 (1965): 189-227.

General

Ackerknecht, E. H. "Psychopathology, Primitive Medicine, and Primitive Culture." *Bulletin of the History of Medicine* 14 (1943): 30-67.

Ahern, Emily. *The Cult of the Dead in a Chinese Village*. Stanford, Calif.: Stanford University Press, 1973.

Baer, Gerhard. "Ein besonderes Merkmal des Süd-Amerikanischen Schamanen." *Zeitscrift für Ethnologie* 94 (1969): 284-92.

————. "Auskunfte eines Srahuano über Schamanistische Vorstellungen seiner Gruppe (Ost-Peru)." *Anthropos* 66 (1970).

Bahr, Donald M. et al., *Piman Shamanism and Staying Sickness*. Yuscan, Ariz.: University of Arizona Press, 1974.

Balikci, Asen. "Shamanistic Behavior Among the Netsilik Eskimos." *Southwestern Journal of Anthropology* 19 (1963): 380-96.

————. *The Netsilik Eskimo*. Garden City, N.Y.: Doubleday, 1970.

Beck, Robert J. "Some Proto-psychotherapeutic Elements in the Practice of Shamanism." *History of Religions* 6 (1967): 303-327.

Berreman, G. D. "Brahmins and Shamans in Pahari Religion." *Journal of Asian Studies* 23 (1964): 53-69.

Benedict, Ruth. *The Concept of the Guardian Spirit in North America*. American Anthropological Association Memoir, no. 29. Menasha, Wis.: 1923.

Berry, Rose. "The Shaman and His Sacred Sandpaintings." *Art and Archaeology* (January, 1929): 3-16.

Beuchett, E. "Die Rückrufung der Ahnen auf Chejudo (Süd Korea): ein Ritual zur Psychischen Stabilisierung." *Anthropos* 70 (1975): 145-79.

Birket-Smith, Kaj. *Eskimos*. New York: Crown, 1971.

Blacker, Carmen. *The Catalpa Bow: A Study of Shamanistic Practices in Japan*. London: George Allen & Unwin Ltd., 1970.

Blau, H. "Function and the False Faces: A Classification of Onondaga Masked Rituals and Themes." *Journal of American Folklore* 79 (1966): 564-80.

Bleibtreau-Ehrenberg, Gisela. "Homosexualität und Tranvestition im Shamanismus." *Anthropos* 65 (1971): 189-228.

Boas, Franz. "The Central Eskimo." In *Sixth Annual Report of the Bureau of American Ethnology*. Washington, D.C.: Government Printing Office, 1891.

————. *The Religion of the Kwakiutl*. Columbia University Contributions to Anthropology, no. 10. New York, 1930.

————. *Race, Language and Culture.* New York: Macmillan, 1940.

Bower, B. "Notes on Shamanism Among the Tepehua Indians." *American Anthropologist* 48 (1946): 680-83.

Boyer, L. Bryce. "Remarks on the Personality of Shamans, with Special Reference to the Apache of the Mescalero Indian Reservation." *Psychoanalytic Study of Society* 2 (1962): 233-54.

————. "Further Remarks Concerning Shamans and Shamanism." *Israel Annals of Psychiatry and Related Disciplines* 2 (1964): 235-57.

————, et al. "Comparison of the Shamans and Pseudoshamans of the Apaches of the Mescalero Indian Reservation: A Study with Rorschach." *Journal of Projective Techniques and Personality Assessment* 28 (1964): 173-80.

Brown, Joseph. *The Sacred Pipe: The Seven Rites of the Oglalla Sioux,* Norman: University of Oklahoma Press, 1953.

Brown, Norman. *Hermes the Thief: The Evolution of a Myth.* New York: Vintage Books, 1969.

Butterworth, E. A. S. *Some Traces of the Pre-Olympian World in Greek Literature and Myth.* Berlin: W. deGruyter, 1966.

Campbell, Joseph. *The Masks of God: Primitive Mythology.* New York: Penguin, 1976.

Carlyle, Mary L. "A Survey of Glossolalia and Related Phenomena in Non-Christian Religions." *American Anthropologist* 58 (1956): 75-96.

Cassirer, Ernst. *The Philosophy of Symbolic Forms.* 3 vols. New Haven: Yale University Press, 1955.

Centlivres, M. "Muslim Shaman of Afghan Turkestan." *Ethnology* 10 (1971): 160-73.

Charles, Lucille H. "Drama in Shaman Exorcism." *Journal of American Folklore* (66): 95-122.

Clements, Forrest E. *Primitive Concepts of Disease.* Berkeley: University of California Press, 1932.

Closs, Alois. "Der Religiöse in Schamanismus." *Kairos* 2 (1960): 29-38.

Cloutier, David. *Spirit: Shaman Songs and Incantations.* Providence, R.I.: Cooper, 1973.

Coe, Michael. "Shamanism in the Bunun Tribe, Central Formosa." *Ethnos* 20 (1955): 181-98.

Cole, David. *The Theatrical Event.* Middletown, Conn.: Wesleyan University Press, 1975.

Dawson, Christopher. *Progress and Religion.* New York: Sheed and Ward, 1933.

Devereux, George. "The Origin of Shamanistic Powers as Reflected in a Neurosis." *Revue Internationale D'Ethnopsychologie Normale et Pathologique* 1 (1956): 19-29.

———. "Dream Learning and Individual Ritual Differences in Mohave Shamanism." *American Anthropologist* 59 (1957): 1036-45.

———. "Shamans as Neurotics." *American Anthropologist* 63 (1961): 1088-93.

Dodds, E. R. *The Greeks and the Irrational.* Berkeley: University of California Press, 1951.

Dole, Gertrude E. "Shamanism and Political Control among the Kuikuru." In *Völkerkundeliche Abhandlung Band I, Beiträge Zur Völkerkunde,* edited by Hans Bacher, pp. 53-62. Hanover: Kommissionverlag Munstermann-Diuck, 1964.

Earhart, H. Byron. *A Religious Study of the Mount Haguro Sect of Shugendo.* Tokyo: Sophia University Press, 1970.

Eckstorm, Fannie Hardy. *Old John Neptune and other Maine Indian Shamans.* Portland, Me.: Southworth-Anthoensen Press, 1945.

Eder, Matthias. "Schamanismus in Japan." *Paideuma* 6 (1958): 367-80.

Edsman, Carl-Martin, ed. *Studies in Shamanism.* Stockholm: Almquist and Wiksell, 1967.

Eliade, Mircea. "Shamanism." In *Forgotten Religions,* edited by Vergilius Ferm, pp. 299-308. New York: Philosophical Library, 1950.

———. *Birth and Rebirth: The Religious Meaning of the Initiation in Human Culture.* New York: Harper Torchbooks, 1958.

———. "Recent Works on Shamanism." *History of Religions* 1 (Summer, 1961): 152-86.

———. *Shamanism: Archaic Techniques of Ecstasy.* Bollingen Series, no. 76. Princeton, N.J.: Princeton University Press, 1964.

Elkin, Adolphus P. *Aboriginal Men of High Degree.* Sydney: Australian Publishing Co., 1946.

Elliot, Alan J. A. *Chinese Spirit-Mediums Cult in Singapore.* Monographs on Social Anthropology, n.s., no. 14. London: 1955.

Erkes, Edward. "Der Schamanistiche Ursprung des Chinesischen

Ahnenkultus." *Sinologica* 2 (1950): 153-62.

Fabrega, Horacio, Jr. and Daniel Silver. "Some Social and Psychological Properties of Zinacanteco Shamans." *Behavioral Science* 15 (1970): 471-86.

Fairchild, William P. "Shamanism in Japan." *Folklore Studies* 21 (1962): 1-122.

Faron, Luis C. "Shamanism and Sorcery Among the Mapuche (Araucanians) of Chile." In *Process and Pattern in Culture,* edited by Robert Manners, pp. 123-46. Chicago: University of Chicago Press, 1964.

Fortune, Reo. *Omaha Secret Societies.* Columbia University Contributions to Anthropology, no. 14. New York: 1932.

Fowler, Gene. *Shaman Songs.* El Cerrito, Calif.: Dust Books, 1967.

Freeman, Derek. "Shaman and Incubus." *Psychoanalytic Study of Society* 4 (1967): 315-43.

Freidel, David. "Shamanism in the Maya Area." *Seminar on the Maya* (Department of Anthropology, Harvard University) 260 (1971): 56ff.

French, A. "Nezual's Amazing Magician: A Czech Shamanistic Epic." *Slavic Review* 32 (1973): 358-69.

Fuhner, H. "Solanazeen als Berauschungsmittel: eine historischethnologische Etudie." *Archiv für experimentelle Pathologie und Pharmakologie* (Leipzig) 3 (1926): 281-94.

Furst, Peter T., ed. *Flesh of the Gods: The Ritual Use of Hallucinogens.* New York: Praeger, 1972.

———. "The Roots and Continuities of Shamanism." 30th-anniversary issue of *Arts Canada* (Toronto), Dec., 1973-Jan., 1974, pp. 34-56.

Gayton, Anna Hadwick. "Yokuts-Mono Chiefs and Shamans." *University of California Publications in American Anthropology/Archaeology and Ethnology* 24 (1930): 361-420.

Geertz, Clifford. *Islam Observed.* Chicago: University of Chicago, 1971.

———. "Religion as a Cultural System," In *Anthropological Approaches to the Study of Religion,* A.S.A. Monograph no. 3, edited by Michael Banton, pp. 1-46. 1971.

Haeberlin, Herman K. "SbEtEtda'q, A Shamanic Performance of the Coast Salish." *American Anthropologist* 20 (1918): 249-57.

Handelman, Don. "Aspects of the Moral Compact of a Washo

Shaman." *Anthropological Quarterly* 45 (1972): 84-101.

———. "The Development of a Washo Shaman." *Ethnology* 6 (1967): 444-64.

———. "Transcultural Shamanic Healing: A Washo Example." *Ethnos* 32 (1967): 49-66.

Harner, Michael, ed. *Hallucinogens and Shamanism.* Oxford: Oxford University Press, 1973.

Harper, Edward B. "Shamanism in South India." *Southwestern Journal of Anthropology* 13 (1957): 267-87.

Harvey, Edwin D. "Shamanism in China." In *Studies in the Science of Society Presented to Albert Galloway Keller,* edited by George Peter Murdoch, pp. 247-66. New Haven: Yale University Press, 1937.

Hitchcock, John T., and Rex L. Jones, eds. *Spirit Possession in the Nepal Himalayas.* New Delhi: Vikas Publishing House, 1976.

Herbert, Jean. *Shinto: At the Fountain-head of Japan.* New York: Stein and Day, 1967.

Hodge, Frederick Webb, ed. *Handbook of the American Indians North of Mexico.* Bureau of American Ethnology, Bulletin no. 30. 2 vols. Washington, D.C.: Government Printing Office, 1907, 1910.

Hogbin, H. Ian. "Spirits and the Healing of the Sick in Ontong Java." *Oceania* 1 (1930): 146-66.

Honigman, J. J. "Parallels in the Development of Shamanism Among Northern and Southern Athapaskans." *American Anthropologist* 51 (1949): 512-14.

Hopkins, L. C. "The Shaman or Chinese Wu: His Inspired Dancing and Versatile Character." *Journal of the Royal Asiatic Society* (1945): 3-16.

Hori, Ichiro. "Penetration of Shamanic Elements into the History of Japanese Folk Religion." In *Festschrift für Adolf E. Jensen,* edited by Eike Haberland, pp. 245-65. Munich: 1964.

———. "Shamanism in Japan." *Japanese Journal of Religious Studies* 2, no. 4 (1975): 131-87.

———. *Folk Religion in Japan.* Chicago: University of Chicago Press, 1968.

Hultkrantz, Ake. *Conceptions of the Soul Among North American Indians: A Study in Religious Ethnology.* Ethnographical Museum of Sweden, Monograph Series 1. Stockholm: 1953.

———. "Spirit Lodge: A North American Shamanistic Seance."

In *Studies in Shamanism*, edited by Carl-Martin Edsman, pp. 32-68. Stockholm: 1967.

————. "Book Reviews: 'Anthropological Approaches to Religion.'" *History of Religions* 9 (1970): 337-52.

Hyde, George E. *Indians of the Woodlands from the Prehistoric Times to 175*. Norman: University of Oklahoma Press, 1962.

Irwin, Violet Mary. *The Shaman's Revenge: based on the Arctic Diaries of Vilhjalmur Stefansson*. New York: Macmillan, 1926.

Jennings, Jesse D., and Edward Norbeck, eds. *Prehistoric Man in the New World*. Rice University Semicentennial Publications. Chicago: University of Chicago Press, 1964.

Johnson, Frederick. "Notes on Micmac Shamanism." *Primitive Man* 16 (1943): 53-80.

Johnson, Ronald. *The Art of the Shaman*. Iowa City: Iowa University Museum of Art Publications, 1973.

Jordan, David K. *Gods, Ghosts and Ancestors: Folk Religion in a Taiwanese Village*. Berkeley: University of California Press, 1972.

Jung, C. G. *Collected Works*. Bollingen Series, no. 20. Princeton, N.J.: Princeton University Press, 1967-72.

Keith, Arthur B. *The Religion and Philosophy of the Veda and Upanishads*. Harvard Oriental Series 31/32. 1925.

Kelly, Isabel T. "Southern Paiute Shamanism." *California University Publications in Anthropology* 2 (1939): 151-67.

Kerenyi, Karl. *Pythagoras und Orpheus*. 3rd ed. Zurich: 1950.

Kirby, E. T. "The Origin of No Drama." *Educational Theatre Journal* 25 (1973): 269-84.

————. *Ur-Drama: The Origin of Theatre*. New York: New York University Press, 1975.

Kirchner, Horst. "Ein archäologischer Beitrag zur Urgeschichte des Schamanismus." *Anthropos* 47 (1952): 244-86.

Knoll-Greiling, Ursula. "Rauschinduzierende mittel bei Naturvölkern und ihre individuelle und sociale Wirkung." *Sociologus* 9 (1959): 47-60.

————. "Berufung und Berufungserlebnis bei den Schamanen." *Tribus* (Stuttgart) 2/3 (1952-53): 227-38.

Kollantz, Arnulf. "Der Schamanismus der Awaren." *Palaeologic* (Osaka) 4 (1955): 63-73.

Krige, J. D. "The Social Function of Witchcraft." *Theoria* (1947): 8-21.

Kroeber, Alfred. "The Eskimo of Smith Sound." *American Mu-*

seum of Natural History Bulletin 12 (1899): 265-327.

──────. *Handbook of the Indians of California.* Bureau of American Ethnology Bulletin no. 78. 1925.

La Barre, Weston. *The Ghost Dance. The Origins of Religion.* New York: Dell Publishing, 1970.

Larsen, Stephen. *The Shaman's Doorway.* New York: Harper and Row, 1976.

Laufer, Berthold. "Origin of the Word 'Shaman.'" *American Anthropologist* 19 (1917): 361-71.

Layard, John W. "Malekula: Flying Tricksters, Ghosts, Gods and Epileptics." *Journal of the Royal Anthropological Institute* 60 (1930): 501-524.

──────. "Shamanism: An Analysis Based on Comparison with the Flying Tricksters of Malekula." *Journal of the Royal Anthropological Institute* 60 (1930): 525-50.

Lebra, William P. *Okinawan Religion: Belief, Ritual and Social Structure.* Honolulu: University of Hawaii Press, 1966.

Lee, J. Y. "Communal Rituals of Korean Shamanism." *Journal of Asian and African Studies* 9 (1974): 82-90.

Leeuw, Gerardus van der. *Religion in Essence and Manifestation.* London: Allen and Unwin, 1938; Harper Paperbacks, 1963.

Lévi-Strauss, Claude. *Structural Anthropology.* New York: Basic Books, 1963; Anchor Books, 1967.

Levy, Gertrude. *Religious Conceptions of the Stone Age.* Published in 1948 as *The Gate of Horn.* New York: Harper and Row, 1963.

Lewis, I. M. *Ecstatic Religion: An Anthropological Study of Spirit Possession and Shamanism.* Baltimore: Penguin, 1971.

Lid, Nils. "North European Shamanism," In *Men and Cultures,* edited by A. F. C. Wallace, pp. 305-308. Philadelphia: University of Pennsylvania Press, 1960.

Loeb, E. M. "The Shaman of the Niue." *American Anthropologist,* n.s., 26 (1924): 393-402.

──────. "Shaman and Seer." *American Anthropologist* 31 (1929): 60-84.

Lommel, Andreas. *Shamanism: The Beginnings of Art.* New York: McGraw-Hill, 1967.

Lopatin, Ivan A. "A Shamanic Performance to Regain the Favor of the Spirit." *Anthropos* 35-36 (1940-41): 352-55.

Lowie, Robert. *Primitive Religion.* New York: Liveright, 1948.

———. *Lowie's Selected Papers in Anthropology.* Edited by C. DuBois. Berkeley: University of California Press, 1960.

McClellan, C. "Shamanistic Syncretism in Southern Yukon." *New York Academy of Sciences* 19 (1956): 130–37.

Maddox, J. L. *The Medicine Man: A Sociological Study of the Character and Evolution of Shamanism.* New York: Macmillan, 1923.

Madsen, William. "Shamanism in Mexico." *Southwestern Journal of Anthropology* 11 (1955): 48–57.

Malinowski, Bronislaw. *Magic, Science and Religion.* Edited by Robert Redfield. New York: Doubleday Co., 1954.

Mallery, Garrick. "Picture Writing of the American Indian." In *Tenth Annual Report of the Bureau of American Ethnology* (1888–89). Reprint. New York: Dover, 1970.

Marquis, Arnold. *A Guide to America's Indians.* Norman: University of Oklahoma Press, 1978.

Morgan, Lewis H. *League of the Ho-De-No Sau-Nee or Iroquois.* Edited by Herbert M. Lloyd. New York: Dodd, Mead and Co., 1901. Reprint. New Haven: Human Relations Area Files Press, 1954.

Mooney, James. "The Ghost Dance Religion and the Sioux Outbreak of 1890." In *Fourteenth Annual Report of the Bureau of American Ethnology,* pp. 641–1136. Washington, D.C.: Government Printing Office, 1896.

Muster, Wilhelm. "Der Schamanismus bei den Etruskern." *Frühgeschichte und Sprachwissenschaft* (Vienna) 1 (1948): 60–77.

Murdock, G. P. "Tenino Shamanism." *Ethnology* 4 (1965): 60–77.

Murphy, Jane M. "Psychotherapeutic Aspects of Shamanism on St. Lawrence Island." In *Magic, Faith and Healing: Studies in Primitive Psychiatry Today,* edited by Ari Kiev, pp. 53–83. New York: Free Press, 1964.

Nadel, S. F. "A Study of the Shamanism in the Nuba Mountains." *Journal of the Royal Anthropological Institute* 76 (1946): 25–37.

Narr, Karl J. "Bärenzeremoniell und Schamanismus in der Alteren Steinzeit Europas." *Saeculum* 10 (1959): 233–72.

Neihardt, John. *Black Elk Speaks.* 1932. University of Nebraska Press, 1961.

Neu, J. "Levi-Strauss on Shamanism." *Man* 10 (1975): 285–92.

Neumann, Franke J. "The Flayed God and His Rattle-Stick: A Shamanic Element in Pre-Hispanic Mesoamerican Religion." *History of Religions* 15 (1976): 251-63.

Nomland, G. A. "Bear River Shaman's Curative Dance." *American Anthropologist* 33 (1931): 38-41.

Oesterreich, T. K. *Possession, Demoniacal and Other, Among Primitive Races in Antiquity, the Middle Ages and Modern Times.* New York: R. R. Smith, 1930.

Ohlmarks, Ake. *Studien zum Problem des Schamanismus.* Kopenhagen: Ejnar Munksgaard, 1939.

Olson, Ronald L. "Tlingit Shamanism and Sorcery." *Kroeber Anthropological Society Papers* 25 (1961): 207-20.

Opler, Morris Edward. "The Creative Role of Shamanism in Mescalero Apache Mythology." *Journal of American Folklore* 59 (1946): 268-81.

――――. "Notes on Chiricahua Apache Culture: Supernatural Powers and the Shaman." *Primitive Man* 20 (1947): 1-14.

――――. "Renumeration to Supernaturals and Man in Apache Ceremonialism." *Ethnology* 7 (1968): 356-93.

Otto, Rudolph. *The Idea of the Holy.* Translated by John Harvey. New York: Galaxy, 1958.

Owen, R. C., J. J. Deetz, and A. D. Fischer, eds. *The North American Indians.* New York: Macmillan, 1967.

Park, Willard. "Paviotso Shamanism." *American Anthropologist* 36 (1934): 98-113.

――――. *Shamanism in Western North America: A Study in Cultural Relationships.* Reprint. New York: Cooper Square, 1974.

Parsons, Elsie Clews, ed. *American Indian Life.* Lincoln: University of Nebraska Press, 1967.

Posinsky, S. "Yurok Shamanism." *Psychiatric Quarterly* 39 (1965): 227-43.

Potter, Jack M. "Cantonese Shamanism." In *Religion and Ritual in Chinese Society,* edited by Arthur P. Wolf. Stanford: Stanford University Press, 1974.

Powell, Peter J. *Sweet Medicine: The Continuing Role of the Sacred Arrows, the Sun Dance, and the Sacred Buffalo Hat in Northern Cheyenne History.* 2 vols. Norman: University of Oklahoma Press, 1969.

Pulver, Max. *The Experience of Light in the Gospels of St. John, in the Corpus hermeticum, in Gnosticism and in the Eastern*

Church. Bollingen Series, no. 30. Princeton, N.J.: Princeton University Press, 1960.

Rahmann, Rudolf. "Shamanistic and Related Phenomena in Northern and Middle India." *Anthropos* 54 (1959): 681-760.

Rasmussen, Knud. *Intellectual Culture of the Hudson Bay Eskimos.* Report of the 5th Thule Expedition 7, no. 1. Copenhagen, 1930.

————. *Observations on the Intellectual Culture of the Caribou Eskimos.* Report of the 5th Thule Expedition 7, no. 2. Copenhagen, 1930.

————. *Iglulik and Caribou Eskimo Texts.* Report of the 5th Thule Expedition 7, no. 3. Copenhagen, 1930.

————. *The Netsilik Eskimos: Social Life and Spiritual Culture.* Report of the 5th Thule Expedition 8, nos. 1 and 2. Copenhagen, 1931.

Ricketts, MacLinscott. "The North American Trickster." *History of Religions* 5 (1966): 327-50.

Reichard, Gladys. *Navaho Medicine Man.* New York: J. J. Augustin, 1939.

————. *Navaho Religion: A Study in Symbolism.* Bollingen Series, no. 18. Princeton, N.J.: Princeton University Press, 1970.

Ridington, William Rubbins, Jr. "The Inner Eye of Shamanism and Totemism." *History of Religions* 10 (1970): 49-61.

Roheim, Geza. "Hungarian Shamanism." *Psychoanalysis and the Social Sciences* 3 (1951): 131-69.

Roux, Jean-Paul. "Elements chamaniques dans les textes premongols." *Anthropos* 53 (1958): 440-56.

————. "Le Nom du chaman dans les textes turco-mongols." *Anthropos* 53 (1958): 33-42.

Rogers, Spencer L. "The Methods, Results and Values in Shamanistic Therapy." *Ciba Symposia* 4 (1942): 1215-24.

Ruben, Walter. "Schamanismus im alten Indien." *Acta Orientalia* 17 (1939): 164-205.

Salmony, Alfred. *Antler and Tongue: An Essay on Ancient Chinese Symbolism and Its Implications.* Ascona, Switzerland: Artibus Asiae, 1954.

Schafer, E. H. "Ritual Exposure in Ancient China." *Harvard Journal of Asiatic Studies* 14 (1951): 130-84.

Sebag, Lucien. "Le chamanisme ayoreo." *L'Homme* 5 (1965): 5-32, 92-122.

Silvermann, Julian. "Shamans and Acute Schizophrenia." *American Anthropologist* 69 (1967): 21-31. Further discussion of this article in *American Anthropologist* 70:252-56, 71:307-309, 72:1093-94.

Stadling, J. "Shamanism." *Contemporary Review* 79 (1901): 86-97.

Stevenson, Matilda Coxe. "The Zuni Indians: Their Mythology, Esoteric Fraternities, and Ceremonies." In *Twenty-Third Annual Report of the Bureau of American Ethnology*. Washington, D.C.: Government Printing Office, 1904.

Steward, Julian. *Handbook of South American Indians*. Bureau of American Ethnology Bulletin no. 143. 8 vols. Washington, D.C.: Government Printing Office, 1946-59.

Stewart, Kenneth. "Spirit Possession in Native America." *Southwestern Journal of Anthropology* 2 (1946): 323-39.

Stirling, M. W. "Jivaro Shamanism." *American Philosophical Society Proceedings* 72 (1933): 137-45.

Swanton, John. "Social Conditions, Beliefs and Linguistic Relationship of the Tlingit Indians." In *Twenty-sixth Annual Report of the Bureau of American Ethnology*. Washington, D.C.: Government Printing Office, 1907.

Textor, R. B. "Statistical Method for the Study of Shamanism: A Case Study from Fieldwork in Thailand." *Human Organization* 21 (1962): 56-60.

Thompson, Stith. *European Tales Among the North American Indians*. Colorado College Publications: General Series, nos. 100 and 101; Language Series 2, no. 34. Colorado Springs, 1919.

Thorndike, Lynn. *A History of Magic and Experimental Science*. New York: Columbia University Press, 1923.

Trimingham, J. Spencer. *The Sufi Orders in Islam*. Oxford: Clarendon Press, 1971.

Turner, Victor. *The Ritual Process*. Chicago: Aldine Pub. Co., 1969.

Underhill, Ruth M. *Red Man's Religion*. Chicago: University of Chicago, 1965.

Vogel, Virgil J. *American Indian Medicine*. Norman: University of Oklahoma Press, 1970.

Voght, M. "Shamans and Padres: The Religion of the Southern

Californian Missions' Indians." *Pacific Historical Review* 36 (1967): 363-73.

Vogt, E. Z. "Ceremonial Organization in Zinacantan." *Ethnology* 4 (1965): 39-52.

Wallace, Anthony. "Revitalization Movements." *American Anthropologist* 58 (1956): 260-82.

Wasson, R. Gordon. *Soma: Divine Mushroom of Immortality.* Ethno-Mycological Studies, no. 1. New York: Harcourt, Brace and World, 1968.

Zaretsky, Irving I., and Mark P. Leone, eds. *Religious Movements in Contemporary America.* Princeton, N.J.: Princeton University Press, 1974.

INDEX